Jim Crow America

Jim Crow America

A Documentary History

EDITED BY

CATHERINE M. LEWIS AND J. RICHARD LEWIS

The University of Arkansas Press
Fayetteville
2009

ISBN-10: (cloth) 1-55728-894-1
ISBN-13: (cloth) 978-1-55728-894-3

ISBN-10: (paper) 1-55728-895-X
ISBN-13: (paper) 978-1-55728-895-0

13   12   11   10   09   5   4   3   2   1

Designed by Liz Lester

⊖ The paper used in this publication meets the minimum requirements of the American
National Standard for Permanence of Paper for Printed Library Materials Z39.48-1984.

LIBRARY OF CONGRESS CATALOGING-IN-PUBLICATION DATA

Jim Crow America : a documentary history / edited by Catherine M. Lewis and
    J. Richard Lewis.
            p.   cm.
        Includes bibliographical references and index.
        ISBN-13: 978-1-55728-894-3 (cloth : alk. paper)
        ISBN-13: 978-1-55728-895-0 (pbk. : alk. paper)
        ISBN-10: 1-55728-894-1 (cloth : alk. paper)
        ISBN-10: 1-55728-895-X (pbk. : alk. paper)
        1. African Americans—Segregation—History—Sources. 2. African
    Americans—Civil rights—History—Sources. 3. Racism—United States—
    History—Sources. 4. United States—Race relations—Sources.
    I. Lewis, Catherine M., 1967– II. Lewis, J. Richard, 1936–
        E185.61.J527   2009
        305.896'073009041—dc22
                                                            2008045166

For Betty Bishop Lewis,
wife and mother,
with all of our love,
now, and then

CONTENTS

ACKNOWLEDGMENTS

This book, like all such projects, involved the assistance, hard work, and support of numerous people. We would like to begin by thanking Larry Malley, Julie Watkins, Brian King, Melissa King, and Thomas Lavoie at the University of Arkansas Press. Their enthusiasm and support for *Jim Crow America* has made the process all the more enjoyable.

Marie Stanton warrants special recognition as she took on the seemingly endless task of converting many of the documents into an electronic format for the second time. She played the same role in our first collaborative book, *Race, Politics, and Memory,* published by University of Arkansas Press in 2007 for the fiftieth anniversary of the desegregation of Central High School in Little Rock, Arkansas. This can often be a tedious and cumbersome process, and her diligence helped make this book possible.

Jeff Bridgers at the Library of Congress Prints and Photographs Division helped us locate and download photographs from that vast collection. His continual good humor and support are much appreciated. Dr. Dana M. Sally, former dean of University Libraries, University of West Florida, and his staff were always helpful, patient, and accommodating in our search for documents. There are numerous individuals who helped us secure permissions to use many of the documents included in this volume, and they include India Artis (*The Crisis*), Rachel Leven (*Foreign Affairs*), Sheila Darryl (Central State University), Beth Howse (Fisk University), Judy Choi (University of Chicago Press), Tanya Milton (*Savannah Tribune*), Gail DaLoach and Steven W. Engerrand (Georgia Archives), Naomi Nelson (Manuscript, Archives, and Rare Book Library, Robert W. Woodruff Library, Emory University), Habiba Alcindor (*The Nation*), Marilyn Benaderet (The Afro-American Newspapers), and Gay Walker (Special Collections and Archives, Eric V. Hauser Memorial Library, Reed College). Finally, we would like to thank Karen Johnson for her fine work as copyeditor.

INTRODUCTION

While the exact origin of the term "Jim Crow" is unknown, most historians point to performer Thomas Dartmouth "Daddy" Rice's 1832 song and dance by the same name as an early source. It became a common adjective by 1838, and "Jim Crow law" was first cited in the *Dictionary of American English* in 1904.[1] In popular culture, the Jim Crow farcical performance became a staple routine in minstrel shows, a popular form of entertainment in the nineteenth century.[2] Mark Twain said in an autobiographical reminiscence that "the genuine nigger show, the extravagant nigger show" was "the show which has no peer" and was "a thoroughly delightful thing."[3] Although blackface musical acts appeared as early as the 1790s, minstrel shows, with their crude parody of African American life, gained popularity in the 1840s. Stock characters such as Jim Dandy, Zip Coon, and Jim Crow (white actors with darkened faces) sang, shuffled, cavorted, and bantered in comic, stereotypical dialect. Remnants of their influence have been present in other media, notably the popular radio series *Amos and Andy* (1928) and the film *The Jazz Singer* (1927).[4] Mainstream performers such as Judy Garland and Bing Crosby occasionally appeared in blackface. Even as minstrel shows waned, songs like "Dixie," "Blue Tail Fly," and "Polly, Wolly, Doodle" remain part of American popular culture.

Jim Crow has had multiple meanings and a dark and complex past, detailed by W. T. Lhamon in his book *Jump Jim Crow*. He explains that "before the concept of 'Jim Crow' stood for America's justly despised segregation laws, it first referred to a very real cross-racial energy and recalcitrant alliance between blacks and lower class whites. That's what the trickster Jim Crow organized and represented: a working-class integration —a jumping, dizzy Jim Crow movement. And that's what those who proposed segregation laws were determined to outlaw."[5] After the Civil War, the term came to refer to the legal, customary, and often extralegal system that segregated and isolated African Americans from mainstream American life.

Over the past half-century, historians have debated the very nature of Jim Crow. C. Vann Woodward's "forgotten alternatives" theory held that the years after the Civil War were a period of experimentation in

Southern race relations before segregation took a firm hold. Others, such as Howard N. Rabinowitz, countered that African Americans were simply excluded from numerous aspects of public life; and before laws were passed (*de jure*), custom and tradition (*de facto*) ensured segregation in the post-war period.[6] More recently, Jennifer Ritterhouse articulated the later position by arguing that "before segregation was written into southern law in the 1890s and early 1900s, exclusion was the norm, making segregation something of an improvement for blacks."[7] Both theories contribute to the understanding of the complex and often fluid nature of race relations in American life.

Contrary to popular opinion, Jim Crow laws did not originate in the South. Indeed, there was no need for such restrictions on black freedom in the region, as slavery provided ample control. The small numbers of free blacks were bound by similar strictures, with small modifications.[8] Historian C. Vann Woodward argued that "the very nature of the institution made separation of the races for the most part impractical. The mere policing of slaves required that they be kept under more or less constant scrutiny, and so did the exaction of involuntary labor. The supervision, maintenance of order, and physical and medical care of slaves necessitated many contacts and encouraged a degree of intimacy between the races unequaled, and often held distasteful, in other parts of the country. The system imposed its own type of interracial contact, unwelcome as it might be to both sides."[9] The end of slavery, which had demanded a great degree of interracial intimacy, now demanded a stricter separation of the races in the South. But long after the end of the Civil War it was still possible to see integrated eating establishments and white infants suckled by African American nurses.[10]

In the urban North, interracial intimacy was uncommon, and most whites were committed to the notion of white supremacy and black inferiority.[11] Segregated housing was the norm, and competition for jobs brought restrictions regarding trades and professions, with many unions limiting apprenticeships and membership to whites only. Access to the courts as well as voting was severely limited, and other legal and extra-legal restrictions on freedom were imposed. Leon F. Litwack's book *North of Slavery* provides evidence that, by 1860, blacks were segregated on or excluded from railroad cars, steamboats, and stagecoaches and were restricted from restaurants, bars, lecture halls, hotels, and the like in almost all of the Northern and border states. They were even separated during communion in churches, as well as restricted to certain pews or the balcony.[12] Even Abraham Lincoln, who signed the Emancipation Proclamation in 1863, was a spokesman for the racist political consensus, stating: "A universal feeling, whether well or ill-founded, can not be safely ignored. We can not, then, make them equals."[13] As free blacks moved farther west, restrictions became more acute. The constitutions of Indiana, Illinois, and Oregon even limited the entrance of African Americans into their borders. Almost nowhere in the West, even in those places where he was allowed to settle, was the black man allowed to vote. Black and white women, of course, were denied this fundamental right. Those restrictions were common in the North as well.[14]

Inventing Jim Crow

At the end of the Civil War, Congress hotly debated and then passed, on December 18, 1865, the Thirteenth Amendment to the Constitution, thus abolishing "the peculiar institution" throughout the United States and its jurisdictions.[15] The federal government established military control of the South but took little immediate action as to the governance of the conquered states. That governance at the state and municipal levels was initially left in the hands of the leaders of the conquered region, and in some cases, like Tennessee and Louisiana, before the end of the war. With President Andrew Johnson's approval, they were quick to establish conventions and, later, provisional legislatures. During Reconstruction, both the South and North struggled to reorder society to address the status of former slaves, whom they believed to be inferior and dangerous.[16] An immediate concern was how to assure a ready supply of workers for the largely agricultural needs of the South. There was also a great deal of uncertainty about the new state of social relations. Mark M. Smith, in *How Race Is Made*, argues: "As freedpeople began claiming rights to education and geographic movement, as they began to behave independently, so white southerners reacted by passing a series of Black Codes in 1865 and 1866."[17] While the laws varied, each state included vagrancy laws (under which unemployed blacks could be hired out as forced labor), apprenticeship laws (under which children whom the courts deemed under improper care could be bound out to white employers), and severe limitations on black occupations and property holding.[18]

Mississippi, which had the largest black population in the South, established some of the first codes. The state forced blacks to enter into a yearlong contract, which stated that "every Negro must have lawful home or employment, and shall have written evidence thereof."[19] Failure to meet the terms of the contract resulted in harsh penalties, including arrest and indenture. It was often impossible to obtain new employment unless one could prove he or she had already been under such a contract. Failure to do so might lead one to be declared a vagrant.[20] By 1865, Mississippi had enacted restrictions on African Americans owning or leasing property outside towns. This essentially prevented them from farming independently, thus forcing them to seek employment on white farms and plantations. The laws in Mississippi were, in some cases, intentionally vague and open to interpretation; one could be accused of vagrancy for being a thief, drunkard, or pauper or for having given offense of "speech and behavior."[21] Mississippi was quickly copied by almost all the Southern states, as well as many Northern and Western ones, in passing laws forbidding marriage between blacks and whites.

Some towns and cities passed even more restrictive laws than those in Mississippi. The Louisiana towns of Opelousas and Franklin and the Parish of St. Landry had various ordinances preventing African Americans from renting or keeping a house if not already in possession by January 1. Additionally, blacks who lived in the country could not visit town without their employer's permission. They were also restricted from selling anything without their employer's or the mayor's permission. These towns even required the evacuation of blacks not in the service of townspeople by 3:00 p.m. on Sunday.[22] Of course, not every Southern town was as harsh, and the Black Laws varied in their punitive nature. For example, a law that provided some protection and justice for blacks was the apprentice law of South Carolina, but even it contained unfair regulations.[23]

But freedmen and women were not completely abandoned. Established on March 3, 1865, and under the U.S. Department of War, the Freedmen's Bureau was a controversial component of Reconstruction from its inception. Despised by the South, under-funded and partly neglected by the federal government, and poorly organized and managed, it still managed to provide some social services to freedmen and women. It built schools, hospitals, and churches and supervised the distribution of rations, clothing, and medicine. The Bureau also helped former slaves locate lost relatives and mediated some domestic disputes in its own court system. Perhaps it was most successful in preventing the South from establishing peonage through its review of labor contracts. Major General Oliver Howard, for whom Howard University was named, was a Civil War hero who served as the Bureau's commissioner. Two years later, though, Congress ended funding for the Bureau's work in all areas except education. Even that would shortly disappear. Despite its limited influence, the Bureau did briefly give African Americans an advocate at the federal level. But some of the policies of the Bureau and the military authorities supported or condoned certain Black Laws, providing tacit approval of the actions of the Southern legislatures.[24]

Coverage in Northern newspapers, as well as pressure from Congress and military governors in the South, led to the nullification by 1867 of most of the Black Laws. This change helped set the stage for the ascension of the Radical Republicans (a group of American politicians who became a force in Congress in 1860) during Reconstruction.[25]

Republican members of Congress, Union supporters, and journalists for Northern newspapers, such as Horace Greeley of the New York *Tribune,* debated and reported on conditions in the South and widespread abuse caused by the Black Laws. Reports of racially motivated violence, riots, and segregationist policies often made headlines. The forgiving policies of President Lincoln and, later, President Johnson, especially the mass amnesty granted to key Confederate figures such as Robert E. Lee and Alexander Stephens, angered members of the Radical Republicans, as those who came to take an even harsher attitude toward the South came to be known. The Thirty-Ninth Congress was prepared to act, and in the 1866–67 session many members refused to seat legislators from the Southern states. The Committee of Fifteen, mainly Republicans who opposed Johnson, advocated legislation reaffirming the role and power of both the Freedman's Bureau and the Union forces in the South, which was passed by overriding a presidential veto. In April of 1866, Congress passed over a veto the Civil Rights Act, extending citizenship to "all persons born in the United States and not subject to any foreign power . . .

of every race and color, without regard to any previous condition of slavery, or involuntary servitude."[26] This became the basis for the Fourteenth Amendment (ratified on July 9, 1868).

Radical Republicans were soon in control of the direction of Reconstruction in the South and managed, in 1867, to pass a series of Reconstruction Acts that created five military districts under general officers. Johnson became less and less able to exert his influence in the matter of Reconstruction, and Radicals tried to impeach him for attempting to dismiss Secretary of War William Stanton and for other alleged misdeeds. However, the stridency of the Republicans' attacks resulted in a failed vote. Still, by the end of 1868, and with the election of a Republican president, Civil War hero Ulysses S. Grant, the Radical agenda continued to prevail.

The status of freedmen and women remained one of the nation's most pressing problems. While the passage of the Fourteenth Amendment overturned the *Dred Scott* decision, the issue of black suffrage was still being debated.[27] It was not until 1870, with the passage of the Fifteenth Amendment, which prohibited states or the federal government from using race, color, or previous status as a basis for voting, that blacks were afforded the right to vote. Though an important step, it did not prevent states from imposing literacy tests or poll taxes to severely restrict black suffrage. For the first time in American history, African Americans briefly played a significant role in the governance of the South. Elected at every level, local, state, and national, black men became judges, governors, and members of both houses of Congress. Despite popular legend —perpetuated by Southern newspapers and magazines well into the twentieth century and the writings of men like Charles Carroll (*The Negro a Beast*) and Thomas Dixon (whose *The Clansman* became the source for W. D Griffith's film *Birth of a Nation*)—these officials were for the most part well-educated and temperate men.[28]

For a brief period in American history, three groups exerted some influence over the South: freedmen, Northern immigrants (called carpetbaggers), and pro-Union Southerners (called scalawags). State constitutions were adopted in the new legislatures, and laws were passed with great debate and conflict. Conservative Democratic Southerners often withdrew from government, while Northern capital flooded into the region. But Southern resistance finally overpowered efforts to affect positive change in most of the former Confederate states. Through political maneuvering, intimidation, and violence, and Northern fatigue with the South and its problems, gradually the general tenor of Reconstruction changed.

Some important Supreme Court cases, such as the *Slaughter-House Cases (1873), Strauder v. West Virginia* (1880), *Plessy v. Ferguson* (1896), *Williams v. Mississippi* (1898), *Cummings v. Richmond County Board of Education* (1899), *Giles v. Harris* (1903), and *Berea College v. Kentucky* (1908), upheld the doctrine of separate but equal, effectively making Jim Crow the law of the land.[29] In his thoroughly researched examination of the court's decisions from the Jim Crow era through the modern civil rights era, Michael J. Klarman states, "the Court's race decisions reflected, far more than they created, the regressive racial climate of the era."[30] This attitude was echoed in the writings of Democratic congressmen Frank Clark (*A Politician's Defense of Segregation),* Thomas W. Hardwick (*A Defense of Negro Disfranchisement),* Episcopal Bishop Theodore DuBose Bratton (*Christian Principals and the Race Issue),* Robert Bennett Bean *(The Negro Brain),* Hubert Howe Bancroft (*A Historian's View of the Negro*), and Howard Odum (*Social and Mental Traits of the Negro).*[31] Magazines such as *Harper's Weekly, Scribner's Monthly Magazine,* and the *Atlantic* disseminated this school of thought broadly throughout the nation.

Reconstructionist state governments gradually became less and less able to resist the onslaught of the conservative Democrats, and by 1876 Reconstruction was effectively over. The contested presidential election of that year between Republican Rutherford B. Hayes and Democrat Samuel J. Tilden was resolved in Hayes's favor when a deal was brokered, involving economic aid to the South and the withdrawal from Louisiana and South Carolina of the last of the federal troops. Power in the South transferred from the Radical Republicans to the Redeemers, the self-styled saviors of the South. The federal government largely abandoned African Americans, and the era of Jim Crow was just beginning.

It would be naive to assume the ascendancy of the Redeemers meant the immediate and complete establishment of Jim Crow in the South. C. Vann Woodward argues, in his seminal book *The Strange Career of Jim Crow,* that "race relations after Redemption were an unstable interlude before the passing of these old and new traditions and the arrival of the Jim Crow code and disfranchisement."[32] In some cases, housing patterns in the South remained mixed, black suffrage was still practiced, and some African Americans still held office at the local and state level. In addition, transportation systems were not yet fully segregated. Charles E. Wynes points out that the "most distinguishing factor in the complexity of social relations between the races was that of inconsistency. From 1870 to 1900, there was no generally accepted code of racial mores and at no time was it the general demand of the white populace that the Negro be disfranchised and white supremacy made the law of the land."[33]

White supremacy was further institutionalized and perpetuated by what historian Jennifer Ritterhouse calls "racial etiquette"—a series of social practices imposed by whites on blacks to maintain their ascendancy.[34] Customs varied from place to place, but most included such practices as requiring all blacks, regardless of age, to address whites as "Mister," "Missus," "Miss," or some variant such as "Missy," "Young Master," or "Boss." These honorifics, except in a few cases such as "Doctor" or "Professor," were denied to African Americans. Most were addressed as "Boy," "Uncle," or "Auntie," if not by their first name. Failure to answer whites without a "Yes, sir" or "Yes, ma'am" was taken as an offense. This held true for eye contact for an extended period of time or failing to yield the sidewalk to a white person. An African American man who spoke to a white woman ran the risk of being accused of being "uppity" or, worse, of having sexual intentions. Arguing with whites, especially in an angry voice, was a serious breech of etiquette that in some cases could be fatal. While whites readily accepted food cooked by African Americans, to eat at the same table was taboo. Black children were taught at a young age that such racial etiquette was not a reflection of good manners but a strategy that might save one's life.[35]

Southern politicians of this era could roughly be divided into three groups. The least influential were the liberals, whose position was best articulated by former Confederate officer and popular author James Branch Cabel and Virginia aristocrat Lewis Harvie Blair, who argued for equal rights and protection for all citizens. The second group, the conservatives (or Redeemers), received broad support in the South and argued that liberals were false friends to African Americans, raising expectations that could never be met. Best represented by South Carolina's Wade Hampton, the Redeemers took, at most, a paternalistic attitude toward

African Americans.[36] The third group were the Populists, an odd mix of agrarians, working-class whites, and artisans who billed themselves as "exponents of a new realism on race, free of the delusions of doctrinaire and sentimental liberalism on the one hand, and the illusions of romantic paternalism on the other."[37] Tom Watson, their foremost spokesman, once said: "Gratitude may fail; so may sympathy, and friendship, and generosity, and patriotism, but, in the long run, self-interest always controls. Let it once appear plainly that it is to the interest of the colored man to vote with the white man and he will do it."[38] Before too long, all three groups had lost much of their influence. The liberals gained no more than a toehold in Southern politics; the ruling conservatives, after a spate of widespread acts of corruption and their perceived alliances with Northern industrialists at the expense of the agrarians, lost much of their political power; and the Populists, never able to overcome their true aversion to blacks and seeking other political alliances, finally lost almost all of their influence. The reality is that the attitudes and beliefs of the lowest element of Southern society (often called "Crackers") would come to dominate Southern racial policies for the next seventy years.

Building and Living Jim Crow

An editor in the 1898 issue of the Charleston *News and Courier,* in arguing against the establishment of Jim Crow laws on railroads in his state, laws that had already swept most of the Southern states to the west, ironically said, "If there must be Jim Crow cars on the railroads, there should be Jim Crow cars on the street railways. Also on all passenger boats. . . . If there should be Jim Crow cars, moreover, there should be Jim Crow waiting saloons at all stations, and Jim Crow eating houses. . . . There should be Jim Crow sections of the jury box, and a separate Jim Crow dock and witness stand in every court—and a Jim Crow Bible for colored witnesses to kiss. It would be advisable also to have a Jim Crow section in county auditor's and treasure's offices for the accommodation of colored taxpayers. . . . There should be a Jim Crow department for making returns and paying for the privileges and blessing of citizenship. Perhaps the best plan would be . . . establishing two or three Jim Crow counties at once, and turning them over to our colored citizens for their special and excusive accommodations."[39] Confident that this *reductio ad absurdum* had dealt the railroad matter a telling blow, the editor must have rested on this accomplishment. Regrettably, after a short while, all those absurd things came to pass, except for the establishment of Jim Crow counties. After a few years, the same newspaper was applauding the fact and urging additional Jim Crow legislation.

What happened was not that the South had new convictions of extreme racism that were now becoming law and practice, but that the forces that had kept them in check were now largely absent. Hatred, fear, and fanaticism had always been present in the South, but the forces that restrained them—moderate Southern opinion, liberal Northern opinion, the nationwide press, the courts, the federal government— were now largely absent from the scene.

Not only were Jim Crow practices realized in the laws and statutes enacted at the local and national level, but the decisions of the Supreme Court had a profound effect on shaping the practices of segregation. Furthermore, America's Republican-led imperialistic efforts in places like the Philippines and Cuba, with the conquest of millions of "people of the lesser races," made protection of American "inferiors" even less of an imperative. The Boston *Evening Transcript* admitted in 1899 that Southern race policy was "now the policy of the Administration of the very party which carried the country into and through a civil war to free the slave."[40]

By 1900, the near-total disfranchisement of blacks through legal and non-legal means was complete. Access to the legal system was denied or severely restricted. African Americans were separated or denied access on railroads and steamships and in hotels, restaurants, and places of entertainment and restricted to separate unions and working conditions. Housing was restricted, and many were prevented from entering certain cities and towns. Prisons, hospitals, and homes for the indigent were likewise segregated to a degree never before known in the South. Racially motivated violence and brutality was commonplace, most but not all within the borders of the South. Lynchings throughout the nation numbered 2,929 between 1882 and 1918, with no end in sight.[41] Two events in 1915—the rebirth of the Ku Klux Klan on Stone Mountain in Georgia and the nationwide acclaim of D. W. Griffith's film *Birth of a Nation*—signaled the nearly complete embrace of this racial status quo.

Jim Crow found a powerful advocate in the Virginia-born and

Georgia-raised president in 1912. Woodrow Wilson's overtly racist views and almost entirely southern cabinet promoted Jim Crow; the postmaster general, Treasury Department, and navy all ordered that their offices be segregated. Wilson segregated Washington, D.C., and began requiring that applicants for government job submit photographs. When confronted by black leaders, Wilson replied: "The purpose of these measures was to reduce the friction. It is as far as possible from being a movement against the Negroes. I sincerely believe it to be in their interest."[42] The House of Representatives, during Wilson's first term, passed a law that made intermarriage a felony in D.C.

Film, newspapers, and magazines in the early twentieth century embraced the theories of racial superiority as a justification for Jim Crow, reflecting Wilson's views. Thomas Dixon's novel *The Clansman* became the basis for D. W. Griffith's popular 1915 film *Birth of a Nation*. To ensure the film's widespread distribution and to give his ideology credibility, Dixon held a private screening for Wilson, his former classmate at Johns Hopkins, at the White House. Wilson is alleged to have reacted with the words, "It is like writing history with lightning; my only regret is that it is so terribly true."[43] Dixon held similar screenings for Supreme Court justices and members of Congress.[44] Dixon's was not the only voice. Historians like Robert W. Schufeldt, who published *The Negro: A Menace to American Civilization* in 1907, also found wide readership.

Resisting Jim Crow

African Americans in the North and South were not passively watching these new developments; they vigorously criticized the racist laws and responded by establishing new institutions and organizations. In response to the increasing loss of the rights of citizenship and the rising tide of violence, the National Association for the Advancement of Colored People (NAACP, first called the National Negro Committee) was founded in 1909.[45] The influential educator W.E.B. Du Bois served as editor of its magazine, the *Crisis*. The NAACP largely rejected Tuskegee Institute founder Booker T. Washington's accommodationist stance, popularized during his "Atlanta Compromise" speech of 1895: "In all things that are purely social we can be as separate as the fingers, yet one as the hand in all things essential to mutual progress."[46] The 360,000 black men who returned from World War I expected to be recognized for their sacrifices, despite being forced to serve in segregated units with almost no black officers. Instead, they faced violence and intimidation; some were even lynched in their uniforms. Especially alarming were the race riots of 1919's "Red Summer" in cities like Chicago, Houston, Little Rock, Harlem, New York, Baltimore, New Orleans, and Washington, D.C.

Numerous African American leaders lent their voices to protesting the economic, political, and social strictures of Jim Crow. Born to slavery in Mississippi, Ida B. Wells became an early and vocal opponent of segregation. In 1884, foreshadowing the action that would catapult Rosa Parks into the national spotlight, Wells refused to vacate her seat in a railroad car. Three men forcibly ejected her. She later founded the Memphis newspaper *Free Speech* and worked tirelessly for the rest of her life against lynching. It is in this area that she had the most influence, publishing important books and pamphlets such as *Southern Horrors: Lynch Law in All Its Phases* (1892), *A Red Record: Tabulated Statistics and Alleged Causes of Lynchings in the United States, 1892–1893–1894* (1895), and *Mob Rule in New Orleans: Robert Charles and His Fight to Death, the Story of His Life, Burning Human Beings Alive, Other Lynching Statistics* (1900). Like Wells, A. Phillip Randolph was among the most aggressive and accomplished civil rights leaders of this era. An early organizer of the Brotherhood of Sleeping Car Porters, he organized the 1941 March on Washington, which resulted in President Franklin Delano Roosevelt issuing the Fair Employment Act for defense industries. Randolph played a crucial role in President Harry S. Truman's decision to desegregate the armed forces. His work extended into the civil rights movement, and he remained a tireless voice for voting rights and an end to segregation in public accommodations.

Passing, where African Americans posted as white, became another form of resistance. Mark M. Smith argues that passing "became an enormous problem for segregation." He goes on to explain: "If race was innate and if white southerners could always identify it, how could blacks fool whites? Failure to locate passers meant that race was not genetic but environmental, and blacks who passed made a mockery of segregation."[47] As late as the 1940s, scholars estimate that more than 2,500 men and women passed into white society. As a practical way to avoid segregation laws, passing was not without its risks. Many who passed risked discovery and were often isolated from their family and community.[48]

In the 1920s, art and culture became a powerful form of protest. Chicago, Detroit, and Memphis all saw a blossoming of black literary and artistic endeavor, but Harlem became the epicenter. Talented and energetic artists came together in this New York City neighborhood and sparked one of the most significant intellectual movements in American history. The Harlem Renaissance, with its heyday sandwiched between the end of World War I and the Great Depression, brought James Weldon Johnson, Duke Ellington, Zora Neale Hurston, Paul Robeson, Langston Hughes, Nella Larsen, Countee Cullen, and Robert Hayden onto the national stage. Harlem was home to the NAACP, the Urban League, and the Universal Negro Improvement Association. Magazines such as the *Crisis, Opportunity,* the *Messenger,* and *Negro World,* all of which sought to publish the writers' work, were headquartered there. Jazz venues like the Cotton Club and the Apollo Theater, which regularly featured Ellington, Billie Holiday, Cab Calloway, and Ella Fitzgerald, gave African American musicians and their largely white audiences a chance to celebrate cultural achievement and the possibility of change.

Perhaps it was the mutual sufferings brought on by the Great Depression that altered the political landscape. For the first time, working-class blacks and whites joined the same political party in support of Franklin Delano Roosevelt. The party traditionally associated with white supremacy was gradually becoming the party of civil rights, as Democrats and Republicans began to trade positions on the issue. For the first time since Reconstruction, Roosevelt set a new direction in racial matters, often spurred on by his wife, Eleanor, who was far more liberal.

Increasing awareness of African American accomplishments spilled into other arenas as well. In 1935, Joe Louis won the heavyweight boxing championship of the world; he would successfully defend his title for thirteen years. In 1936, Jesse Owens's track and field accomplishments at the Berlin Olympic Games exposed the hypocrisy of Adolf Hitler's Aryan superiority. During World War II, the Tuskegee Airmen (African American pilots and support personnel) became among the most decorated units of the entire Army Air Corps. They later distinguished themselves in separate postwar squadrons until President Truman's Executive Order 9981 integrated them into other units. After the war, Jackie Robinson desegregated major league baseball when he joined the Brooklyn Dodgers in 1947. In nearly all areas of public life, segregation was becoming harder to justify. Many felt that Langston

Hughes's 1938 poem, "Let America Be America Again" served as an anthem of the era, with the stanza:

> O, let America be America again—
> The land that never has been yet—
> And yet must be—the land where every man is free.
> The land that's mine—the poor man's, Indian's, Negro's, ME—
> Who made America,
> Whose sweat and blood, whose faith and pain,
> Whose hand at the foundry, whose plow in the rain,
> Must bring back our mighty dream again.[49]

America under Jim Crow, as it was becoming increasingly clear, was not one of freedom or justice.

All too recently absent from the battle for justice, religious organizations began to take a more active role in fighting Jim Crow. Methodists, Episcopalians, Catholics, and others began to recognize the disparities between their creed and custom and began to lobby for greater human rights for blacks, founding such organizations as the Commission on Interracial Cooperation. Liberal newspapermen and editors, such as Ralph McGill of the Atlanta *Constitution* and Harry S. Ashmore of the *Arkansas Gazette*, gradually reappeared in the South and became a force for change. Slowly and clumsily, Jim Crow began his slow demise.

Dismantling Jim Crow

The federal government took an active role in dismantling Jim Crow toward the end of the Great Depression. In 1937 and 1938, there were ten civil rights bills introduced in Congress; by 1950, that number had increased to seventy-two. With the election of Harry S. Truman, Democrats adopted a civil rights plank in their platform that finally ended the Solid South.[50] This ultimately led the Dixicrats (a segregationist and socially conservative splinter party of the Democratic Party that saw federal intervention as a threat to southern values) to join the Republican Party. Truman, hailing from a border state with strong Confederate ties, surprised many when he urged the elimination of the poll tax and lynching, fairness in elections, integration of interstate transportation, and the establishment of a permanent civil rights commission. The Korean War and Republican victories in Congress prevented many of these measures from being enacted, but Truman dealt one major blow to Jim Crow. In 1948, by Executive Order 9981, he ordered the desegregation of the armed forces, where almost all African Americans served in segregated units led by white officers. The U. S. Navy restricted blacks to mess duty, serving in such jobs as waiters and cooks. Harry S. Ashmore, an army colonel who would go on to play a starring role in the desegregation crisis at Little Rock's Central High School, quoted a fellow officer from the South in response to the decision: "It shakes them up at first, but they begin to realize that they can work and fight alongside a Nigra, or under one, without having any close personal contact if that's the way they want it. The main thing is what it does for the Nigras. It gives them a kind of self-confidence a soldier has got to have if he is going to put his ass on the line."[51]

Unfortunately the momentum for civil rights realized by both Roosevelt and Truman came to a virtual halt with the election of Dwight D. Eisenhower. Eisenhower largely reflected the prevailing southern attitudes regarding blacks, accepting the existing social structure as appropriate. He "was very much a product of his times and culture, and his racial politics were far from progressive."[52] Stephen Ambrose, who generally admired Eisenhower, argued that the president's failure to take a firm position against segregation "did incalculable harm to the civil-rights crusade and to America's image."[53] While Eisenhower appointed E. Fredric Morrow as the only black member of his administration, he seldom sought his advice. He finally sponsored a very weak civil rights bill in 1957, largely at the urging of his attorney general, Herbert Brownell. He did, however, undo much of the Wilson-era mandates by desegregating the city of Washington, D.C., as well as the navy yards and veterans' hospitals. When the issue moved beyond the federal realm into that of the states, he was largely silent. His attitude was usually, "I don't believe you can change the hearts of men with laws or decisions."[54] His view of civil rights was brought into bold relief when the Supreme Court dealt what was to be arguably the most significant blow to Jim Crow in American history—*Brown v. Board of Education of Topeka, Kansas* (1954).[55] At first, some southern newspapers reported favorably of the decision, while most dissented. Reaction in the North was largely positive, but not overwhelmingly so. Some few school systems in the Deep South and border states took immediate action to desegregate their schools, including several in Arkansas. Others made plans to comply with the decision. Nothing much happened elsewhere until the Court, acting on what has become known as *Brown II,* in 1955 gave more direction to implementation, albeit with the vague "with all deliberate speed."[56] This second decision helped galvanize resistance to *Brown,* which would last for almost twenty years. Neither decision ended violence against African Americans. That same year, Emmit Till, a teenage boy, was brutally murdered for his violation of racial "etiquette" by whistling at a white woman in Money, Mississippi.

An event that began on December 1, 1955, in Birmingham, Alabama, would help loosen Jim Crow's stranglehold on the South. A respected seamstress and community organizer, Rosa Parks, captured the nation's attention when she, tired after a day's work, refused to vacate her seat to a white man on a Montgomery public bus. She was arrested for violating Montgomery's segregation laws. Thus began the Montgomery Bus Boycott, which brought a twenty-six-year-old, obscure, recently arrived Baptist minister, Martin Luther King Jr., onto the world stage. His Southern Christian Leadership Conference, along with the NAACP, galvanized resistance to Jim Crow. As media attention, especially television, focused on Montgomery, the issue became more intense and began what C. Vann Woodward called a "Second Reconstruction."[57]

The results of the Supreme Court's decisions on *Brown* exploded in Little Rock, Arkansas, in 1957, when nine black students attempted to enter all-white Central High School. Arkansas, with a moderate record on civil rights in comparison to other southern states, was the least likely city for serious confrontation. Governor Orval Faubus was a moderate among southern governors, and the state had already integrated several school districts. Little Rock superintendent Virgil Blossom had a widely accepted desegregation plan, which would have integrated all the schools in about nine years. After a series of events, including a visit by segregationist Georgia governor Marvin Griffin and White Citizens Council head Roy Harris, Faubus saw that his only avenue to reelection was to join the segregationist camp. A series of confrontations resulted in Eisenhower calling in the 101st Airborne Division to Little Rock. The entire proceedings were reported daily in newspapers and magazines throughout America and the world and, perhaps most powerfully, shown through the medium of television worldwide in everyone's living room. Orval Faubus was elected by the people of Arkansas for five more terms as governor and was chosen as one of *Time* magazine's "Ten Most Admired Men in America." He became a role model for subsequent southern governors like George Wallace.

Eisenhower's belated action had little to do with his acceptance of integrated schools and much to do with the negative worldwide press America was receiving and his concern for the encroachment on federal authority by the state of Arkansas. Eisenhower later said his biggest mistake was "the appointment of that dumb son of a bitch [Chief Justice] Earl Warren."[58] He also refused to receive the nine students and their mentor, Daisy Bates, at the White House because he feared it would offend his southern supporters.

The Montgomery Bus Boycott and Little Rock events galvanized civil rights supporters and made civil rights part of the national discourse. By 1960, student-led sit-in campaigns, most famously in Greensboro, North Carolina, erupted throughout the South. Additional protests against common Jim Crow practices swept the South, with some in the North and West, led by students affiliated with the Student Nonviolent Coordinating Committee (SNCC). Widely reported in the press and on television, the students' silent and nonviolent courage had a profound effect on the American public, which was increasingly realizing the injustices perpetrated on their fellow countrymen.

Encouraged by these and other events, civil rights organizations seem to take on new energy, continuing to practice nonviolent direct action. Martin Luther King Jr.'s words, "We will soon wear you down by our capacity to suffer and in winning our freedom we will so appeal to your heart and conscience that we will win you in the process," moved all but the most rabid segregationists.[59] The 1960 election of John F. Kennedy was seen as a turning point. In his inaugural address, Kennedy affirmed his support for *Brown,* calling it both legally and morally right. With his encouragement, desegregation of schools saw some progress, but mainly resistance and even violence. The vast majority of black students attended segregated schools, and in some places resistance reached lofty heights. By 1962, Alabama, Mississippi, and South Carolina still had no integrated schools. James W. Silver described Mississippi, the poorest state and the most profoundly isolated from national life, as "a closed society" which "comes as near to approximating a police state as anything we have yet seen in America."[60] The 1962 registration of James Meredith at the University of Mississippi erupted into a riot, which killed 2 and injured 375.

The next several years were characterized by acts of resistance and violence, large public demonstrations, and belated federal intervention. On June 11, 1963, Governor George Wallace stood in the doorway of Foster Auditorium and refused to admit black students to the University of Alabama. He relented only after confrontation with federal marshals, sent by President Kennedy. On September 15, 1963, Birmingham saw the bombing of the Sixteenth Street Baptist Church, where four girls, Denise McNair, Cynthia Wesley, Carole Robertson, and Addie Mae Collins, died. These instances of interracial violence were echoed in cities outside the South, such as Philadelphia, Pennsylvania, and Cambridge, Maryland. The August 28, 1963, March on Washington, attended by more than 250,000 people, put additional pressure on both the president and Congress to act. Kennedy, who had already sent a civil rights bill to Congress on June 19, was opposed to the march. He said, "We want success in Congress, not just a big show at the Capitol. Some of these people are looking for an excuse to be against us; and I don't want to give any of them a chance to say 'Yes, I'm for the bill, but I am damned if I will vote for it at the point of a gun.'"[61] His plea went unheeded, and Martin Luther King's "I Have a Dream" speech became the anthem for the movement. The legislation that covered equal access to public accommodations, state programs receiving federal aid, employment, and labor unions and authorized the federal government to sue for desegregation of public schools was drafted by the administration. Kennedy threw all his personal influence into the effort toward bipartisan backing of the bill. He was assassinated on November 22, 1963, before its passage, but his commitment signaled a new era.

It was left to a southerner, Lyndon B. Johnson, to shepherd through Congress the most far-reaching civil rights legislation that effectively ended Jim Crow. Unlike Kennedy, Johnson had personal experience with poverty and injustice, and he felt considerable sympathy for the plight of blacks. With years of legislative service behind him in the rough and tumble of both Texas and Washington politics, Johnson was one of the most persuasive politicians in American history. Upon taking office, he immediately activated the black leadership and bullied, intimidated, and persuaded members of Congress. After seven months' delay, he signed the Civil Rights Bill into law on July 2, 1964. It banned segregation in restaurants, hotels, places of entertainment, and all places of public accommodation. The passage of the bill coincided with the June 1964 Mississippi Summer Project, commonly known as Freedom Summer. During that month, civil rights leaders affiliated with the Council of Federated Organizations (COFO) recruited more than one thousand volunteers, including many Jewish and other white young adults from the North, to register voters in Mississippi.

Barry Goldwater, Johnson's opponent in the 1964 presidential election, savagely attacked the Civil Rights Act, but the majority of the country supported Johnson. He would go even farther and sign the Voting Rights Act into law on August 6, 1965. Jim Crow was legally dead. Its demise, however, did not ensure equal treatment before the law. Racially motivated violence and discrimination continued, and the promise of Johnson's "Great Society" became mired in the Vietnam War, which took attention and resources away from solving the nation's increasingly widening racial chasm that still exists today. Historians need look no further than the drama surrounding six black students in Jena, Louisiana, that erupted in September 2007.[62]

Doubtless, the journey toward racial justice is still a dream, but that is another story. The incontrovertible fact is that the Johnson years, and all the work leading up to them—that of Roosevelt, Truman, Kennedy, and, to a lesser degree, Eisenhower, as well as the work of countless persons of good will—saw an end to Jim Crow. Even with the November 4, 2008, election of Barack Obama, the task is far from complete. The "dream of a land where men will not argue that the color of a man's skin determines the content of his character," in the words of Dr. Martin Luther King, had not yet been fully realized.[63]

How to Use This Volume

The primary documents (newspaper articles, political cartoons, letters, speeches, photographs, and editorials) collected in this volume are organized thematically to help readers understand what the Jim Crow era reveals about how historians practice their craft. The documents have not been altered; original spelling, grammatical errors, and typographical errors have been retained. The goal is for the reader to understand the historical process by (1) seeing how disparate materials are gathered, (2) reading conflicting accounts or differing perspectives, (3) arriving at conclusions based upon the evidence presented, and (4) determining how historical events are remembered over time.

Five sections that include primary documents representing multiple perspectives follow this introduction. The appendixes and an annotated bibliography include a list of key players in the desegregation crisis, a timeline, questions for consideration, and sample assignments. The documents for each section were selected for one of three reasons: (1) they have never been published, (2) they reveal something significant about the long history of Jim Crow, or (3) they offer an unconventional or unexpected perspective on this era. The documents encourage scholars to examine how Jim Crow was codified into American law and society and then, many generations later, dismantled. This approach situates the era squarely in discussions about how race and the legacy of segregation continue to shape current events.

Notes

1. C. Vann Woodward, *The Strange Career of Jim Crow* (New York: Oxford University Press, 2002), 7.

2. Numerous scholars have written about the rise and significance of minstrel shows and the stock characters upon which they depend. See Joseph Boskin *Sambo: The Demise of an American Jester* (New York: Oxford University Press, 1988); Annemarie Bean, James V. Hatch, and Brooks McNamara, eds., *Inside the Minstrel Mask: Readings in Nineteenth-Century Blackface Minstrelsy* (Hanover: Wesleyan University Press, 1996); and W. T. Lhamon Jr., *Jump Jim Crow: Lost Plays, Lyrics, and Street Prose of the First Atlantic Popular Culture* (Cambridge: Harvard University Press, 2003).

3. Quoted in "A True Story Just as I Heard It," from *Sketches, New and Old,* reprinted in *The Oxford Mark Twain,* edited by Shelley Fisher Fishkin (New York: Oxford University Press, 1996), 202.

4. *Amos and Andy* ran as a television series until 1963.

5. Lhamon, *Jump Jim Crow,* viii.

6. Howard N. Rabinowitz, "From Exclusion to Segregation: Southern Race Relations, 1865–1890," *Journal of American History* 63 (September 1976): 325–50.

7. Jennifer Ritterhouse, *Growing Up Jim Crow* (Chapel Hill: University of North Carolina Press, 2006), 8.

8. Woodward, *Strange Career of Jim Crow,* 15.

9. Ibid., 12.

10. Ibid., 26, 31, 34–7. See also Edward L. Ayres, *The Promise of the New South: Life after Reconstruction* (New York: Oxford University Press, 1992), 33, 136; and Rabinowitz, "From Exclusion to Segregation."

11. Woodward, *Strange Career of Jim Crow*, 18.

12. Leon F. Litwick, *North of Slavery* (Chicago: University of Chicago Press, 1961).

13. Lincoln, quoted in Woodward, *Strange Career of Jim Crow*, 21.

14. Woodward, *Strange Career of Jim Crow*, 20.

15. The Thirteenth Amendment was ratified by most states almost immediately, though Mississippi did not do so until 1995.

16. John Hope Franklin, *Reconstruction after the Civil War* (Chicago: University of Chicago Press, 1994), 33.

17. Mark M. Smith, *How Race Is Made* (Chapel Hill: University of North Carolina Press, 2006), 51.

18. Theodore Brantner, *The Black Codes of the South* (Tuscaloosa: University of Alabama Press, 1965), 66–67.

19. Ibid., 66.

20. Ibid., 66.

21. Theodore B. Wilson, *The Black Codes of the South* (Birmingham: University of Alabama Press, 1965), 68.

22. Ibid., 74.

23. Ibid., 74

24. Ibid., 83.

25. Ibid., 71.

26. Franklin, *Reconstruction after the Civil War*, 60.

27. *Dred Scott v. Sanford*, 60 U.S. 393, 1857, declared that "no slave or his descendent could be or ever has been a U.S. citizen, and as such, has no rights, could not sue in federal court, and must remain a slave."

28. Franklin, *Reconstruction after the Civil War*, 90; Charles Carroll, *The Negro a Beast, or in the Image of God* (St. Louis: American Book and Bible House, 1900).

29. *The Slaughter House Cases* (83 U.S. 36, 1873) were three similar cases blended into one: (1) *The Butchers' Benevolent Association of New Orleans v. The Crescent City Live-Stock Landing and Slaughter-House Company*; (2) *Paul Esteben, L. Ruch, J. P. Rouede, W. Maylie, S. Firmberg, B. Beaubay, William Fagan, J. D. Broderick, N. Seibel, M. Lannes, J. Gitzinger, J. P. Aycock, D. Verges, The Live-Stock Dealers' and Butchers' Association of New Orleans, and Charles Cavaroc v. The State of Louisiana, ex rel. S. Belden, Attorney-General*; (3) *The Butchers' Benevolent Association of New Orleans v. The Crescent City Live-Stock Landing and Slaughter-House Company. Strauder v. West Virginia*, 100 U.S. 303 (1880); *Plessy v. Ferguson*, 163 U.S. 537 (1896); *Williams v. State of Mississippi*, 170 U.S. 213 (1898); *Cummings v. Richmond County Board of Education*, 175 U.S. 528 (1899); *Giles v. Harris*, 189 U.S. 475 (1903); *Berea College v. Kentucky*, 211 U.S. 45 (1908).

30. Michael J. Klarman, *From Jim Crow to Civil Rights: The Supreme Court and the Struggle for Racial Equality* (Oxford and New York: Oxford University Press, 2004), 9.

31. See Frank Clark, "A Politician's Defense of Segregation," *U.S. Congressional Record*, vol. 42, part 8, 60th Cong., 1st sess. (Washington, D.C.: GPO, February 22, 1908), Appendix, 38–40; Thomas W. Hardwick, "A Defense of Negro Disenfranchisement," *U.S. Congressional Record*, vol. 38, part 2, 58th Cong., 2nd sess. (Washington,

D.C.: GPO, January 27, 1904), 1276–1278; Theodore DuBose Bratton, "The Christian South and Negro Education," *Sewanee Review* 16 (July 1908): 290–297; Robert Bennett Bean, "The Negro Brain," *Century Magazine* 72 (October 1906): 778–764; Hubert Howe Bancroft, "A Historian's View of the Negro," in *Retrospection* (New York: Bancroft Co., 1912), 367–374; Howard Odum, *Social and Mental Traits of the Negro* (New York: Columbia University Press, 1910), 37–50.

32. Woodward, *Strange Career of Jim Crow,* 36.

33. Wynes, quoted in Woodward, *Strange Career of Jim Crow,* 33.

34. Ritterhouse, *Growing Up Jim Crow.*

35. Ibid., 22–54.

36. Woodward, *Strange Career of Jim Crow,* 48.

37. Ibid., 61.

38. Watson, quoted in Woodward, *Strange Career of Jim Crow,* 61.

39. Editor, quoted in Woodward, *Strange Career of Jim Crow,* 68.

40. Quoted in Woodward, *Strange Career of Jim Crow,* 73.

41. Tuskegee University statistics, published on the University of Missouri–Kansas City School of Law Web site, *http://www.law.umke.edu/faculty/projects/ftrials/shipp/lynchingyear.html* (accessed March 1, 2008).

42. Wilson, quoted in Public Broadcasting Corporation, "Woodrow Wilson: A Portrait," *http://www.pbs.org/wgbh/amex/wilson/portrait/wp_african.html* (accessed January 1, 2008).

43. Wilson, quoted in Arthur S. Link, *Wilson: The New Freedom,* vol. 2 (Princeton: Princeton University Press, 1956). Link denies that Wilson made such a remark. He may not have, but it would be consistent with his thinking about race.

44. Glenda Elizabeth Gilmore, *Gender and Jim Crow: Women and the Politics of White Supremacy in North Carolina* (Chapel Hill: University of North Carolina Press, 1996), 137.

45. On the eve of World War II, there were more that five hundred local chapters of the NAACP. The National Urban League had forty-eight chapters in cities and was increasingly active.

46. Booker T. Washington, "Atlanta Exposition Address," in *Discovering the American Past,* ed. William Bruce Wheeler and Susan Becker Wheeler (Boston: Houghton Mifflin Company, 2002), 40.

47. Smith, *How Race Is Made,* 69.

48. See E. W. Eckard, "How Many Negroes 'Pass'?" *American Journal of Sociology* 52 (May 1947): 498; and John H. Burma "The Measurement of Negro 'Passing,'" *American Journal of Sociology* 52 (July 1946): 18–22.

49. The poem was originally published in *Esquire* (1938) and in the International Worker Order pamphlet *A New Song* (1938).

50. After the Civil War, former Confederate states maintained a cohesive voting pattern for nearly a century that became known as the Solid South. For more information, see Dewey Grantham, *The Life and Death of the Solid South: A Political History* (Lexington: University of Kentucky Press, 1992). See also *http://www.pbs.org/now/politics/solidsouth.html* (accessed March 1, 2008).

51. Harry S. Ashmore, *Civil Rights and Wrongs* (New York: Pantheon, 1994), 88.

52. Catherine M. Lewis and J. Richard Lewis, *Race, Politics, and Memory* (Fayetteville: University of Arkansas Press, 2007), xiv.

53. Stephen A. Ambrose, *Eisenhower, Soldier and President* (New York: Simon and Schuster, 1984), 620.

54. Eisenhower, quoted in Woodward, *Strange Career of Jim Crow,* 139.

55. *Brown v. Board of Education, Topeka Kansas,* 347 U.S. 483 (1954).

56. *Brown v. Board of Education II,* 349 U.S. 294 (1955).

57. See C. Vann Woodward, *The Strange Career of Jim Crow* (New York: Oxford University Press, 2001).

58. Eisenhower, quoted in Ambrose, *Eisenhower, Soldier and President,* 190.

59. King, quoted in Woodward, *Strange Career of Jim Crow,* 170

60. Silver, quoted in Woodward, *Strange Career of Jim Crow,* 173.

61. John F. Kennedy, quoted in Howard Sitkoff, *The Struggle for Black Equality, 1954–80* (New York: Hill and Wang, 1981), 160.

62. Tom Mangold, "Racism goes on trial again in America's Deep South," Observer, May 20, 2007; see http://www.guardian.co.uk/world/2007/may/20/usa.theobserver (accessed July 30, 2007).

63. Clayborne Carson, ed., *The Papers of Martin Luther King, Jr.: Threshold of a New Decade, January 1959–December 1960,* vol. 5 (Berkeley: University of California Press, 2005), 507.

CHAPTER 1

Inventing Jim Crow

The documents in this first section examine the origins of the term "Jim Crow," the legal means by which slavery was ended in the United States, and early attempts to formalize and justify segregation throughout the nation after the Civil War.

DOCUMENT 1:
Song lyrics, "Jump Jim Crow," by Thomas Dartmouth (T. D.) "Daddy" Rice, 1828.

"Daddy Rice," a nineteenth-century blackface performer, introduced the song and dance "Jump Jim Crow" in 1828 in a minstrel show. The first printed version of the song was published by E. Riley in the early 1830s. Supposedly inspired by an African man from Cincinnati, Jim Crow became a popular American trickster figure. Several terms in the song need clarification: (1) "Tuckyhoe" might refer to the plantation where Thomas Jefferson spent his childhood; (2) "Pagannini" is a reference to Italian violinist, guitarist, and composer Niccolò Paganini (1782–1840); (3) "Pakenham" likely refers to Major General Edward Pakenham, who commanded the British forces that invaded New Orleans during the War of 1812; (4) "Wiper" refers to viper; (5) hoecake is unleavened cornmeal batter that is cooked on a hoe in an open fire. The song below includes eleven of the forty-four verses. The full version is available in W. T. Lhamon Jr.'s *Jump Jim Crow: Lost Plays, Lyrics, and Street Prose of the First Atlantic Popular Culture* (Cambridge: Harvard University Press, 2003), 95–102.

Come listen all you galls and boys
I's jist from Tuckyhoe,
I'm going to sing a little song,
My name is Jim Crow.
        CHORUS: Weel about and turn about and do jis so,
        Eb'ry time I weel about and jump Jim Crow

Oh I'm a roarer on de Fiddle,
And down in old Virginny,
They say I play de skyentific
Like Massa Pagannini.

I git 'pon a flat boat
I cotch de Uncle Sam,
Den I went to see dep place
Where dey kill'd Packenham.

I went down to de riber,
I did'nt mean to stay,
But dere I see so many galls,
I could'nt get away.

An den I go to Orleans
An feel so full of fight
Dey put me in de Calaboose,
An keep me dare all night.

When I got out I hit a man,
His name I now forget,
But dere was nothing left
'Sept a little grease spot.

I wip my weight in wildcats
I eat an Alligator,

And tear up more ground
Dan kifer 50 load of tater.

I sit upon a Hornet's nets,
I dance upon my head,
I tie a Wiper round my neck,
And den I goes to bed.

Dere's Possum up de gumtree
An Raccoon in de hollow,
Wake snakes for June bugs
Stole my half dollar.

A ring tail'd monkey
An a rib nose Babboon,
Went out de odder day
To spend de arternoon.

Oh de way dey bake de hoecake
In old Virginny neber tire
Dey put de doe upon de foot
An hole it to de fire.

DOCUMENT 2:
Sheet music cover, "Jim Crow Jubilee," 1847.

Courtesy Library of Congress.

The cover of this sheet music is illustrated with caricatures of ragged African American musicians and dancers, suggesting that, in a short period of time, Jim Crow had become a stock, stereotypical comedic figure in American popular culture.

DOCUMENT 3:

Excerpt, H. G. Adams, ed., *God's Image in Ebony: Being a Series of Biographical Sketches, Facts, Anecdotes, etc. Demonstrative of the Mental Powers and Intellectual Capacities of the Negro Race* (London: Partridge and Oakley, 1854).

This anti-slavery volume features a series of sketches of prominent African Americans such as Toussaint L'Overture, Frederick Douglass, William Wells Brown, and Phillis Wheatley. In this excerpt from the introductory chapter, Adams challenges the notion that

the "Negro race" is "essentially and unalterably inferior to any other
of the distinct races."

GOD'S IMAGE IN EBONY.
CHAPTER I.—INTRODUCTORY.

**"So God created man in his own image; in the image of God cre-
ated he him; male and female created he them."—GENESIS, i. 27.**

ETHNOLOGY, or the science of races, has of late years occupied
much of the attention of the learned. Many books have been written
on the subject, and many theories propounded, to account for the diversities observable in the physical and mental characteristics of the
dwellers upon the various portions of the habitable globe. Some, in
direct opposition to scripture, have asserted that these distinct tribes and
nations, so diverse in stature, in colour, in language, and in physical conformation, could not all have descended from one common parent—
that the peculiarities now observable in the structural anatomy of the
different human races, have always existed, and separated those races as
distinctly, as one tribe of animals is divided from another. Climate and
circumstances are not believed to have had any influence in these matters, and yet the very author who advances this opinion,*

Those who contend that the Negro race is essentially and unalterably inferior to any other of the distinct races, to use the ethnologist's

---

*Dr. Knox, vide "The Races of Men." tells us afterwards that race is permanent, only
so long "as the existing media and order of things prevail." What are we to understand by this, if not that climate and circumstances *have* power to effect changes in the
human frame, and to produce all those diversities of character and conformation now
observable in the great divisions of the family of man? We merely mention this to
show the inconsistencies into which scientific men are often led, when in pursuit of a
favourite theory, the more especially when that theory is at variance with revealed
truth; and to show also that those who contend for a natural and unchangeable inferiority of race, are not altogether so perfect in their wisdom, that we should listen to
them in preference to the word of God, who tells us that He hath "made of one
blood all the nations of men, to dwell upon the face of the earth." Is it not plain from
this declaration, that all men are brothers—children of one common parent, aye, of
one *earthly* parent; for, if by this is meant our Heavenly Creator only, then are we
brothers with the soulless brutes also, and we look in vain for the symbol and pledge
of our humanity; which, although fallen and degraded, has still lingering about it
some faint traces of the god-like and divine.

term, which occupy the different divisions of the globe, do so in the face of proofs to the contrary, which one would think ought to convince them of their error; some of these proofs it will presently be our task to adduce; just now we have a few more observations to offer upon the general bearing of our subject, and aspect of the slavery question.

That slave-holders, and all who would trample on and oppress their weaker fellow-men, are advocates for this theory, is not to be wondered at, they find in it an excuse for their acts of cruelty and oppression; it places the slave upon the same low ground as that occupied by their dogs and horses, and, although the humane man (and we do not mean to deny that there are many such proprietors of human chattels) would not overtask or torture even these, yet, the consideration and respect which is due to every being with an immortal soul, is lost sight of, and so that the physical wants of his slaves are satisfied, the master has little care for the imperishable part of their nature. And this is the most crying evil of the whole system: bodily torture, cold, hunger, taunts, revilings, toil beneath the lash of the overseer, nay, death itself, are as nothing in comparison with this annihilation of every glimmering spark of the divine light within, (which should be as a lamp to lead the soul to a Saviour's feet,) which generally ensues in that state of brutal ignorance in which the slave is allowed to remain, if he be not, as in most instances he is, kept and bound there.

Education for the slave is a thing not to be thought of, not to be tolerated; and so we hear of heavy fines and penalties, and other punishments, inflicted on those who attempt to teach the benighted African, dwelling in a so-called christian land, the way of salvation; and why? because the freedom of the soul from the thraldom of ignorance and superstition, and sensuality, must soon be followed by the freedom of the body. If once your slave gets but a revelation of divine truth, he is a slave no longer; he knows that other than an earthly master hath bought him at a high price; and bind him as securely, watch him as closely, and torture him as severely as you may; oh, haughty southern planter! there is a part of him—the more noble part—which you cannot hold, nor frighten, nor maltreat. This truth is nowhere more forcibly demonstrated than in Mrs. Stowe's admirable work: poor Tom dying under the lash of the fiend-like Legree, was more free than the sin-bound and embruted creature who owned his body, because

"He could read his title clear,
To mansions in the skies."

And he knew full well, that the trouble and suffering through which it was his lot to pass, was but as a rugged gloomy passage to a bright and blissful hereafter. It is Bryant who bids us

"Deem not the just by heaven forgot!
Though life its common gifts deny—
Though with a crushed and bleeding heart,
And spurned of man, he goes to die!
For God hath marked each sorrowing day,
And numbered every bitter tear;
And heaven's long years of bliss shall pay
For all his children suffer here."

The educated and spiritually enlightened slave, we say, knows all this, and fears not the stripes and injuries which man can inflict; if he attempt not to escape from his earthly bondage, which he generally will do, being conscious of his *right* to freedom, he will shew by his aspect and demeanour, that he claims a recognition of that common humanity which he shares with his owner; he is no longer a brute, but a man. And what so galling to the pride of a tyrannical master, as for that being of an assumed inferior nature to rise up and claim brotherhood with him, the delicately-nurtured, the highly- educated, and refined lord of broad lands, and human chattels.

To us it seems that no science can be true science, no philosophy other than spurious, that does not recognise in every human being, whether his skin be white or sable, a man and a brother. "The christian philosopher," says Dr. Chalmers, "sees in every man a partaker of his own nature, and a brother of his own species. He contemplates the human mind in the generality of its great elements. He enters upon a wide field of benevolence, and disdains the geographical barriers by which little men would shut out one half of the species from the kind offices of the other. Let man's localities be what they may, it is enough for his large and noble heart, that he is bone of the as a bone."

Let us add to this the testimony of the pious Richard Watson, which we find quoted in Wilson Armistead's "Tribute for the Negro," a noble volume, to which we are indebted for much of the information contained in the following pages; pointing to the scripture passage which tells how our Saviour became incarnate, "that he by the grace of God should taste death for every man." Watson says, 'Behold then the foundation of the fraternity of our race, however coloured, and however scattered. Essential distinctions of inferiority and superiority had been, in almost every part of the Gentile World, adopted as the palliation or the justification of the wrongs inflicted by man on man; but against this notion, christianity, from its first promulgation, has lifted up its voice. God hath made the varied tribes of men 'of one blood.' Dost thou wrong a human being? He is thy brother. Art thou a murderer by war, private malice, or a wasting and exhausting oppression? 'The voice, of thy brother's blood crieth to God from the ground.' Dost thou, because of some accidental circumstance of rank, opulence, or power, on thy part treat him with scorn and contempt? He is thy 'brother for whom Christ died;' the incarnate Redeemer assumed his nature as well as thine. He came into the world to seek and to save him, as well as thee; and it was in reference to him also, that he went through the scenes of the garden and the cross. There is not then a man on earth who has not a father in heaven, and to whom Christ is not an advocate and patron; nay, more, because of our common humanity, to whom he is not a brother."

Hear this, ye slave-holding churches of America! and tremble for the account which you will have to render at the great day of judgment, when the question shall be asked—What hast thou done with that poor benighted African—that talent that was given thee to improve? Hast thou squandered it? Hast thou hidden it in a napkin; or hast thou used it in any way so that it shall redound to the glory of God and the good of man? Alas, no! to use thou hast put it; but to how base a use! Thou hast made it subservient to thine own pride, and avarice, and sensuality; and thus bast hast done thy best to efface the glorious image of its and thy Maker, with which it was stamped in the mint of heaven, and to substitute a figure and a superscription which shall make it pass current in the exchange of hell. This thou hast done; oh, false professor of a creed of brotherhood! This thou continuest to do; and what avails it in the sight of heaven, that thou makest long prayers, and givest alms to the poor, and teachest and preachest with such fervency and unction, the holy precepts of christianity, with which thine *actions* have so little agreement?

How fearful, when thou standest before thy Father, and thy Judge, to give an account of all that thou hast done in the flesh, will be the question—"Cain where is thy brother Abel?" Will thy trembling lips then dare to ask—"Am I my brother's keeper?" No, for thou wilt know that thou oughtest to have been his helper, and instructor, and protector. Will you babble then about the Old Testament law? Will ye point to the Gospel, and say that Paul sent Onesimus back to bondage; ye, who have dwelt in the full blaze of a new dispensation, and who knew, or ought to have known, that the only bondage referred to by the Apostle, was, that of christian fellowship, into which the poor disciple was to be received *"as a brother."* How vain will be all such subterfuges; and how vain do they seem even now; well may the poor slave exclaim—

"Deem our nation brutes no longer,
Till some reason ye shall find,
Worthier of regard and stronger,
Than the colour of our kind.

Slaves of gold! whose sordid dealings
Tarnish all your boasted powers,
Prove that you have human feelings,
Ere you proudly question ours!"

It would be well for those who contend for the inferiority of the Negro race, and point to the present degraded condition of the poor Africans, as a proof of that inferiority, to glance for a moment at Caesar's description of their own ancestors.—"In their domestic and social habits, the Britons are as degraded as the most savage nations. They are clothed with skins; wear the hair of their heads unshaven and long, and shave the rest of their bodies except their upper lip; and stain themselves a blue colour, with woad, which gives them a horrible aspect in battle." Deeply sunken as they were in ignorance and superstition, uncouth in appearance, rude in manners, savage in war, and in their religious rites cruel and bloody, if we wish for a parallel picture, we must look to the countries watered by the Senegal or the Gambia; we shall see there but the reflex of our own primitive state, and it may well be questioned whether, if the same opportunities of civilization and improvement which the aborigines of Britain enjoyed, were given to the woolly-headed tribes of

Africa, they would not make more rapid advances than did the woad-stained dwellers in these islands, proud as is the position which they now occupy in the scale of intellect and morality.

The Roman orator, Cicero, urges his friend Atticus "not to buy slaves from Britain, on account of their stupidity, and their inaptitude to learn music and other accomplishments." And he adds, that the ugliest and most stupid slaves came from this country. No doubt, to the highly civilized and powerful Romans, the barbarous Angles appeared like an inferior race, whom it was alike philosophical and humane to keep in a state of dependence and degradation. In the correspondence of Dr. Philip, there is an instructive passage on this head, which we cannot refrain from quoting—"Seated one day in the house of a friend, at Cape Town, with a bust of Cicero on my right hand, and of Sir Isaac Newton on my left, I accidentally opened a book on the table, at that passage in Cicero in which the philosopher speaks so contemptuously of the natives of Great Britain. Struck with the curious coincidence arising from the circumstances in which I found myself; pointing to the bust of Cicero, and then to that of Sir Isaac Newton, I could not help exclaiming—Hear what that man says of that man's country." Dr. Philip goes on to observe, very truly, that ,"The Romans might have found an image of their own ancestors in the representation they have given of ours. And we may form not an imperfect idea of what *our* ancestors were at the time when Caesar invaded Britain, by the present condition of some of the African tribes. By them we may perceive, as in a mirror, the features of our progenitors; and by our own history, we may learn the extent to which such tribes may be elevated by means favourable to their improvement." To this, we may add, the testimony of Dr. Pritchard who in his celebrated "Researches into the Physical History of Mankind," says, "The ancient Britons were nearly on a level with the New Zealanders, or Tahitians of the present day or perhaps not very superior to the Australians." And again, "Of all pagan nations, the Gauls and Britons appear to have had the most sanguinary rites. They may well be compared, in this respect, to the Ashante, Dahomehs, and other nations of Western Africa." Let us talk no longer then of inferiority of race.—

> "Let us not then the negro slave despise;
> just such our sires appeared in Caesar's eyes."

Instances might be cited, in which, what are generally considered as the distinctive marks of the negro race, have become greatly modified under the influence of a change of climate and circumstances, in the course of one or two generations; and even in the same individual a wonderful change has been observed to take place, after his shackles have been loosed, his mind enlightened, his physical wants satisfied, and his natural feelings and affections studied and respected. Frederick Douglass, cowering under the lash of Covey, the slave-breaker, half-starved and scantily clothed, and beaten like a dog, is a very different being from he who lately stood up before a British audience, in a land of freedom, himself as free as any there, and electrified thousands by his thrilling eloquence. Gilbert, like a true artist as he is, has finely depicted this difference in "Uncle Tom's Cabin Almanack." Let our readers look on the two pictures, and ask themselves, admirably as the likeness is preserved, if it *can* be the same individual, here grovelling on the earth, and terror-stricken at the expected punishment, like the mere animal; there upright, as a *man* should be, with flashing eyes, and a countenance lighted with intelligence.

Look again at poor Pennington, the scared run-away, when he entered with a trembling heart and hesitating steps, the presence of the benevolent quaker, who sheltered and fed him for awhile; and again ask yourselves—Can this be he who afterwards became so efficient a minister of the Gospel of Christ; who stood up on the platform at the Paris Peace Convention, and delivered so beautiful and impressive a speech; "whose amiable and gentlemanly deportment, pliant and elegant mind, and culture and power of intellect, have won for him the esteem of very many, while his eloquence and pathos have touched the hearts of multitudes who have been privileged to hear him;" and on whom, a German University, from whose venerable walls have gone forth masters in the loftiest departments of human lore, has conferred the honourable distinction of D. D.?

Look again at Josiah Henson, at William Wells Brown, and others, whose biographies will be presently given, in their enslaved and free state; mark the difference, and then ask yourselves another question:— Can these noble specimens of God's handiworks—these enlightened, high-souled christian men, belong to an inferior race? Can we believe this? no, the rather let us agree with the wise and benevolent Dr. Channing, who addresses his countrymen thus:—

"We are holding in bondage one of the best races of the human family. The Negro is among the mildest and gentlest of men. He is singularly susceptible of improvement from abroad. His children, it is said, receive more rapidly than ours the elements of knowledge. How far he can originate improvements, time alone can teach. His nature is affectionate, easily touched; and hence he is more open to religious impressions than the white man. The European races have manifested more courage, enterprise, invention; but in the dispositions which Christianity particularly honours, how inferior are they to the African! When I cast my eyes over our southern region, the land of bowie knives, Lynch law and duels—of chivalry honour, and revenge—and when I consider that Christianity is declared to be a spirit of charity, "which seeketh not its own, is not easily provoked, thinketh no evil, and endureth all things,'— can I hesitate in deciding to which of the races in that land Christianity is most adapted and in which its noblest disciples are likely to be reared."

Elsewhere this eloquent advocate of the oppressed Negro makes the following forcible observations:—"The moral influence of slavery is to destroy the proper consciousness and spirit of a man. The slave, regarded and treated as property, bought and sold like a brute, denied the rights of humanity, unprotected against insult, made a tool, and systematically subdued, that he may be a manageable useful tool, how can he help regarding himself as fallen below his race? How must his spirit be crushed? How can he respect himself? He becomes bowed to servility. This word, borrowed from his condition, expresses the ruin wrought by slavery within him. The idea that he was made for his own virtue and happiness scarcely dawns on his mind. To be an instrument of the physical, material good of another, whose will is his highest law, he is taught to regard as the great purpose of his being. The whips and imprisonment of slavery, and even the horrors of the middle passage from Africa to America, these are not to be named in comparison with this extinction of the proper consciousness of a human being, with the degradation of a man into a brute.

It may be said that the slave is used to his yoke; that his sensibilities are blunted; and that he receives, without a pang or a thought, the treatment which would sting other men to madness. And to what does this apology amount? It virtually declares that slavery has done its perfect work—has quenched the spirit of humanity—that the Man is dead within the Slave. It is not, however, true that this work of abasement is ever so effectually done as to extinguish all feeling. Man is too great a creature to be wholly ruined by Man. When he seems dead he only sleeps. There are occasionally some sullen murmurs in the calm of slavery, showing that life still beats in the soul, that the idea of rights cannot be wholly effaced from the human being. It would be too painful, and it is not needed, to detail the process by which the spirit is broken in slavery. I refer to one only, the selling of slaves. The practice of exposing fellow-creatures for sale, of having markets for men as for cattle, of examining the limbs and muscles of a man and woman as of a brute, of putting human beings under the hammer of an auctioneer, and delivering them, like any other article of merchandise, to the highest bidder, all this is such an insult to our common nature, and so infinitely degrading to the poor victim, that it is hard to conceive of its existence except in a barbarous country. The violation of his own rights to which he is inured from birth, must throw confusion over his ideas of all human rights. He cannot comprehend them; or, if he does, how can he respect them, seeing them, as he does, perpetually trampled on in his own person?"

Other demoralizing, we had almost said demonizing, influences, which the system of slavery calls into play, might be dwelt upon, were they not of too dark and impure a character to admit of more than a passing hint. Any properly constituted and instructed mind must shrink with horror at even a distant contemplation of those violations of virtue and decency, and the best and holiest affections of humanity, which are of daily, hourly occurrence in the slave states of America, if the testimony of a "thousand witnesses" many of them favourable to this accursed system, is to be believed.

We may now quote a few remarks apropos to our subject, by an authority of some weight in this country. In an article in "Chambers' Edinburgh Journal," on a work published some years since in one of the slave states, the professed object of which was to prove that Negroes are not human beings in the full sense of the term, but a sort of intermediate link between the larger of the ape tribe and the white races of man, it is said in conclusion, "The answer to all these arguments is, we think, not difficult. Supposing the Negroes differ in all the alleged respects from the whites, the difference we would say, is not such as to justify, the whites in making a property of them, and treating them with cruelty.

But the Negroes are not, in reality, beyond the pale of humanity, either physically or mentally, Their external conformation is not greatly different from that of whites. Their being the same mentally, is shewn by the fact, that many Negroes have displayed intellectual and moral features equal to those of whites of high endowment. We might instance Carey, Jenkins, Cuffee, Gustavus Vasa, Toussaint, and many others.

If any one Negro has shewn a character identical with that of the white race, the whole family must be the same, though in general inferior. The inferiority is shewn to be not in kind, but in degree; and it would be just as proper for the clever whites to seize and enslave the stupid ones, as for the whites in general to enslave the blacks in general. The blacks, moreover, have shewn a capacity of improvement. They have shewn that, as in many districts of even our island of Great Britain, many parts of mind appear absent only when not brought out or called into exercise, and that by education the dormant faculties can be awakened and called into strength, if not in one generation, at least in the course of several. The tendency slavery is to keep down, at nearly the level of brutes, beings who might be brightened into intellectual and moral beauty."

Further, in their "Tract on Intelligent Negroes," the Messrs. Chambers either give utterance, or the sanction of their names, to this sentiment—"Such men as Jenkins and Carey at once close the mouths of those who, from ignorance or something worse, allege an absolute difference, or specific character, between the two races, and justify the consignment of the black to a fate which only proves the lingering barbarism of the white."

Yes, we are all stones from one quarry, dark of hue and rugged of form as some may be, while others are white and beautifully polished; coloured and shapen in accordance with the will of the Divine Architect, we shall form eventually one grand and symmetrical whole—a temple that shall redound to the glory of Him who designed and fashioned it. What, then; shall the richly sculptured capital of the slender column, or the embossed key-stone of the stately arch, despise the dark and rugged mass which helps to form the basement? nay, not so; for it performs an important work in the economy of the whole structure, and might by labour and skill have been rendered worthy a place in its more ornamental parts. But dropping the metaphor, truly may we say to the Negro—

"Bone of our bone, flesh of our flesh, thou art,

Co-heritor of kindred being thou;

From the full tide that warmed one mother's heart,

Thy veins and ours received the genial flow."

DOCUMENT 4:
Petition, 1859.

Reprinted in Society for the Study of the Negro in Dentistry, Inc., "Roderick D. Badger: Atlanta's First Afro-American Dentist," Newsletter (October–December 1989). Subject File: Afro-Americans–Civil Rights—Afro-Americans–History (1877–1964). Folder: Negro Community. Courtesy Kenan Research Center, Atlanta History Center.

This newsletter includes the text from a May 1859 Atlanta City Council petition urging the city to not tolerate the presence of a "Negro dentist." The petition reveals the tenuous position of free blacks, particularly professionals, in the South on the eve of the Civil War.

In May, 1859, a Petition was presented to the Atlanta City Council which stated "We feel aggrieved as Southern citizens, that your honorable body tolerates a Negro dentist (Roderick Badger) in our midst, and in justice to ourselves and the community, it ought to be abated. We the residents of Atlanta appeal to you for justice". The petition resulted in an ordinance which required all free black persons coming to live within the Atlanta city limited to pay $200.00 to the council clerk. Again in February, 1861, another petition was presented to the City Council "calling attention of Council to the professional pretensions of a colored man styling himself R.D. Badger."*

Apparently, no repressive measures were taken regarding Badger's practice. He overcame the prejudices of his fellow Atlanta dentists and acquired a very successful practice. His patients were among the leading citizens of Atlanta.

Dr. Roderick D. Badger was born on July 4, 1834 in DeKalb County, Georgia. He was the son of Dr. Joshua Bostic Badger, prominent white dentist of DeKalb County, and a slave named Martha. He began the study of dentistry at age 16 under the supervision of his father, who also trained Roderick's brothers, Ralph and Robert, to be dentists. Roderick is listed as a practicing dentist in the city directory of 1859–60, giving him the distinction of being the First Afro-American to practice dentistry in Atlanta. He married Mary A. Murphy in 1855, who bore him eight children.

Roderick Badger served in the Civil War as an aide to a Confederate Army Colonel. During the siege of Atlanta, July to September, 1864, the citizens were compelled to evacuate the city. Roderick, Robert and their families settled temporarily in Chicago, Illinois until 1866 when they moved back to Atlanta. He re-opened his dental office at 39 Peachtree Street. Badger owned extensive properties in Atlanta. He was thrifty, prosperous, and highly respected. The *Atlanta Constitution* and *Atlanta Journal* commented extensively on the occasion of his death on 27 December 1890.

A myriad of Badgers preceded Roderick. All descended from Giles and Elizabeth Greenleaf Badger who were early settlers of South Carolina and Northwest Georgia. They were all very talented and industrious individuals and were represented in all of the learned professions. Several Badger males had successful dental careers. Living descendents of the Badgers can trace their lineage to two signers of the Declaration of Independence: Eldridge Gerry (Massachusetts) and William Whipple (New Hampshire). The relationship is through Gerry's mother, a relative of Elizabeth Greenleaf Badger, and William Whipple's cousin, Sara Worth, who married Captain Daniel Badger.

Dr. Roderick D. Badger is buried in the Historic Oakland Cemetery in Atlanta.

SSND is indeed grateful to DR. Henry S. Robinson of Washington, D.C., Professor of History at Morgan State University, for sending us this information on his great-grandfather.

Editor's Note: This petition is indicative of the racial climate during the pre-Emancipation period in the slave-holding states. Black people were not given nor permitted to use surnames.

DOCUMENT 5:
Abraham Lincoln, "The Emancipation Proclamation," January 1, 1863.

The Emancipation Proclamation, issued during the third year of the Civil War, freed slaves in the Confederate states. Though significant, it did not apply to slaves in border states or to areas of the Confederacy under Union control. Freedom was also contingent upon a Union victory. Despite these restrictions, the proclamation allowed slaves to join the Union army and navy; ultimately 200,000 served.

By the President of the United States of America:
A Proclamation.

Whereas, on the twenty-second day of September, in the year of our Lord one thousand eight hundred and sixty-two, a proclamation was issued by the President of the United States, containing, among other things, the following, to wit:

"That on the first day of January, in the year of our Lord one thousand eight hundred and sixty-three, all persons held as slaves within any State or designated part of a State, the people whereof shall then be in rebellion against the United States, shall be then, thenceforward, and forever free; and the Executive Government of the United States, including the military and naval authority thereof, will recognize and maintain the freedom of such persons, and will do no act or acts to repress such persons, or any of them, in any efforts they may make for their actual freedom.

"That the Executive will, on the first day of January aforesaid, by proclamation, designate the States and parts of States, if any, in which the people thereof, respectively, shall then be in rebellion against the United States; and the fact that any State, or the people thereof, shall on that day be, in good faith, represented in the Congress of the United States by members chosen thereto at elections wherein a majority of the qualified voters of such State shall have participated, shall, in the absence of strong countervailing testimony, be deemed conclusive evidence that such State, and the people thereof, are not then in rebellion against the United States."

Now, therefore I, Abraham Lincoln, President of the United States, by virtue of the power in me vested as Commander-in-Chief, of the Army and Navy of the United States in time of actual armed rebellion against the authority and government of the United States, and as a fit and necessary war measure for suppressing said rebellion, do, on this first day of January, in the year of our Lord one thousand eight hundred and sixty-three, and in accordance with my purpose so to do publicly proclaimed for the full period of one hundred days, from the day first above mentioned, order and designate as the States and parts of States wherein the people thereof respectively, are this day in rebellion against the United States, the following, to wit:

Arkansas, Texas, Louisiana, (except the Parishes of St. Bernard, Plaquemines, Jefferson, St. John, St. Charles, St. James Ascension, Assumption, Terrebonne, Lafourche, St. Mary, St. Martin, and Orleans, including the City of New Orleans) Mississippi, Alabama, Florida, Georgia, South Carolina, North Carolina, and Virginia, (except the forty-eight counties designated as West Virginia, and also the counties of Berkley, Accomac, Northampton, Elizabeth City, York, Princess Ann, and Norfolk, including the cities of Norfolk and Portsmouth[)], and which excepted parts, are for the present, left precisely as if this proclamation were not issued.

And by virtue of the power, and for the purpose aforesaid, I do order and declare that all persons held as slaves within said designated States, and parts of States, are, and henceforward shall be free; and that the Executive government of the United States, including the military and naval authorities thereof, will recognize and maintain the freedom of said persons.

And I hereby enjoin upon the people so declared to be free to abstain from all violence, unless in necessary self-defence; and I recommend to them that, in all cases when allowed, they labor faithfully for reasonable wages.

And I further declare and make known, that such persons of suitable condition, will be received into the armed service of the United States to garrison forts, positions, stations, and other places, and to man vessels of all sorts in said service.

And upon this act, sincerely believed to be an act of justice, warranted by the Constitution, upon military necessity, I invoke the considerate judgment of mankind, and the gracious favor of Almighty God.

In witness whereof, I have hereunto set my hand and caused the seal of the United States to be affixed.

Done at the City of Washington, this first day of January, in the year of our Lord one thousand eight hundred and sixty three, and of the Independence of the United States of America the eighty-seventh.

By the President: ABRAHAM LINCOLN
WILLIAM H. SEWARD, Secretary of State.

DOCUMENT 6:
Thirteenth Amendment, 1865.

Concerned about the validity of the Emancipation Proclamation, twenty-seven of the thirty-six states ratified the Thirteenth Amendment, the first of the Reconstruction Amendments, to end slavery in America in 1865. Illinois was the first state to ratify on February 1. The entire process was finally completed on December 6, 1865. The amendment, which was authored by Congressmen James Mitchell Ashley (R-Ohio) and James Falconer Wilson (R-Iowa) and Senator John B. Henderson (D-Missouri), was rejected by Mississippi until March 16, 1995.

---

1. Neither slavery nor involuntary servitude, except as a punishment for crime where of the party shall have been duly convicted, shall exist within the United States, or any place subject to their jurisdiction.

2. Congress shall have power to enforce this article by appropriate legislation.

DOCUMENT 7:

Broadside, "The Freedman's Bureau: An Agency to Keep the Negro in Idleness at the Expense of the White Man," 1866.

Courtesy Library of Congress.

Published during the Pennsylvania gubernatorial election of 1866, the broadside was one of many racist posters challenging the Radical Republicans on the issue of the black vote.

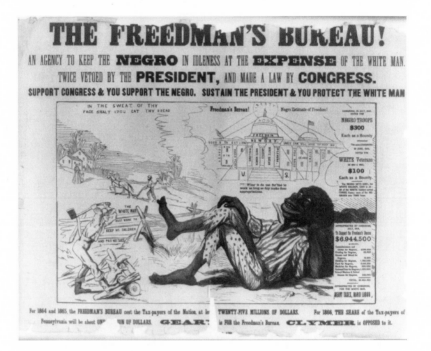

DOCUMENT 8:

Civil Rights Act of 1866.

This act, passed by Congress on April 9 over a veto of President Andrew Johnson, provided one of the first statutory definitions of the rights of U.S. citizens. The first article, included here, extended citizenship to all native-born blacks regardless of their previous condition of servitude. Persons who denied these rights to former slaves were guilty of a misdemeanor and upon conviction faced a fine not exceeding one thousand dollars, or imprisonment not exceeding one year, or both. The Ku Klux Klan and other white supremacist organizations undermined the act, making it difficult to guarantee civil rights to African Americans. It became the basis for the Fourteenth Amendment.

Be it enacted by the Senate and the House of Representatives of the United States of America in Congress assembled, That all persons born in the United States and not subject to any foreign power, excluding Indians not taxed, are hereby declared to be citizens of the United States; and such citizens, of every race and color, without regard to any previous condition of slavery or involuntary servitude, except as a punishment for crime whereof the party shall have been duly convicted, shall have the same right, in every State and Territory in the United States, to make and enforce contracts, to sue, be parties, and give evidence, to inherit, purchase, lease, sell, hold, and convey real and personal property, and to full and equal benefit of all laws and proceedings for the security of person and property, as is enjoyed by white citizens, and shall be subject to like punishment, pains, and penalties, and to none other, any law, statute, ordinance, regulation, or custom, to the contrary notwithstanding.

DOCUMENT 9:
"Schools for Freedmen," *Harper's Weekly,* March 30, 1867, 1.

Subject File: Afro-Americans-Civil Rights—Afro-Americans-History (1877–1964). Folder: Black Community. Courtesy Kenan Research Center, Atlanta History Center.

This short article celebrates the proliferation of schools in the former Confederacy for former slaves, often sponsored by northern philanthropists. Based in New York City, *Harper's Weekly (A Journal of Civilization)* was published by Harper and Brothers from 1857 to 1916. Its influence is reflected in its circulation, which reached two hundred thousand on the eve of the Civil War.

SCHOOLS FOR FREEDMEN.

We have had occasion heretofore to notice the earnestness with which the freedmen of the South have availed themselves of the opportunities for education offered by the fortunate result of the war. They have even contributed material aid out of their scanty means to the building of schools for the colored children, and evinced an encouraging desire to secure the benefits heretofore denied them. Very great good has already been accomplished in this way, and great results are promised by the philanthropic efforts of men and women engaged in this labor of love. We have no means of estimating the number of colored children enjoying the privilege of attending school in all parts of the South at this moment, but information from Alabama states that General WAGER SWAYNE, Commissioner for Freedmen in that State, reports that there are over thirty thousand colored children in attendance at school in his district alone. Great efforts are being made all over the South by Northern missionaries and philanthropists, like PEABODY, HOWARD, TILLSON, SWAYNE, and others, to promote education among the poorer classes of whites and freedmen; and we may assert with perfect truthfulness that there are more public schools in the South in its present disorganized and demoralized state that there were at any period under the old *régime*.

FIRST FREEDMEN'S SCHOOL IN GEORGIA.

We give herewith a picture of the first schoolhouse for freedmen ever built in the State of Georgia. This house, which is located in Atlanta, was completed and dedicated to Education and Religion on the 8th of December, 1866, with appropriate and impressive ceremonies, by Rev. E. M. CRAVATH, Secretary of the American Missionary Association, and other gentlemen friendly to impartial and universal education. It contains, in front, four rooms, each of sufficient capacity to accommodate seventy-five pupils, and an office for the Superintendent.

The projection to the rear in the left of the picture is the chapel, which is used for day and Sunday school and religious services, and seats comfortably an audience of 450 persons. The school-rooms, in finish, inside and out, are in all appointments equal to any first-class school-house either North or South. The entire cost was about $6000. Of that amount $1000 was given by Rev. Dr. STORRS'S Congregation in Cincinnati, and, in honor of their pastor, is called the *"Stoors School."* The remaining $5000 was paid jointly by the Freedmen's Bureau and the American Missionary Association, under whose direction the house was erected, and by whom the schools in it are sustained. The Association has twelve teachers in Atlanta, under whose daily tuition there are now over 1100 colored pupils.

DOCUMENT 10:
Fourteenth Amendment, 1868.

The Fourteenth Amendment, known commonly as the second of the Reconstruction Amendments, was passed by Congress June 13, 1866, and ratified July 9, 1868. It includes important due process and equal protection clauses that result in significant structural changes to the U.S. Constitution. By offering a broad definition of citizenship, the amendment overturns the 1857 case *Dred Scott v. Sanford* that declared that slaves and free blacks were not and could never become citizens of the United States.

SECTION 1. All persons born or naturalized in the United States, and subject to the jurisdiction thereof, are citizens of the United States and of the State wherein they reside. No State shall make or enforce any law which shall abridge the privileges or immunities of citizens of the United States; nor shall any State deprive any person of life, liberty, or property, without due process of law; nor deny to any person within its jurisdiction the equal protection of the laws.

SECTION 2. Representatives shall be *apportioned* among the several States according to their respective numbers, counting the whole number of persons in each State, excluding Indians not taxed. But when the right to vote at any election for the choice of electors for President and Vice President of the United States, Representatives in Congress, the Executive and Judicial officers of a State, or the members of the Legislature thereof, is denied to any of the male inhabitants of such State, being twenty-one years of age, and citizens of the United States, or in any way abridged, except for participation in rebellion, or other crime, the basis of representation therein shall be reduced in the proportion which the number of such male citizens shall bear to the whole number of male citizens twenty-one years of age in such State.

SECTION 3. No person shall be a Senator or Representative in Congress, or elector of President and Vice President, or hold any office, civil or military, under the United States, or under any State, who, having previously taken an oath, as a member of Congress, or as an officer of the United States, or as a member of any State legislature, or as an executive or judicial officer of any State, to support the Constitution of the United States, shall have engaged in insurrection or rebellion against the same, or given aid or comfort to the enemies thereof. But Congress may by a vote of two-thirds of each House, remove such disability.

SECTION 4. The validity of the public debt of the United States, authorized by law, including debts incurred for payment of pensions and bounties for services in suppressing insurrection or rebellion, shall not be questioned. But neither the United States nor any State shall assume or pay any debt or obligation incurred in aid of insurrection or rebellion against the United States, or any claim for the loss or emancipation of any slave; but all such debts, obligations and claims shall be held illegal and void.

SECTION 5. The Congress shall have power to enforce, by appropriate legislation, the provisions of this article.

DOCUMENT 11:
Cartoon, "This Is a White Man's Government," 1868.

Courtesy Library of Congress.

This Reconstruction cartoon depicts a man with a Confederate States of America (CSA) belt buckle holding a knife labeled "the lost cause." A stereotyped Irishman, holding a club labeled "a vote," and another man, wearing a button labeled "5 Avenue" and holding a wallet labeled "capital for votes," have their feet on an African American soldier sprawled on the ground. In the background, a "colored orphan asylum" and a "southern school" are in flames. African American children have been lynched near the burning buildings.

"THIS IS A WHITE MAN'S GOVERNMENT."

"We regard the Reconstruction Acts (so called) of Congress as usurpations, and unconstitutional, revolutionary, and void."—*Democratic Platform.*

DOCUMENT 12:
Fifteenth Amendment, 1870.

The third of the Reconstruction Amendments, the Fifteenth Amendment focused on eliminating race or previous condition of servitude as a qualification for suffrage. The first person to vote under the new provision was Thomas Mundy Peterson on February 4, 1870. During the Jim Crow era, states enacted literacy tests, poll taxes, and other measures to restrict African American voting. Not until the Voting Rights Act of 1965 did the amendment finally reach its intended purpose.

SECTION 1. The right of citizens of the United States to vote shall not be denied or abridged by the United States or by any State on account of race, color, or previous condition of servitude.

SECTION 2. The Congress shall have power to enforce this article by appropriate legislation.

DOCUMENT 13:
Lithograph, Fifteenth Amendment, 1871.

Courtesy Library of Congress.

This image depicts President Ulysses S. Grant at a large table signing the Fifteenth Amendment surrounded by vignettes showing African Americans in school, on the farm, and at the voting booth.

DOCUMENT 14:
Cartoon, Jim Crow, ca. 1870s.

Courtesy Library of Congress.

This cartoon presents a common depiction of Jim Crow as a minstrel figure, a white man in blackface who mimicked stereotypical and comedic behavior of blacks. Minstrel shows, which began in the 1830s and remained popular through the turn of the century,

Document 13

were one of the first forms of musical theater created in America. African Americans were often portrayed as bumbling fools who were unproductive members of society because they passed time by singing and dancing. In his book *Blackface,* Michael Rogin argues that minstrel shows not only dehumanized blacks, but also allowed whites to explore fantasies such as sexual desire, laziness, and leisure that were largely shunned by the middle classes.

DOCUMENT 15:
Lithograph, "The Shackle Broken by the Genius of Freedom," 1874.

Courtesy Library of Congress.

This lithograph commemorates South Carolina congressman Robert B. Elliott's speech in favor of the Civil Rights Act, which

Document 14

was delivered in the House of Representatives on January 6, 1874. Born in Liverpool, England, Elliott was an African American member of the forty-second and forty-third U.S. House of Representatives from South Carolina. He had served in the South Carolina House of Representatives, as assistant adjutant-general, and as the South Carolina attorney general. After Reconstruction, he moved to New Orleans and established a private law practice.

Document 15

DOCUMENT 16:
Civil Rights Act of 1875, 18 Stat. 335.

This legislation, guaranteeing the same treatment in public accommodations regardless of race, color, or previous condition of servitude, was introduced by Senator Charles Sumner and Congressman Benjamin F. Butler in 1870 and passed five years later on March 1, 1875. In 1883, the Supreme Court declared that Congress could not regulate conduct and transactions between private individuals, thus declaring the act unconstitutional.

An Act to Protect All Citizens in Their Civil and Legal Rights.

Whereas it is essential to just government we recognize the equality of all men before the law, and hold that it is the duty of government in its dealings with the people to mete out equal and exact justice to all, of whatever nativity, race, color, or persuasion, religious or political; and it being the appropriate object of legislation to enact great fundamental principles into law: Therefore,

Be it enacted by the Senate and House of Representatives of the United States of American in Congress assembled, That all persons within the jurisdiction of the United States shall be entitled to the full and equal enjoyment of the accommodations, advantages, facilities, and privileges of inns, public conveyances on land or water, theaters, and other places of public amusement; subject only to the conditions and limitations established by law, and applicable alike to citizens of every race and color, regardless of any previous condition of servitude.

SECTION 2. That any person who shall violate the foregoing section by denying to any citizen, except for reasons by law applicable to citizens of every race and color, and regardless of any previous condition of servitude, the full enjoyment of any of the accommodations, advantages, facilities, or privileges in said section enumerated, or by aiding or inciting such denial, shall, for every offence, forfeit and pay the sum of five hundred dollars to the person aggrieved thereby, to be recovered in an action of debt, with full costs; and shall also, for every such offense, be deemed guilty of a misdemeanor, and, upon conviction thereof, shall be fined not less than five hundred nor more than one thousand dollars, or shall be imprisoned not less than thirty days nor more than one year: Provided, that all persons may elect to sue for the State under their rights at common law and by State statutes; and having so elected to proceed in the one mode or the other, their right to proceed in the other jurisdiction shall be barred. But this proviso shall not apply to criminal proceedings, either under this act or the criminal law of any State: And provided further, That a judgment for the penalty in favor of the party aggrieved, or a judgment upon an indictment, shall be a bar to either prosecution respectively.

SECTION 3. That the district and circuit courts of the United States shall have, exclusively of the courts of the several States, cognizance of all crimes and offenses against, and violations of, the provisions of this act; and actions for the penalty given by the preceding section may be prosecuted in the territorial, district, or circuit courts of the United States wherever the defendant may be found, without regard to the other party; and the district attorneys, marshals, and deputy marshals of the United States, and commissioners appointed by the circuit and territorial courts of the United States, with powers of arresting and imprisoning or bailing offenders against the laws of the United States, are hereby specially authorized and required to institute proceedings against every person who shall violate the provisions of this act, and cause him to be arrested and imprisoned or bailed, as the case may be, for trial before such court of the United States, or territorial court, as by law has cognizance of the offense, except in respect of the right of action accruing to the person aggrieved; and such district attorneys shall cause such proceedings to be prosecuted to their termination as in other cases: Provided, That nothing contained in this section shall be construed to deny or defeat any right of civil action accruing to any person, whether by reason of this act or otherwise; and any district attorney who shall willfully fail to institute and prosecute the proceedings herein required, shall, for every such offense, forfeit and pay the sum of five hundred dollars to the person aggrieved thereby, to be recovered by an action of debt, with full costs, and shall, on conviction thereof, be deemed guilty of a misdemeanor, and be fined not less than one thousand nor more than five thousand dollars: And provided further, That a judgment for the penalty in favor of the party aggrieved against any such district attorney, or a judgment upon an indictment against any such district attorney, shall be a bar to either prosecution respectively.

SECTION 4. That no citizen possessing all other qualification which are or may be prescribed by law shall be disqualified for service as grand or petit juror in any court of the United States, or of any State, on account of race, color, or previous condition of servitude; and any officer or other person charged with any duty in the selection or summoning of jurors who shall exclude or fail to summon any citizen for the cause aforesaid shall, on conviction thereof, be deemed guilty of a misdemeanor, and be fined not more than five thousand dollars.

SECTION 5. That all cases arising under the provisions of this act in the courts of the United States shall be reviewable by the Supreme Court of the United States, without regard to the sum in controversy, under the same provisions and regulations as are now provided by law for the review of other causes in said court.

Approved, March 1, 1875.

DOCUMENT 17:
Civil Rights Cases, Supreme Court 109 U.S. 3, 1883.

The Civil Rights Cases, as the five legal cases in which African Americans sued for access to public facilities came to be known, were combined and reviewed by the Supreme Court in 1883. The majority decision, written by Justice Joseph P. Bradley, claimed that equal protection promised by the Fourteenth Amendment did not allow Congress power to regulate private acts. Writing for the dissent, Justice John Marshall Harlan, who would later write the dissent for *Plessy v. Feguson,* argued: "The one underlying purpose of congressional legislation has been to enable the black race to take the rank of mere citizens." This decision ushered in the Jim Crow era by allowing segregation in employment, housing, and public facilities.

---

1. The 1st and 2d sections of the Civil Rights Act passed March 1st, 1876, are unconstitutional enactments as applied to the several States, not being authorized either by the XIIIth or XIVth Amendments of the Constitution

2. The XIVth Amendment is prohibitory upon the States only, and the legislation authorized to be adopted by Congress for enforcing it is not direct legislation on the matters respecting which the States are prohibited from making or enforcing certain laws, or doing certain acts, but is corrective legislation such as may be necessary or proper for counteracting and redressing the effect of such laws or acts. [p4]

3. The XIIIth Amendment relates only to slavery and involuntary servitude (which it abolishes), and, although, by its reflex action, it establishes universal freedom in the United States, and Congress may probably pass laws directly enforcing its provisions, yet such legislative power extends only to the subject of slavery and its incidents, and the denial of equal accommodations in inns, public conveyances, and places of pub-

lic amusement (which is forbidden by the sections in question), imposes no badge of slavery or involuntary servitude upon the party but at most, infringes rights which are protected from State aggression by the XIVth Amendment.

4. Whether the accommodations and privileges sought to be protected by the 1st and 2d sections of the Civil Rights Act are or are not rights constitutionally demandable, and if they are, in what form they are to be protected, is not now decided.

5. Nor is it decided whether the law, as it stands, is operative in the Territories and District of Columbia, the decision only relating to its validity as applied to the States.

6. Nor is it decided whether Congress, under the commercial power, may or may not pass a law securing to all persons equal accommodations on lines of public conveyance between two or more States.

These cases were all founded on the first and second sections of the Act of Congress known as the Civil Rights Act, passed March 1st, 1875, entitled "An Act to protect all citizens in their civil and legal rights." 18 Stat. 335. Two of the cases, those against Stanley and Nichols, were indictments for denying to persons of color the accommodations and privileges of an inn or hotel; two of them, those against Ryan and Singleton, were, one on information, the other an indictment, for denying to individuals the privileges and accommodations of a theatre, the information against Ryan being for refusing a colored person a seat in the dress circle of Maguire's theatre in San Francisco, and the indictment against Singleton was for denying to another person, whose color was not stated, the full enjoyment of the accommodations of the theatre known as the Grand Opera House in New York, "said denial not being made for any reasons by law applicable to citizens of every race and color, and regardless of any previous condition of servitude."

The case of Robinson and wife against the Memphis & Charleston R.R. Company was an action brought in the Circuit Court of the United States for the Western District of Tennessee to recover the penalty of five hundred dollars [p5] given by the second section of the act, and the gravamen was the refusal by the conductor of the railroad company to allow the wife to ride in the ladies' car, for the reason, as stated in one of the counts, that she was a person of African descent. The jury rendered a verdict for the defendants in this case upon the merits, under a charge of the court to which a bill of exceptions was taken by the plaintiffs. The case was tried on the assumption by both parties of the validity of the act of Congress, and the principal point made by the exceptions was that the judge allowed evidence to go to the jury tending to show that the conductor had reason to suspect that the plaintiff, the wife, was an improper person because she was in company with a young man whom he supposed to be a white man, and, on that account, inferred that there was some improper connection between them, and the judge charged the jury, in substance, that, if this was the conductor's *bona fide* reason for excluding the woman from the car, they might take it into consideration on the question of the liability of the company. The case was brought here by writ of error at the suit of the plaintiffs. The cases of Stanley, Nichols, and Singleton came up on certificates of division of opinion between the judges below as to the constitutionality of the first and second sections of the act referred to, and the case of Ryan on a writ of error to the judgment of the Circuit Court for the District of California sustaining a demurrer to the information.

The Stanley, Ryan, Nichols, and Singleton cases were submitted together by the solicitor general at the last term of court, on the 7th day of November, 1882. There were no appearances, and no briefs filed for the defendants.

The Robinson case was submitted on the briefs at the last term, on the 9th day of March, 1883.

DOCUMENT 18:
Act passed by the General Assembly of the State of Louisiana, No. 111, July 10, 1890.

This act required separate accommodations for blacks and whites on railroads, with the provision that they remain equal. As a result, black and white residents of New Orleans established the Citizen's Committee to Test the Separate Car Act to fight to repeal the law. Radical Republican jurist Albion W. Tourgee took the case on the committee's behalf and enlisted Homer Plessy, who was one-

eighth black, to serve as plaintiff. They selected Plessy to challenge
the law because his race was ambiguous. They lost the case, *Plessy
v. Ferguson,* with a seven to one Supreme Court decision in 1896.

To promote the comfort of passengers on railway trains; requiring all
railway companies carrying passengers on their trains, in this State, to
provide equal but separate accommodations for the white and colored
races, by providing separate coaches or compartments so as to secure
separate accommodations; defining the duties of the officers of such
railways; directing them to assign passengers to the coaches or compartment set aside for the use of the race to which such passengers belong;
authorizing them to refuse to carry on their train such passengers as
may refuse to occupy the coaches or compartments to which he or she
is assigned; to exonerate such railway companies from any and all blame
or damages that might proceed or result from such a refusal; to prescribe
penalties for all violations of this act; to put this act into effect ninety
days after its promulgation, and to repeal all other laws or parts of laws
contrary to or inconsistent with the provisions of this act.

SECTION 1. *Be it enacted by the General Assembly of the State of Louisiana,*
That all railway companies carrying passengers in their coaches in this
State, shall provide equal but separate accommodations for the white,
and colored races, by providing two or more passenger coaches for each
passenger train, or by dividing the passenger coaches by a partition so
as to secure separate accommodations; *provided* that this section shall
not be construed to apply to street railroads. No person or persons, shall
be permitted to occupy seats in coaches, other than, the ones, assigned,
to them on account of the race they belong to.

SECTION 2. *Be it further enacted etc.,* That the officers of such passenger
trains shall have power and are hereby required to assign each passenger
to the coach or compartment used for the race to which such passenger
belongs; any passenger insisting on going into a coach or compartment
to which by race he does not belong, shall be liable to a fine of twenty-
five dollars or in lieu thereof to imprisonment for a period of not more
than twenty days in the parish prison and any officer of any railroad insisting on assigning a passenger to a coach or compartment other than the

one set aside for the race to which said passenger belongs shall be liable to a fine of twenty-five dollars or in lieu thereof to imprisonment for a period of not more than twenty days in the parish prison; and should any passenger refuse to occupy the coach or compartment to which he or she is assigned by the officer of such railway, said officer shall have power to refuse to carry such passenger on his train, and for such refusal neither he nor the railway company which he represents shall be liable for damagers in any of the courts of this State.

SECTION 3. *Be it further enacted etc.*, That all officers and directors of railway companies that shall refuse or neglect to comply with the provisions and requirements of this act shall be deemed guilty of a misdemeanor and shall upon conviction before any court of competent jurisdiction be fined not less than one hundred dollars nor more than five hundred dollars; and any conductor of other employees of such passenger train, having charge of the same, who shall refuse or neglect to carry out the provisions of this act shall on conviction be fined not less than twenty-five dollars nor more than fifty dollars for each offense; all railroad corporations carrying passengers in this State other than street railroads shall keep this law posted up in a conspicuous place in each passenger coach and ticket office, provided that nothing in this act shall be construed as applying to nurses attending to children of the other race.

SECTION 4. *Be it further enacted etc.*, That all laws or parts of laws contrary to or inconsistent with the provisions of this act be and the same are hereby repealed, and that this act shall take effect and be in full force ninety days after its promulgation.

S. P. HENRY,
Speaker of the House of Representatives.

JAMES JEFFRIES,
Lieut. Governor and President of the Senate.

Approved July 10th, 1890.

Frances T. Nichols
Governor of the State of Louisiana.

A true copy for the original:
L. F. MASON,
Secretary of State.

DOCUMENT 19:
Plessy v. Ferguson, 163 U.S. 537, 1896.

This landmark decision upheld the doctrine of "separate but equal" that codified segregation and Jim Crow in America. With a vote of seven to one, Justice Henry Billings Brown wrote the majority opinion supporting the Louisiana statue, stating that segregated railroad cars did not violate the Fourteenth Amendment. The dissent came from Justice John Marshall Harlan, a former slaveholder, who argued that segregation undermined the color-blind spirit of the Constitution. The *Plessy* decision, excerpted here, remained the standard until *Brown v. Board of Education* in 1954, which desegregated public schools and helped end the Jim Crow era. For the full text of the decision, visit http://www.ourdocuments.gov/doc.php?flash=true&doc=52&page=transcript.

Supreme Court of the United States,
No. 210, October Term, 1895.

Homer Adolph Plessy,
Plaintiff in Error,
vs.
J.H. Ferguson, Judge of Section "A"
Criminal District Court for the Parish of Orleans

In Error to the Supreme Court of the State of Louisiana

This cause came on to be heard on the transcript of the record from the Supreme Court of the State of Louisiana, and was argued by counsel.

On consideration whereof, It is now here ordered and adjudged by this Court that the judgement of the said Supreme Court, in this cause, be and the the same is hereby, affirmed with costs.

per Mr. Justice Brown,
May 18, 1896.

Dissenting:
Mr. Justice Harlan

(Transcription of Opinion of the Supreme Court of the United States in Plessy v. Ferguson.)

U.S. Supreme Court
PLESSY v. FERGUSON, 163 U.S. 537 (1896)

163 U.S. 537
PLESSY v. FERGUSON.
No. 210.

May 18, 1896.
This was a petition for writs of prohibition and certiorari originally filed in the supreme court of the state by Plessy, the plaintiff in error, against the Hon. John H. Ferguson, judge of the criminal district court for the parish of Orleans, and setting forth, in substance, the following facts:

That petitioner was a citizen of the United States and a resident of the state of Louisiana, of mixed descent, in the proportion of seven-eighths Caucasian and one-eighth African blood; that the mixture of colored blood was not discernible in him, and that he was entitled to every recognition, right, privilege, and immunity secured to the citizens of the United States of the white race by its constitution and laws; that on June 7, 1892, he engaged and paid for a first-class passage on the East Louisiana Railway, from New Orleans to Covington, in the same state, and thereupon entered a passenger train, and took possession of a vacant seat in a coach where passengers of the white race were accommodated; that such railroad company was incorporated by the laws of Louisiana as a common carrier, and was not authorized to distinguish between citizens according to their race, but, notwithstanding this, petitioner was required by the conductor, under penalty of ejection from said train and imprisonment, to vacate said coach, and occupy another seat, in a coach assigned by said company for persons not of the white race, and for no other reason than that petitioner was of the colored race; that, upon petitioner's refusal to comply with such order, he was, with the aid of a police officer, forcibly ejected from said coach, and hurried off to, and imprisoned in, the parish jail of New Orleans, and there held to answer a charge made by such officer to the effect that he was guilty of having criminally violated an act of the general assembly of the state, approved July 10, 1890, in such case made and provided.

The petitioner was subsequently brought before the recorder of the city for preliminary examination, and committed for trial to the criminal district court for the parish of Orleans, where an information was filed against him in the matter above set forth, for a violation of the above act, which act the petitioner affirmed to be null and void, because in conflict with the constitution of the United States; that petitioner interposed a plea to such information, based upon the unconstitutionality of the act of the general assembly, to which the district attorney, on behalf of the state, filed a demurrer; that, upon issue being joined upon such demurrer and plea, the court sustained the demurrer, overruled the plea, and ordered petitioner to plead over to the facts set forth in the information, and that, unless the judge of the said court be enjoined by a writ of prohibition from further proceeding in such case, the court will proceed to fine and sentence petitioner to imprisonment, and thus deprive him of his constitutional rights set forth in his said plea, notwithstanding the unconstitutionality of the act under which he was being prosecuted; that no appeal lay from such sentence, and petitioner was without relief or remedy except by writs of prohibition and certiorari. Copies of the information and other proceedings in the criminal district court were annexed to the petition as an exhibit.

Upon the filing of this petition, an order was issued upon the respondent to show cause why a writ of prohibition should not issue, and be made perpetual, and a further order that the record of the proceedings had in the criminal cause be certified and transmitted to the supreme court.

To this order the respondent made answer, transmitting a certified copy of the proceedings, asserting the constitutionality of the law, and averring that, instead of pleading or admitting that he belonged to the colored race, the said Plessy declined and refused, either by pleading or otherwise, to admit that he was in any sense or in any proportion a colored man.

The case coming on for hearing before the supreme court, that court was of opinion that the law under which the prosecution was had was constitutional and denied the relief prayed for by the petitioner (Ex parte Plessy, 45 La. Ann. 80, 11 South. 948); whereupon petitioner prayed for a writ of error from this court, which was allowed by the chief justice of the supreme court of Louisiana.

Mr. Justice Harlan dissenting.

A. W. Tourgee and S. F. Phillips, for plaintiff in error.

Alex. Porter Morse, for defendant in error.

Mr. Justice BROWN, after stating the facts in the foregoing language, delivered the opinion of the court.

This case turns upon the constitutionality of an act of the general assembly of the state of Louisiana, passed in 1890, providing for separate railway carriages for the white and colored races. Acts 1890, No. 111, p. 152.

The first section of the statute enacts 'that all railway companies carrying passengers in their coaches in this state, shall provide equal but separate accommodations for the white, and colored races, by providing two or more passenger coaches for each passenger train, or by dividing the passenger coaches by a partition so as to secure separate accommodations: provided, that this section shall not be construed to apply to street railroads. No person or persons shall be permitted to occupy seats in coaches, other than the ones assigned to them, on account of the race they belong to.'

By the second section it was enacted 'that the officers of such passenger trains shall have power and are hereby required to assign each passenger to the coach or compartment used for the race to which such passenger belongs; any passenger insisting on going into a coach or compartment to which by race he does not belong, shall be liable to a fine of twenty-five dollars, or in lieu thereof to imprisonment for a period of not more than twenty days in the parish prison, and any officer of any railroad insisting on assigning a passenger to a coach or compartment other than the one set aside for the race to which said passenger belongs, shall be liable to a fine of twenty-five dollars, or in lieu thereof to imprisonment for a period of not more than twenty days in the parish prison; and should any passenger refuse to occupy the coach or compartment to which he or she is assigned by the officer of such railway, said officer shall have power to refuse to carry such passenger on his train, and for such refusal neither he nor the railway company which he represents shall be liable for damages in any of the courts of this state.'

The third section provides penalties for the refusal or neglect of the officers, directors, conductors, and employees of railway companies to comply with the act, with a proviso that 'nothing in this act shall be construed as applying to nurses attending children of the other race.' The fourth section is immaterial.

The information filed in the criminal district court charged, in substance, that Plessy, being a passenger between two stations within the state of Louisiana, was assigned by officers of the company to the coach used for the race to which he belonged, but he insisted upon going into a coach used by the race to which he did not belong. Neither in the information nor plea was his particular race or color averred.

The petition for the writ of prohibition averred that petitioner was seven-eights Caucasian and one-eighth African blood; that the mixture of colored blood was not discernible in him; and that he was entitled to every right, privilege, and immunity secured to citizens of the United States of the white race; and that, upon such theory, he took possession of a vacant seat in a coach where passengers of the white race were accommodated, and was ordered by the conductor to vacate said coach, and take a seat in another, assigned to persons of the colored race, and, having refused to comply with such demand, he was forcibly ejected, with the aid of a police officer, and imprisoned in the parish jail to answer a charge of having violated the above act.

The constitutionality of this act is attacked upon the ground that it conflicts both with the thirteenth amendment of the constitution, abolishing slavery, and the fourteenth amendment, which prohibits certain restrictive legislation on the part of the states. . . .

CHAPTER 2

Building Jim Crow

Jim Crow was not a single federal law, but a series of state, local, and county statutes, as well as unwritten codes of conduct, that evolved into a restrictive, punitive system of widespread segregation, created in the North and later concentrated in the American South. The documents in this section present a wide range of perspectives on the laws themselves and the social, scientific, and cultural ideas that gave them widespread support.

DOCUMENT 20:
Cartoon, "Out in the Cold," *The Judge,* March 22, 1884.

Courtesy Library of Congress.

This cartoon was printed on the cover of *The Judge,* a magazine founded in 1881 by artists who had left the popular comic magazine *Puck.* It struggled in competition with *Puck,* and the Republican Party ultimately offered the magazine financial support. *The Judge* thrived in the 1880s and 1890s. *Puck* ceased publication in 1918, while *The Judge* survived into the 1930s. This particular cartoon reminded readers that suffrage was not universal; in fact, Chinese immigrants and women in the 1880s were still isolated from the political process, while the Irish, African American men, and other immigrant groups enjoyed this right of citizenship. Women would not gain the vote until the Nineteenth Amendment was passed in 1920.

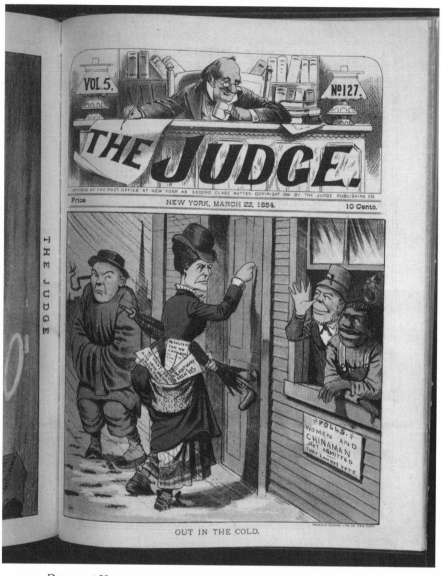

OUT IN THE COLD.

Document 20

DOCUMENT 21:
Edmund Kirke, "How Shall the Negro Be Educated?" *North American Review* 360 (November 1886): 421–426.

Prolific writer and abolitionist James R. Gilmore, writing under the pseudonym Edmund Kirke, was a noted author and man of letters. His best-known work is *Among the Pines*. In this article, he extols the virtue of freedom for blacks, but goes on to describe how freedom has contributed among many to indolence and idleness. Critical of classical education for former slaves, Kirke claims for blacks, "They learn the words as a parrot learns them, but of the ideas the words convey they have no comprehension." His remedy is vocational training in sewing, carpentry, mechanics, and cooking.

THERE is no better position from which to observe the present condition of the Southern negroes than Knoxville, Tennessee, and there, I think, the problem has been solved of how they should be educated. They flock to that city from all quarters, house-servants from Virginia and plantation-hands from Georgia and the Carolinas, drawn, doubtless, by reports that in this Republican region they will be able to work out their material salvation in the utmost freedom, and without any unfriendly interference from the white man. In no Northern town have they larger liberty, or more perfect freedom to develop whatever of manhood or womanhood is in them. They do not lack for employment, are generally preferred as house-servants and mechanics to the wretched white labor, and they mingle freely with the whites in the street-cars and in places of public gathering. On the steam railways they are restricted to separate cars or compartments, and they have their own schools and churches; but this last thing is of their own choosing. My observation is that, when left to himself, the negro prefers to keep with his own kind, both in social intercourse and in religious assembling.

About six thousand have gathered together in Knoxville, and from this large number, drawn, as I have said, from all quarters, we should be able to judge of the effect which freedom has upon the race when placed in a condition where their liberty is restricted only by a due regard for the rights of others. I think no candid observer will deny that, with nearly all who have had the previous discipline of slavery, the effect has been to not only improve their physical condition but to elevate their moral character—to make of them better husbands and fathers, and more useful members of the community. But this remark will not so generally apply to the Georgia and Carolina field-hands. When a slave in the far South, the plantation negro was but little better than a brute, and freedom has not lifted him at once above a mere animal condition. He will still mistake other people's property for his own, drink more whisky than is good for him, loll lazily in the sunshine, and do only just enough work to keep his soul and body together. Doubtless he was a better producer when he worked under the lash of an overseer; but I question if he was then so much of a man as he is now in freedom. He gives, no doubt, too free a rein to his natural indolence, but I have noticed that he does this only in his prime, when he need have no great anxiety about the morrow. When he sees old age creeping upon him he bestirs himself, takes to more frugal and industrious ways, and he thinks of a roof to cover him, and a grave in which to lay his bones. For two hundred years he has moved the wheels of the Southern civilization, but it is not likely that the car will stop, or get permanently off the track, if he now indulges himself in a short holiday. His indolence harms no one but himself; and, when he shall realize what work is doing for others he will arouse himself, and develop a better manhood.

But the town negroes, and such plantation-hands as I have seen from Virginia and the upper Carolinas—where they were well trained when in slavery—do work, and work as well as any white people. I have met very many of them who have accumulated comfortable little properties —snug homes, with money laid by for a rainy day, or to educate their children. They are uniformly frugal, industrious, self-respecting, and law-abiding, and I know of some who have developed traits that would be deemed very creditable in a white man. I could name scores of instances, but one is enough to show that there is genuine manhood in the negro. I have in mind a coal-black-fellow, who, when he was about twenty, heard that Lee had surrendered, and he was a freeman. But the event that made him free reduced his mistress to poverty. Her husband had been killed in the war, and all her property being in slaves, she was now left penniless, with a small family dependent upon her. Naturally, she was appalled at the desolate outlook. But this black freeman said to her: "Cheer up, mistress, and doan't griebe. I knows how massa used ter make de nostrums. I'll make 'em, and I'll sell 'em, and 'fore long I'll hab you as well off as you eber was." And he did do it. The master had been a physician who had found the concocting of medicine of more profit than a regular practice. The ex-slave followed in his footsteps, and soon places his mistress in comparative affluence. Almost any week he may now be seen in the streets of Knoxville, with a gaudily-painted wagon and gaily-caparisoned horses, vending nostrums which he warrants to cure "pains and aches, and scalds and burns, and in short, sir, all the ills that flesh is heir to."

This itinerant nostrum-vendor is only one of a multitude I could name, who have demonstrated that freedom has been unalloyed blessing to every black that has known how to use it. To all others it has been anything but a blessing; and among these others must be included nearly the whole of the rising generation. They are coming up idle, thriftless, and with a contempt for work that is deplorable in their circumstances. They are not ashamed to be parasites, feeding upon the sweat-sprinkled bread of some hard-working father or mother, and too often they fall into the dissipation and vice that are fostered by idleness. To them—the very class who were expected to profit most from emancipation—freedom is proving an almost unmitigated evil; and this through no fault of freedom. This unfortunate result is partly owing to the mistaken ambition of the ex-slaves, who, having experienced the evils of ignorance, are passionately desirous that their children shall know, as one expressed it to me, "all dar am in de books, sar;" but it is mainly to be attributed to the ill-directed philanthropy of those excellent Northern people who have founded schools at the South to give the negro the "advantages of a classical education." Because the system operates well in the North they conclude it will work equally well in the South; and they teach Latin, astronomy, geology, and the mathematics to colored boys and girls to whom such knowledge can never be of any practical value, and they neglect giving them instruction in such branches as will be of daily use in their future lives. Upon this wrong system the work was begun, and, the fashion having once been set, it has so continued, till now this "higher education," as it is called, is being applied to a majority of the rising generation, unfitting them for useful work, and giving them ideas altogether unsuited to their condition in life.

The highest education, I take it, is that which fits man and woman to do most worthily and well the duties that pertain to the station in which they are placed. In the very nature of things the larger number of Southern blacks must be house-servants and farm-laborers, or else pursue some form of mechanical industry. Not one of them in one hundred, old or young, is now a good and skillful worker in any of these employments, and it must be evident that, if we would do them genuine service, we should give them instruction in those branches which enter into the duties of their daily lives. Of course, they should be taught the common English branches, and to such as show a capacity for intellectual pursuits should be given a higher instruction; but not many will show this capacity, for it must be borne in the mind that the negro is now but a child. Two hundred years of ignorance and animalism have so beclouded his intellect that not one in a hundred can so much as understand purely intellectual studies. They learn the words as the parrot learns them, but of the ideas the words convey they have no comprehension. This I have found to be true of every one of the "advanced scholars" I have met among the Southern negroes.

To do essential service to the emancipated blacks, some general system of industrial training is needed, that shall fit them for the pursuits they will of necessity have to follow. That such a system is practicable, and can be universally applied, has been demonstrated by a teacher at Knoxville, who has answered the question, "How shall the negro be educated?" and, in doing so, has solved the problem, "What to do with the Southern blacks." This teacher is a woman—a highly-cultivated and accomplished Northern lady—who, though placed above the necessity of exertion, decided, some sixteen years ago, to put her life to some use by devoting it to the education of the Southern negro. She went South and busied herself among the Knoxville blacks, where the atmosphere was dense with negro soot, and she saw scarcely a single white face in a fortnight. She opened a school, and gathered the negroes about her, attending to their physical needs, counseling them in health and ministering to them in sickness, and giving to their children such instruction as she then thought would make of them useful men and women. At first she was ostracized by the better portion of Knoxville society, and even denied communion by the Christian church to which she took letters of discipleship. These good people did not object to the teaching of blacks. They had reversed their old opinion, that any book-knowledge, however small, is dangerous to the negro; but a woman who would engage in such work must be very "low down," and totally unfit to touch the skirts of her saintly sisterhood. Everywhere the cold shoulder was turned upon her, but the noble woman was not disheartened. She found her society in books, and her consolation in the consciousness that she was doing the Master's work among his perishing children. Even some of those for whom she was sacrificing so much were "unthankful and evil," but, sustained by her high purpose, she worked on, year after year, for twelve long years, until the little children she had taught their A, B, C's had grown up to be men and women, and she was looked up to as a guide, counselor, and friend, by the black population of fully six thousand.

At first she worked under the auspices of the Freedman's Bureau, but, when that was dissolved, she supported her school from her own resources and the contributions of friends in the North. This she did till the black children overflowed her borders, and then she put up a school-building which is altogether the best and most spacious in Knoxville. It is of brick, with large, well-lighted rooms, and is an architectural ornament to the city. When it was completed, thinking to interest the authorities more fully in her work, she donated the building to the city, making the sole condition that the "Austin School" should be forever devoted to the education of the blacks, and should share in the common-school fund of Tennessee.

Thus she worked for twelve years, and then she looked about her to see the fruits of her labors. She saw it in many of her best and brightest scholars—girls who had gone to the bad, and boys who were unfitted for useful work, and actually good for nothing. She had taught the blacks as she would have taught the whites—all the higher branches—and the result she saw was harm instead of good; a large population of young people whose heads were crammed with a learning they did not understand, and who had none of the knowledge that is indispensable to their success in the world. All her disinterested effort seemed to have been misdirected; her twelve years of unrequited toil absolutely wasted. It is not surprising that, for the moment, she was discouraged, almost heart-broken. But she is not a woman to give way to despondency. The evil was no sooner clearly seen than she set about applying the remedy, which lay in training her girls to be good housewives, and her boys to be efficient bread-winners for a family. Doing this, she would teach them less about books and more about life and its daily duties, and thereby qualify them to do well the work that would devolve upon them by the necessities of their condition. At once she opened for girls a sewing-school and a kitchen-garden, in which she taught them simple house-work. Then she established a carpenter's shop for boys, and a cooking-school for both boys and girls. The experiment was successful from the outset, and she soon added other branches to her teaching, till now, at the end of four years, her institution covers about every indus-trial pursuit followed by the negro, except agriculture, and she has been forced to erect another large building for her industrial school, mean-while adding hundreds of skillful workers to a community where skilled labor in any department is always in demand at high wages. Her system, generally adopted, would revolutionize labor in the South, and solve the problem which is now puzzling the heads of the wisest statesmen, namely, "What shall be done with the Southern negro?" Through six-teen long years of prejudice and opposition, often sick in body and weary of soul, this heroic woman has worked at this problem, and the solution she has at last wrought out, in most successful experiment, is this: "Train the negro to do skillful work, and you will make him a good citizen."

DOCUMENT 22:
Speech, Booker T. Washington, "Atlanta Compromise," 1895.

Booker T. Washington, a noted African American orator and edu-cator in the late nineteenth and early twentieth century, delivered this speech at the Cotton States and International Exposition at Piedmont Park in Atlanta on September 18, 1895. To a mainly white audience, he advocated industrial education, in sharp con-trast to the liberal education supported by W.E.B. Du Bois. It came to be known as the "Atlanta Compromise," and remains one of the most influential speeches in American history.

Mr. President and Gentlemen of the Board of Directors and Citizens:

One-third of the population of the South is of the Negro race. No enterprise seeking the material, civil, or moral welfare of this section can disregard this element of our population and reach the highest success. I but convey to you, Mr. President and Directors, the sentiment of the masses of my race when I say that in no way have the value and manhood of the American Negro been more fittingly and generously recognized than by the managers of this magnificent Exposition at every stage of its progress. It is a recognition that will do more to cement the friendship of the two races than any occurrence since the dawn of our freedom.

Not only this, but the opportunity here afforded will awaken among us a new era of industrial progress. Ignorant and inexperienced, it is not strange that in the first years of our new life we began at the top instead of at the bottom; that a seat in Congress or the state legislature was more sought than real estate or industrial skill; that the political convention or stump speaking had more attractions than starting a dairy farm or truck garden.

A ship lost at sea for many days suddenly sighted a friendly vessel. From the mast of the unfortunate vessel was seen a signal, "Water, water; we die of thirst!" The answer from the friendly vessel at once came back, "Cast down your bucket where you are." A second time the signal, "Water, water; send us water!" ran up from the distressed vessel, and was answered, "Cast down your bucket where you are." And a third and fourth signal for water was answered, "Cast down your bucket where you are." The captain of the distressed vessel, at last heeding the injunction, cast down his bucket, and it came up full of fresh, sparkling water from the mouth of the Amazon River. To those of my race who depend on bettering their condition in a foreign land or who underestimate the importance of cultivating friendly relations with the Southern white man, who is their next-door neighbor, I would say: "Cast down your bucket where you are"—cast it down in making friends in every manly way of the people of all races by whom we are surrounded.

Cast it down in agriculture, mechanics, in commerce, in domestic service, and in the professions. And in this connection it is well to bear in mind that whatever other sins the South may be called to bear, when it comes to business, pure and simple, it is in the South that the Negro is given a man's chance in the commercial world, and in nothing is this Exposition more eloquent than in emphasizing this chance. Our greatest danger is that in the great leap from slavery to freedom we may overlook the fact that the masses of us are to live by the productions of our hands, and fail to keep in mind that we shall prosper in proportion as we learn to dignify and glorify common labour, and put brains and skill into the common occupations of life; shall prosper in proportion as we learn to draw the line between the superficial and the substantial, the ornamental gewgaws of life and the useful. No race can prosper till it learns that there is as much dignity in tilling a field as in writing a poem. It is at the bottom of life we must begin, and not at the top. Nor should we permit our grievances to overshadow our opportunities.

To those of the white race who look to the incoming of those of foreign birth and strange tongue and habits for the prosperity of the South, were I permitted I would repeat what I say to my own race, "Cast down your bucket where you are." Cast it down among the eight millions of Negroes whose habits you know, whose fidelity and love you have tested in days when to have proved treacherous meant the ruin of your firesides. Cast down your bucket among these people who have, without strikes and labour wars, tilled your fields, cleared your forests, built your railroads and cities, and brought forth treasures from the bowels of the earth, and helped make possible this magnificent representation of the progress of the South. Casting down your bucket among my people, helping and encouraging them as you are doing on these grounds, and to education of head, hand, and heart, you will find that they will buy your surplus land, make blossom the waste places in your fields, and run your factories. While doing this, you can be sure in the future, as in the past, that you and your families will be surrounded by the most patient, faithful, law-abiding, and unresentful people that the world has seen. As we have proved our loyalty to you in the past, in nursing your children, watching by the sick-bed of your mothers and fathers, and often following them with tear-dimmed eyes to their graves, so in the future, in our humble way, we shall stand by you with a devotion that no foreigner can approach, ready to lay down our lives, if need be, in defense of yours, interlacing our industrial, commercial, civil, and religious life with yours in a way that shall make the interests of both races one. In all things that are purely social we can be as separate as the fingers, yet one as the hand in all things essential to mutual progress.

There is no defense or security for any of us except in the highest intelligence and development of all. If anywhere there are efforts tending to curtail the fullest growth of the Negro, let these efforts be turned into stimulating, encouraging, and making him the most useful and intelligent citizen. Effort or means so invested will pay a thousand per cent interest. These efforts will be twice blessed—blessing him that gives and him that takes. There is no escape through law of man or God from the inevitable:

The laws of changeless justice bind Oppressor with oppressed;

And close as sin and suffering joined We march to fate abreast . . .

Nearly sixteen millions of hands will aid you in pulling the load upward, or they will pull against you the load downward. We shall constitute one-third and more of the ignorance and crime of the South, or one-third [of] its intelligence and progress; we shall contribute one-third to the business and industrial prosperity of the South, or we shall prove a veritable body of death, stagnating, depressing, retarding every effort to advance the body politic.

Gentlemen of the Exposition, as we present to you our humble effort at an exhibition of our progress, you must not expect overmuch. Starting thirty years ago with ownership here and there in a few quilts and pumpkins and chickens (gathered from miscellaneous sources), remember the path that has led from these to the inventions and production of agricultural implements, buggies, steam-engines, newspapers, books, statuary, carving, paintings, the management of drug stores and banks, has not been trodden without contact with thorns and thistles. While we take pride in what we exhibit as a result of our independent efforts, we do not for a moment forget that our part in this exhibition would fall far short of your expectations but for the constant help that has come to our educational life, not only from the Southern states, but especially from Northern philanthropists, who have made their gifts a constant stream of blessing and encouragement.

The wisest among my race understand that the agitation of questions of social equality is the extremest folly, and that progress in the enjoyment of all the privileges that will come to us must be the result of severe and constant struggle rather than of artificial forcing. No race that has anything to contribute to the markets of the world is long in any degree ostracized. It is important and right that all privileges of the law be ours, but it is vastly more important that we be prepared for the exercise of these privileges. The opportunity to earn a dollar in a factory just now is worth infinitely more than the opportunity to spend a dollar in an opera-house.

In conclusion, may I repeat that nothing in thirty years has given us more hope and encouragement, and drawn us so near to you of the white race, as this opportunity offered by the Exposition; and here bending, as it were, over the altar that represents the results of the struggles of your race and mine, both starting practically empty-handed three decades ago, I pledge that in your effort to work out the great and intricate problem which God has laid at the doors of the South, you shall have at all times the patient, sympathetic help of my race; only let this [be] constantly in mind, that, while from representations in these buildings of the product of field, of forest, of mine, of factory, letters, and art, much good will come, yet far above and beyond material benefits will be that higher good, that, let us pray God, will come, in a blotting out of sectional differences and racial animosities and suspicions, in a determination to administer absolute justice, in a willing obedience among all classes to the mandates of law. This, coupled with our material prosperity, will bring into our beloved South a new heaven and a new earth.

DOCUMENT 23:
Clarence H. Poe, "Suffrage Restriction in the South: Its Causes and Consequences," *North American Review* 175 (October 1902): 534–563.

In the *Progressive Farmer* (founded in Winston-Salem, North Carolina, in 1886), Clarence H. Poe details the history of the South since the passage of the Fourteenth Amendment. He presents, in this excerpt of a much longer essay, a relatively typical position that whites, though superior to blacks, owe them "a high duty." The *North American Review* was founded in Boston in 1815 and is the oldest literary magazine published in the United States.

THE political history of the Southern States since the adoption of the Fourteenth Amendment to our national Constitution has been completely dominated by one overshadowing problem, negro suffrage. And with regard to that problem, this period of the South's history may be roughly divided into three epochs:

1. The era of unrestricted negro suffrage, ending about 1875;

2. The era of restriction or control by methods not recognized in the law. This lasted, broadly speaking, from 1875 to 1895;

3. The era of disenfranchisement by State laws, prescribing, as much tests of fitness for the suffrage, qualifications possessed by a much smaller proportion of blacks than of whites. Of this period we have hardly yet reached the end of the beginning.

At this time of changing conditions, therefore, it may not be inappropriate or unprofitable to glance at the more salient features of the two periods that seem to have passed into history, and to examine, with more fulness, the present trend of Southern political affairs.

I.

We shall rapidly pass over the Reconstruction Period, but not so rapidly as to leave unnoticed the fact that some of its legacies linger with us, and that to recollections of this period are due the few traces of sectional animosity that yet exist in the South. Of the great war, when brave men met brave men in open battle, it can be truthfully said that its memories arouse no bitterness; but this is not true of that later period when the victors—thousands of them in a spirit of mistaken philanthropy, many of them carelessly and thoughtlessly, some with malice aforethought—allowed a race only a few generations removed from African barbarism to take the reins of government into its own hands, and humiliate the men and women who had built up the splendid civilizations of the Old South. If, as a well-known magazine editor said some time ago, "there is no period of American history at once so poetic and so full of the atmosphere of chivalric romance as that which the South saw for a score of years prior to 1860," there is, on the other hand, no decade of our history so dark with foolish blunders and foul wrongs as that which this South saw from 1865 to 1875.

Difficult enough for the Southern whites would have been the simpler task of dealing, without outside interference, with the ignorance and recklessness of the newly-enfranchised blacks. A hundredfold more difficult did the task become, when designing plunderers came and found in negro suffrage a cat's-paw admirably adapted to their schemes. Ignorance and Greed having joined hands, corrupt men might make laws, propertyless men might levy taxes, illiterate men might conduct public school work, characterless men might serve as judges. The plunderers cared not; the blacks did not understand; the native whites could not resist the military force that threatened them. The South of Reconstruction days, like the fabled Prometheus, lay chained and helpless while the vultures preyed on her vitals.

Finally, however, time brought the inevitable readjustment. Failure came to the unnatural and irrational scheme of the extremists, from its inception doomed to defeat, and the white man took again the heritage of his fathers.

II.

But if the story of Reconstruction makes unpleasant reading for the Northern man, it is no less true that the Southerner finds much to humiliate him in the story as the succeeding epoch. Irregular election methods were adopted, demagoguery encouraged, bullyism condoned, politics corrupted.

The negroes formed an unchanging political factor. Whatever the politics of the Republican Party or the character of its candidates, the undivided slave-like support of the blacks was assured, and their numbers gave them the power of the majority in that party. Division of the whites, therefore, the Democratic leaders lost no time in pointing out, meant negro rule. Independent voting was denounced; black solidarity was opposed by white solidarity; bigoted partisanship dominated both races. Even when there was no real danger of negro supremacy, the race question, as the "Baltimore Manufacturers' Record" says, "was often made a pretext to keep the white vote solid, and almost to ostracize those who dared to speak their convictions on economic questions, if against the Democratic organization." It was but natural that, out of such conditions, rings and cliques should spring forth; and so it came about that States sorely in need of progressive leadership found themselves in the grasp of oligarchies that stifled freedom and hindered progress. The South lost prestige in national affairs with both political parties, because she no longer considered questions on their merits, but judged them solely by their reaction to the incubus with which she struggled. Such a condition was fatal to statesmanship. In all this period, the South produced no Washington or Jefferson or Marshall or Calhoun or Clay. Such men could not grow in an atmosphere poisoned by such influences, or among a people whose judgment and intellect were kept in subjection by the presence of a negro problem.

Not less demoralizing were the election frauds which bad men practiced and good men often thought it necessary to wink at. Mr. Dixon does not mention it, but I have heard the story of that prominent North Carolina minister known in "The Leopard's Spots" as the Rev. John Durham, saying to the men who were telling him how they propose to overcome the negro majority in his country: "I am a preacher; don't tell me how you're going to win; but remember, you must do it."

I would not extenuate the evils of election frauds; there is probably nothing in our political life more debasing, nothing that strikes more directly at the corner-stone of our liberties. Without fair elections, as ex-Secretary of the Navy Herbert told his Alabama people recently, "the natural outcome of republican government is discontent, unrest, instability, and finally revolution." But, that the reader may get the proper historical perspective, it should be said in passing that the people of the North, as well as those of the South, have at times excused lawlessness as the means to a righteous or popular end. Subsequently, many election frauds were perpetrated in the South for indefensible purposes; but the spirit which caused the people to forget law in their struggle with carpet-bag leaders, was much akin to that which caused Massachusetts Abolitionists of the fifties to nullify fugitive slave laws and justify illegal means of helping runaways. Transferred to the South of the seventies and given a genuine insight into the condition of affairs, these brave New Englanders, moved by their old-time temper, would have joined the Southern white man in the desperate measures adopted by him, answering their critics as before with Lowell's words:

> "We owe allegiance to the State, but deeper, truer, more,
> To the sympathies that God hath set within our spirits' core;

> Our country claims our fealty; we grant it so; but then,
> Before Man made us citizens, great Nature made us men."

At the Charleston Exposition a few months ago, an old man—a man of character and intelligence, a Democrat whose breadth of view was shown by his high praise of President Roosevelt—told me of the Southern Carolina campaign of 1876 that ended the saturnalia of negro rule in that State. "In my precinct," he said, "there was 800 negro or Republican majority, but when the votes were counted it was Wade Hampton who was 800 votes ahead." The old man added, "It had to be done"; and it was clear that he and his co-laborers thought of their work as Cicero thought of his official career, when, asked to take oath that he had done nothing to contrary to the laws, "I swear," said Cicero, "I swear—that I have saved the Republic!"

III.

But there is nothing more uncontrollable than lawlessness. To no certain spheres of activity can you confine it; to no certain periods of time can you limit it. It is subject to no law save that of growth: sow the wind and reap the whirlwind. Wink at your election officer's thievery in times of stress and peril, and next you may have election thievery to aid plundering schemes, or to save the rings and cliques to which the election officer belongs. Give rein to mob violence at a time when you think such action is justifiable, and you will find your reward in a popular contempt for the restraint of law, a permanent injury to public morals.

So thoughtful Southern people soon came to perceive, if they did not understand from the first, the dangerous nature of these methods of dealing with the negro problem. The South had escaped the Black Peril, to be sure; but the baleful spirit of trickery and disorder with which she had leagued herself, and whose aid she had invoked, clave to her with the tenacity of an Old Man of the Sea, haunted and threatened by her like another Mr. Hyde grown too powerful to be controlled by Dr. Jekyll. On the one hand, negro rule endangered peace and safety; on the other hand, the demagogue and trickster were a constant menace.

This was the situation when the Southern whites, taking courage from the waning of Northern bitterness, resolved to steer boldly away from the Scylla and Charybdis between which they had been so long held.

While baser motives actuated some, it was in this spirit that the South, as a whole, began the work of remoulding its suffrage laws. Very rapid has been the progress of this movement; and now, of the Coast States between Maryland and Texas, only two (Georgia and Florida) have not yet adopted so-called "disenfranchised amendments." This, however, is a matter of such recent history, as has been so often explained in the press, that it is unnecessary for me to outline the provisions of these laws or relate the story of their adoption.

What the reader is most interested in is the situation at present and the probably consequences of the new policy.

IV.

The ship so recently launched has hardly yet found herself; the machinery is not yet in good running order. In several States no elections have been held under the new régime, and the dread of national inference has retarded in some degree the coming of the promised good results. Moreover, in some of the States (in South Carolina, for example), the limited legal restriction of the suffrage affords only partial relief, and the old-time Tillmanesque methods remain in force.

Taking a general view, however, the thoughtful observer finds many signs of promise—signs not of a startling or miraculous transformation, but indications of a gradual recovery from our nearly four decades of bondage to the race issue.

First, there are evidences of a healthier public sentiment with regard to dishonest election methods. In this, as in other kindred matters, we cannot expect in a year, nor in five years, complete reform. Fairer election laws have been adopted; but it is not in the letter of the statues, but in the proper popular reverence for the essence of the law, that safety is to be found. That the long-standing abuses will be sloughed off with reasonable rapidity, the awakening of the public conscience, or rather the breaking of the fetters that have bound it, clearly indicates.

Not less surely are the people beginning to exercise greater freedom and tolerance in matters political. The men here and there who say to you, "The negro question is out of the way and I shall vote as I please hereafter," are the pioneers. The newspapers are growing more independent, and many that used to accept with well-feigned grace all men

and measures bearing the image and superscription of the party authorities now manifest a spirit of stubbornness very disheartening to the
bosses. Manufacturers assert their belief in certain political policies and
their readiness to break party ties, if necessary, to further those policies.
Efforts to resuscitate the race issue (evidently for the purpose of stay-
ing the growing spirit of independence) call forth the most emphatic
disapproval. In North Carolina, for example, such an effort recently
made the by acknowledged head of the Democratic Party in the State,
has been coldly received by the Democratic partisan press, and has been
plainly condemned by nearly all the independent and religious papers.
This typical comment is from the *"Raleigh Christian Advocate,"* organ of
the North Carolina Methodist Conference:

"No, there are thousands of white men throughout the State who
are determined to vote hereafter for men and principles rather than by
the color line, and the fact might as well be known. They will not have
the negro question thrust on them again."

DOCUMENT 24:
William I. Thomas, "The Psychology of Race-Prejudice," *American Journal of Sociology* 9, no. 5 (March 1904): 593-611.

Written by an eminent University of Chicago sociologist, this is
but one of the many examples of "scientific racism," a theory that
held that an individual's race determines behavior. Although bas-
ing his theories on faulty science, William I. Thomas was a well-
respected scholar of the day who felt he was merely seeking the
truth and likely had little interest in supporting segregation. This
is an excerpt of the complete article.

I.

IN looking for an explanation of the antipathy which one race feels
toward another, we may first of all inquire whether there are any conditions arising in the course of the biological development of a species
which, aside from social activities, lead to a predilection for those of one's
own kind and a prejudice against organically different groups. And we do,

in fact, find such conditions. The earliest movements of animal life involve, in the rejection of stimulations vitally bad, an attitude which is the analogue of prejudice. On the principle of chemiotaxis, the microorganism will approach a particle of food placed in the water and shun a particle of poison; and its movements are similarly controlled by heat, light, electricity, and other tropic forces. The development of animal life from this point upward consists in the growth of structure and organs of sense adapted to discriminate between different stimulations, to choose between the beneficial and prejudicial, and to obtain in this way a more complete control of the environment. Passing over the lower forms of animal life, we find in the human type the power of attention, memory, and comparison highly developed, so that an estimate is put on stimulations and situations correspondent with the bearing of stimulations or situations of this type on welfare in the past. The choice and rejection involved in this process are accompanied by organic changes (felt as emotions) designed to assist in the action which follows a decision. Both the judgment and the emotions are thus involved on the presentation to the senses of a situation or object involving possible advantage or hurt, pleasure or pain. It consequently transpires that the feelings called out on the presentation of disagreeable objects and their contrary are very different, and there arise in this connection fixed mental attitudes corresponding with fixed or habitually recurrent external situations—hate and love, prejudice and predilection—answering to situations which revive feelings of pain on the one hand, and feelings of pleasure on the other. And such is the working of suggestion that not alone an object or situation may produce a given state of feeling, but a voice, an odor, a color, or any characteristic sign of an object may produce the same effect as the object itself. The sight or smell of blood is an excitant to a bull, because it revives a conflict state of feeling, and even the color of a red rag produces a similar effect.

"Unaccommodated man" was, to begin with, in relations more hostile than friendly. The struggle for food was so serious a fact, and predaciousness to such a degree the habit of life, that a suspicious, hostile, and hateful state of mind was the rule, with exceptions only in the cases where truce, association, and alliance had come about in the course of experience. This was still the state of affairs in so advanced a stage of development as the Indian society of North America, where a tribe was in a state of war with every tribe with which it had not made a treaty of peace; and it is perhaps true, generally speaking, of men today, that they regard others with a degree of distrust and aversion until they have proved themselves good fellows. What, indeed, would be the fate of a man on the streets of a city if he did otherwise? There has, nevertheless, grown up an intimate relation between man and certain portions of his environment, and this includes not only his wife and children, his dog and his blood-brother, but, with lessening intensity, the members of his clan, tribe, and nation. These become, psychologically speaking, a portion of himself, and stand with him against the world at large. From the standpoint here outlined, prejudice or its analogue is the starting-point, and our question becomes one of the determination of the steps of the process by which man mentally allied with himself certain portions of his environment to the exclusion others.

When we come to examine in detail the process by which an associational and sympathetic relation is set up between the individual and certain parts of the outside world to the exclusion of others, we find this at first on a purely instinctive and reflex basis, originating in connection with food-getting and reproduction, and growing more conscious in the higher forms of life. One of the most important origins of association and pre-possession is seen in the relation of parents, particularly of mothers, to children. This begins, of course, among the lower animals. The mammalian class, in particular, is distinguished by the strength and persistence of the devotion of parents to offspring. The advantage secured by the form of reproduction characteristic of man and the other mammals is that a closer connection is secured between the child and the mother. By the intra-uterine form of reproduction the association of mother and offspring is set up in an organic way before the birth of the latter, and is continued and put on a social basis during the period of lactation and the early helpless years of the child. By continuing the helpless period of the young for a period of years, nature has made provision on the time side for a complex physical and mental type, impossible in types thrown at birth on their own resources. Along with the structural modification of the female on account of the intra-uterine form of reproduction and the effort of nature to secure a more complex type and a better chance of survival, there is a corresponding development of the sentiments, and maternal feeling, in particular, is developed as the subjective condition necessary to carrying out the plan of giving the infant a prolonged period of helplessness and play through which its faculties are developed. The scheme would not work if the mother were not more interested in the child than in anything else in the world. In the course of development every variational tendency in mothers to dote on their children was rewarded by the survival of these children, and the consequent survival of the stock, owing to better nutrition, protection, and training. Of course, this inherited interest in children is shared by the males of the group also, though not in the same degree, and there is reason to believe also that the interest of the male parent in children is acquired in a great degree indirectly and socially through his more potent desire to associate with the mother.

This interest and providence on the score of offspring has also a characteristic expression on the mental side. All sense-perceptions are colored and all judgments biased where the child is in question, and affection for it extends to the particular marks which distinguish it. Not only its physical features, but its dress and little shoes, its toys and everything it has touched, take on a peculiar aspect. This tendency of the attention and memory to seize on characteristic aspects, and to be obsessed by them to the exclusion or disparagement of contrasted aspects, is an important condition in the psychology of race-prejudice. It implies a set of conditions in which the attention is practiced in attaching peculiar values to signs of personality—conditions differing also from those arising in the reaction to environment on the food side.

Another origin of a sympathetic attitude toward those of our own kind is seen in connection with courtship. As a result of selection, doubtless, there is a peculiar organic response on the part of either sex to the presence and peculiarities of the other. Among birds the voice, plumage, odor, ornamentation, and movements of the male are in the wooing season powerful excitants to the female. These aspects of the male, which are the most conspicuous of his characteristics, are recognized as the marks of maleness by the female, and she is most deeply impressed, and is in fact won, by the male most conspicuously marked and displaying these marks most skilfully. And in the same way feminine traits and behavior exercise a powerful influence on the male. It is of particular significance just here that the attention is able to single out particular marks of the personality of the opposite sex, and that these marks become the carriers of the whole fund of sexual suggestion. This interest in the characteristic features of the opposite sex has always dominated fashion and ornament to a large extent in human society, and this is particularly true in historical times in connection with women, who are both the objects of sexual attention and the exponents of fashion. The white lady uses rice powder and rouge to emphasize her white-and-pink complexion, and the African lady uses charcoal and fat to enhance the luster of her ebony skin. The most characteristic features of woman—the bust and the pelvis—are brought into greater prominence by lacing, padding, balloon sleeves, pull-backs, hoop-skirts, and other such like devices; and the interest in characteristic expressions of femaleness is even carried over from the person to the objects habitually associated with the person, as when the lover shows a fetishistic regard for the pocket handkerchief or the slipper of his mistress.[1] In this connection Hirn remarks:

> By exaggerating and accentuating in their own appearance the common qualities of the tribe, the individual males or females have thus created a more and more differentiated tribal type. And the inherited predilections and aversions of the opposite sex have, on the other hand, by continuously influencing positive and negative choice, contributed to the fixing of these types as tribal ideals, not of beauty, but of sexual attractiveness.[2]

In both of the conditions growing out of reproduction which we have examined we find a significant tendency to single out characteristic signs of personality and attach an emotional value to them. In still another connection, that of co-operative activity, there is a tendency to knit alliances with others; and here also the attention shows the tendency to fix on characteristic signs and attach emotional values to them. It was pointed out above that the first efforts of the animal to adjust itself to its food environment were on a purely chemical and physical basis, and we find that its first movements toward a combination with other organisms in an associational relation are equally unreflective. This is very well illustrated by the following description of the association of plants and animals growing out of a dearth of water:

> A mesquite springs up on the plain; within two or three years the birds resting in its branches drop the seeds of cacti, some of which, like vines, are unable to stand alone, and the cactus and

---

1. The pathological expressions of this interest are well known to the psychiatrist.

2. HIRN, *Origins of Art*, p. 212.

mesquite combine their armature of thorns for mutual protection. The wind-grown grass seeds lodge about the roots, and grasses grow and seed beneath the sheltering branches; and next small mammals seek the same protection and dig their holes beneath the roots, giving channels for the water to the ensuing rain and fertilizing the spot with *rejectamenta*. Meantime the annual and semi-annual plants which maintain a precarious existence in the desert take root in the sheltered and fertilized soil beneath the growing cactus and mesquite, and in season it becomes a miniature garden of foliage and bloomage. Then certain ants come for seeds, and certain flies and wasps for the nectar, and certain birds to nest in the branches. In this way a community is developed in which each participant retains individuality, yet in which each contributes to the general welfare.[3]

Among mammalian forms, however, an instinctive, if not reflective, appreciation of the presence and personality of others is seen in the fact of gregariousness, and here already a definite meaning is attached to signs of personality. In fact, a certain grade of memory is all that is essential to antipathy or affection. In mankind various practices show a growing "consciousness of kind," there is resort to symbolism to secure and increase the feeling of solidarity, and finally a dependence of emotional states on this symbolism.

Fighting and hunting operations soon make it plain that undertakings otherwise impossible can be accomplished by combining with one's fellows, and that life and safety often depend on friendly aid. A definite and interesting expression of this principle is seen in the widespread rite of blood-brotherhood. Taught by experience the value of a friend in time of danger, man mingles his blood and joins his fortunes with this friend, thus making over into himself a portion of his environment. This rite which may be regarded as a concrete aid to the savage's unpracticed power of abstraction, is in some parts of the world the only sure way of securing the friendship of the natives. Stanley recognized its value fully, and went through the ceremony with above fifty African chiefs. In the universal practice of feud we have another evidence that men engaged in co-operative life come to set the same value on their fellows

3. W. J. McGee, "The Beginnings of Agriculture," *American Anthropologist,* Vol. VIII, p. 350.

as on themselves, and to draw a very sharp line between the social self and not-self. An example will show how strong this contrast becomes in feeling and practice:

> The quarrelsome character of this people [the Berdurani of Afghanistan] and the constant strife that they lead are declared by a mere glance at their villages and fields, which bristle in all directions with round towers. These are constantly occupied with men at enmity with their neighbors in the same or adjoining villages, who, perched in their little shooting boxes, watch the opportunity of putting a bullet into each other's body with the most persevering patience. The fields, even, are studded with these round towers, and the men holding them most jealously guard their lands from anyone with whom they are at feud. If even a fowl strays from its owner into the grounds of another, it is sure to receive a bullet from the adversary's tower. So constant are their feuds that it is a well-known fact that the village children are taught never to walk in the center of the road, but always from the force of habit walk stealthily along under cover of the wall nearest to any tower.[4]

We may be sure that any characteristic of either of these groups, in the way of dress, features, speech, or social practice, would be hateful in the sight of the other; and it is interesting to note that the antipathy extends to the domestic animals.[5]

Tribal marks are another widespread sign of consciousness of community of interest. Scarification, tattooing, bodily mutilations, totemic marks, and other devices of this nature are consciously and unconsciously employed to keep up the feeling of group solidarity; and whether instituted with this end in view or not, any visible marks which become by usage characteristic of the group represent to the group-mind the associational and emotional past of the group. A similar dependence of cultural groups on signs of solidarity is seen in the enthusiasm aroused by the display of the flag of our country or the playing of a national air.

Habit also plays an important role in our emotional attitude toward the unfamiliar. The usual is felt as comfortable and safe, and a sinister view

4. W. W. BILLSON, "The Origin of Criminal Law," *Popular Science Monthly*, Vol. XVI, p. 438, quoting Bellew.

5. Mine enemy's dog, / Though he had bit me, should have stood that night / Against my fire.   —*Lear*, IV, iii, 36.

is taken of the unknown. When things are running along habitual lines, the attention is relaxed and the emotional processes are running low. A disturbance of habit throws a strain on the attention, and the emotional processes are accelerated in the attempt to accommodate. And since the normal attitude, as noted above, is one of distrust toward everything not included in the old run of habits, we find the most sinister meaning attached to signs of unfamiliar personality. The mental disturbance caused in the lower races by the appearance of white has often been noted by travelers:

> There must be something in the appearance of white men frightfully repulsive to the unsophisticated natives of Africa; for on entering villages previously unvisited by Europeans, if we met a child coming quietly and unsuspectingly toward us, the moment he raised his eyes and saw the men in "bags," he would take to his heels in an agony of terror, such as we might feel if we met a live Egyptian mummy at the door of the British Museum. Alarmed by the child's wild outcries, the mother rushes out of the hut, but darts back again at the first glimpse of the fearful apparition. Dogs turn tail and scour off in dismay, and hens, abandoning their chickens, fly screaming to the tops of the houses.[6]

By some such steps as we have outlined a group whose members have a history in common has to some degree a consciousness in common, and common emotional reactions. And before turning to the concrete expressions of its feeling for itself as expressed in its prejudices for aliens, I will illustrate by an instance the degree to which it is true that activities in common and community of interest may imply a common emotional attitude. The reception of news of disaster to a war party of Sioux Indians is thus related by Mr. Eastman, himself a Sioux:

> One frosty morning . . . the weird song of a solitary brave was heard. In an instant the camp was thrown into indescribable confusion. The meaning of this was clear as day to everybody—all of our war party were killed save the one whose mournful song announced the fate of his companions. . . . . . The village was convulsed with grief; for in sorrow as in joy every Indian shares with all the others. The old women stood still wherever they might be

6. LIVINGSTONE, *The Zambesi and its Tributaries*, p. 181.

and wailed dismally, at intervals chanting the praises of the departed warriors. The wives went a little way from their tepees and there audibly mourned; but the young maidens wandered further away from the camp, where no one could witness their grief. The old men joined in the crying and singing. To all appearances the most unmoved of all were the warriors, whose tears must be poured forth in the country of the enemy to embitter their vengeance. These sat silently in their lodges, and strove to conceal their feelings behind a stoical countenance. . . . . The first sad shock over, then came the change of habiliments. In savage usage the outward expression of mourning surpasses that of civilization. The Indian mourner gives up all his good clothing and contents himself with scanty and miserable garments. Blankets are cut in two, and the hair is cropped short. Often a devoted mother will scarify her arms and legs; a sister or a young wife would cut off all her beautiful hair and disfigure herself by undergoing hardships. Fathers and brothers blackened their faces and wore only the shabbiest garments.[7]

II.

If it is assumed, then, that the group comes to have a quasi-personality, and that, like the individual, it is in an attitude of suspicion and hostility toward the outside world, and that, like the individual also, it has a feeling of intimacy with itself, it follows that the signs of unlikeness in another group are regarded with prejudice. It is also a characteristic of the attention that unlikeness is determined by the aid of certain external signs—namely, physical features, dress, speech, social habits, etc.—and that the concrete expressions of prejudice are seen in connection with these. We may therefore examine in more detail the directions taken in the expression of prejudice, and the signs of personality to which it attaches itself, with a view to determining its depth or superficiality, and getting light on the conditions under which it is eradicable or modifiable.

Humboldt was perhaps the first observer to make a general statement on the predilection which every group has for its own peculiarities:

Nations attach the idea of beauty to everything which particularly characterizes their own physical conformation, their national

7. C. A. EASTMAN, *Indian Boyhood*, p. 223.

physiognomy. Hence it ensues that among a people to whom nature has given very little beard, a narrow forehead, and a brownish-red skin, every individual thinks himself handsome in proportion as his body is destitute of hair, his head flattened, his skin more covered with annatto, or chica, or some other copper-red color.[8]

And the more concrete reports of other observers are to the same effect:

Ask a northern Indian what is beauty, and he will answer, a broad flat face, small eyes, high cheek-bones, three or four broad black lines across each cheek, a low forehead, a large broad chin, a clumsy hook nose, a tawny hide, and breasts hanging down to the belt.[9]

Those women are preferred who have the Mandschú form; that is to say, a broad face, high cheek-bones, very broad noses, and enormous ears.[10]

A small round face, full rosy-red cheeks and lips, white forehead, black tresses, and small dark eyes are marks of a Samoyede beauty. Thus in a Samoyedian song a girl is praised for her small eyes, her broad face, and its rosy color.[11]

These three, the most comely among the twenty beauties of Mtesa's court, were of the Wahuma race, no doubt from Ankori. They had the complexion of quadroons, were straight-nosed and thin-lipped, with large lustrous eyes. In the other graces of a beautiful form they excelled, and Hafiz might have said with poetic rapture that they were "straight as palm trees and beautiful as moons." . . . . Mtesa, however, does not believe them to be superior or even equal to his well-fleshed, unctuous-bodied, flat-nosed wives; indeed, when I pointed them out to him one day at a private audience, he even regarded them with a sneer.[12]

8. A. VON HUMBOLDT, *Personal Narrative of Travels to the Equinoctial Regions of America,* ed. BOHN, Vol. I, p. 303.

9. HEARNE, *A Journey from Prince of Wales Fort,* ed. 1796, p. 89.

10. PALLAS, in PRICHARD, *Researches into the Physical History of Mankind,* 4th ed., Vol. IV, p. 519.

11. CASTRÉN, *Nordiska resor och forskningar,* Vol. I, p. 229; in WESTERMARCK, *History of Human Marriage,* p. 262.

12. STANLEY, *Through the Dark Continent,* Vol. I, p. 308.

Taking the physical aspects separately, we find that the color of the skin is among those most obvious to the eye, and consequently one in connection with which prejudice is generally expressed:

> The skin, except among the tribes near Delagoa Bay, is not usually black, the prevailing color being a mixture of black and red, the most common shade being chocolate. Dark complexions, as being most common, are naturally held in the highest esteem. To be told that he is light-colored, or like a white man, would be deemed a very poor compliment by a Kaffir. I have heard of one unfortunate man who was so very fair that no girl would marry him.[13]

> On the western coast, as Mr. Winwood Reade informs me, the negroes admire a very black skin more than one of a lighter tint. But their horror of whiteness may be attributed, according to this same traveler, partly to the belief held by most negroes that demons and spirits are white, and partly to their thinking it a sign of ill-health.[14]

> An Australian woman had a child by a white man: she smoked it and rubbed it with oil to give it a darker color.[15]

> The children that are born [in Mabaar] are black enough, but the blacker they be the more they are thought of; wherefore from the day of their birth their parents do rub them every week with oil of sesamé so that they become as black as devils. Moreover, they make their gods black and their devils white, and the images of their saints they do paint black all over.[16]

... Race-prejudice is an instinct originating in the tribal stage of society, when solidarity in feeling and action were essential to the preservation of the group. It, or some analogue of it, will probably never disappear completely, since an identity of standards, traditions, and physical appearance in all geographical zones is neither possible nor aesthetically desirable. It is, too, an affair which can neither be reasoned with nor legislated about very effectively, because it is connected with the affective, rather

13. SHOOTER, *The Kafirs of Natal and the Zulu Country* p. 1.
14. DARWIN, *Descent of Man,* Part III, chap. 19.
15. WAITZ, *Anthropologie der Naturvölker,* English translation, Vol. I, p. 263.
16. MARCO POLO, *The Book of Marco Polo concerning the Kingdoms and Marvels of the East,* Book III, chap. 18.

than the cognitive, processes. But it tends to become more insignificant as increased communication brings interests and standards in common, and as similar systems of education and equal access to knowledge bring about a greater mental and social parity between groups, and remove the grounds for "invidious distinction." It is, indeed, probable that a position will be reached on the race question similar to the condition now reached among the specialized occupations, particularly among the scientific callings, and also in business, where the individual's ability to get results gives him an interest and a status independent of, and, in point of fact, quite overshadowing, the superficial marks of personality.

DOCUMENT 25:
Robert Bennett Bean, "The Negro Brain," *Century Magazine* 72 (October 1906): 778–784.

Bean, a professor of anatomy at the University of Virginia, espouses a common theory circulated by scientists and social scientists prior to World War I. They argued that African Americans were inferior for physiological reasons, and in Bean's case he argues that the size of the brain distinguishes the races. Despite the spurious nature of his research methodology, his article, excerpted here, was widely hailed by segregationists.

. . . In the ultimate settlement of this imminently critical [race] question the facts of scientific investigation should not be ignored. Not only should an earnest philanthropy and an honest statesmanship be brought to the solution of the negro problem, but the fundamental physical and mental differences of the white and black races should be considered in any rational adjustment of the relations between them, and a just discrimination of the character and genius of each race should be made.

It is an undoubted fact that environment affects the individual more than race, whereas heredity affects the race more than the individual. Individuals may be altered without altering the race. By both heredity and environment we may explain the greatness of certain men like [Alexander] Dumas, Booker Washington, [Bishop Benjamin T.] Tanner, and Professor [W.E.B.] Dubois, who are classed as negroes, but are not pure negroes ethnically. . . .

The subject in all its phases cannot be considered here, but the attention of the reader may be directed to one or two significant facts. The first is that the negro race is now considered to be one of the oldest races in the world, evidences of its existence in prehistoric times having been recently discovered throughout Africa, Australia, and Oceania. In historic times negroes are depicted on the monuments of Egypt thousands of years before the Anglo-Saxon had emerged from barbarism. They have been in contact continually with the highest civilizations of antiquity, but have never risen to the eminence of other nations, having retained their primitive condition, even as is now apparent in the Southern States, where they are isolated in large masses.

Another significant fact is that the negro brain in smaller than the Caucasian, the difference in size being represented in both gray matter (nerve cells) and white matter (nerve fibers), as I will attempt presently to demonstrate. Brain cells are the basis of brain power or mental ability, and their number is known to remain constant throughout life, so that there seems never to be a degree of mental development beyond the possible expression of the brain cells inherited. Development of mental activity by experience, education, etc., is considered to be correlated with the development of sheaths around the nerve fibers as they become active in the transmission of impulses. The efficiency of the brain depends upon the number and position of such nerve fibers, just as the efficiency of a telephone system depends upon the number of its various connections and ramifications. The negro brain having fewer nerve cells and nerve fibers, assuming that gray matter and white matter respectively represent these numerically, the possibilities of developing the negro are therefore limited, except by crossing with other races. This has been done to such an extent in times past that it is difficult to determine whether a pure negro really exists in America. . . .

[My discussion] of the American negro is based upon an intimate study at close range of thousands of individuals in various parts of the South and the North, and it has been confirmed by the careful inspection and measurement of one hundred and three brains, individuals of various classes presenting, according to my observations, recognizable differences in their brain development. I do not purpose to enter into a discussion of these differences here, but desire to consider the larger questions as to differences of brain development in the negro and the white as demonstrated by a comparison of the negro brains mentioned above with forty-nine brains of American Caucasians. . . .

[EDITORS NOTE: Bean then presents his data on black and white brains, based on faulty measurements, analysis, and conclusions.]

The Caucasian has the subjective faculties well developed; the negro, the objective. The Caucasian, and more particularly the Anglo-Saxon, is dominant and domineering, and possessed primarily with determination, will power, self-control, self-government, and all the attributes of the subjective self, with a high development of the ethical and esthetic faculties and great reasoning powers. The negro is in direct contrast by reason of a certain lack of these powers, and a great development of the objective qualities. The negro is primarily affectionate, immensely emotional, then sensual, and under provocation, passionate. There is love of outward show, of ostentation, of approbation. He loves melody and a rude kind of poetry and sonorous language. There is undeveloped artistic power and taste—negroes make good artisans and handicraftsmen. They are deficient in judgment, in the formulation of new ideas from existing facts, in devising hypotheses, and in making deductions in general. They are imitative rather than original, inventive, or constructive. There is instability of character incident to lack of self-control, especially in connection with the sexual relation, and there is lack of orientation, or recognition of position and condition of self and environment, evidenced in various ways, but by a peculiar "bumptiousness," so called by Prof. Blackshear of Texas, that is particularly noticeable.

The white and the black races are antipodal, then, in cardinal points. The one has a large frontal region of the brain, the other a larger region behind; the one is subjective, the other objective; the one a great reasoner, the other preeminently emotional; the one domineering, but having great self-control, the other meek and submission, but violent and lacking self-control when the passions are aroused; the one a very advanced race, the other a very backward one. The Caucasian and the negro are fundamentally opposite extremes in evolution.

Having demonstrated that the negro and the Caucasian are widely different in characteristics, due to a deficiency of gray matter and connecting fibers in the negro brain, especially in the frontal lobes, a deficiency that is hereditary and can be altered only by intermarriage, we are forced to conclude that it is useless to try to elevate the negro by education or otherwise, except in the direction of his natural endowments. The way may be made plain to the black people, and they may be encouraged in the proper direction, but the solution of the question still must come from within the race. Let them win their reward by diligent service.

DOCUMENT 26:

Lithograph, Arthur Ignatius Keller, "I Hurl the Everlasting Curse of a Nation," c. 1905.

Courtesy Library of Congress.

This lithograph, published in Thomas Dixon's novel *The Clansman*, decries the radicalism of the Reconstruction era and celebrates white supremacy.

DOCUMENT 27:

Exchange of Letters, Mr. J. F. Suttle to H. H. Warren, October 10, 1912. J. Freeman Suttle Collection (MSS1017).

Courtesy Special Collections, Robert W. Woodruff Library, Emory University.

This 1912 letter from "J. Freeman Suttle, Merchant, Planter and Live Stock" to H. H. Warren regarded the possible employment of Henry Johnson, a black man, as Warren's assistant. Warren's reluctance to hire Johnson evokes from Suttle an unusual statement that "a negro of the right kind would beat a cheap white man." While that might seem faint praise, for some southerners to affirm a black man's worth was exceptional.

Document 26

Oct. 10, 1912

Mr. H. H. Warren,
  Hattiesburg, Miss.

My dear sir:-

I arrived from Birmingham last evening and found your letter waiting my return.

As to the employment of Henry Johnson instead of a white man, will leave the matter with you, in fact will leave the matter of whether you have any assistance at all with you, I suggested it as I thought the right man would be good deal of help to you and if he was a good active fellow could make his salary for us. I dont doubt but what a negro of the right kind would beat a cheap white man, but to get one who you can trust is the question, and I will leave that with you: but who ever you get I would expect him to take hold and do what came before him to be done.

As to you spending a few days in Mississippi after the first on my expenses will say, that is alright, of course you are working for me and my interest and expect results to give returns.

I think the trip to Daleville or up in that section would be good, if you get some labor from there, it would be very apt to be good and stay with us for a while. I dont know but that I will send Walter Martin over to the Fair one day and let him see some of the people from up the Country.

We must be sure to get some more labor from some place to manage the proposition that you will have on the Edwards place, but at the same time be very carefull about the kind that you get.

I have the letter from Henry Johnson and herewith enclose you copy of my reply.

Yours truly,

[Not signed—from J. Freeman Suttle, Merchant, Planter, and Live Stock Felix, Perry Co., ALA.]

DOCUMENT 28:
Letter from Joseph F. Johnston, U.S. Senate, Committee on Military Affairs, May 31, 1913. J. Freeman Suttle Collection (MSS1017).

Courtesy Special Collections, Robert W. Woodruff Library, Emory University.

This 1913 letter from Joseph F. Johnston (U.S. senator from Alabama from 1907 to 1913) to businessman J. F. Suttle responds to criticism of his political position on several matters. He celebrates his service to the Confederacy and highlights his role in joining in the "ranks of the white people of Alabama . . . to overthrow the rule of the carpetbaggers and the negroes."

JOSEPH F. JOHNSTON, ALA., CHAIRMAN.

GEORGE E. CHAMBERLAIN, OREG.	HENRY A. DUPONT, DEL.
GILBERT M. HITCHCOCK, NEBR.	FRANCIS E. WARREN, WYO.
LUKE LEA, TENN.	JOSEPH L. BRISTOW, KANS.
DUNCAN U. FLETCHER,FLA.	THOMAS B. CATRON, N.MEX.
HENRY L. MYERS, MONT.	JAMES H. BRADY, N.MEX.
CHARLES S. THOMAS, COLO.	WILLIAM S. KENYON, IOWA.
JAMES K. VARDAMAN, MISS.	NATHAN GOFF, W.VA.
JAMES P. CLARKE, ARK.	

THOS. B. STALLINGS, CLERK.

United States Senate,
COMMITTEE ON MILITARY AFFAIRS.

May 31, 1913.

My dear Sir:

I shall send you some brief speeches showing my position in the Senate on certain questions which I learn that some persons are attempting to distort.

Differences of opinion are of little moment, but the deliberate conclusions of my people, made upon the facts, are highly prized to me. I desire to represent the best thought and deliberate judgment of my people on all public matters. Upon which vital questions have I not the support of thoughtful democrats?

I stood with my brethren of the South four bloody years to maintain our rights. My attitude then could not have been contrary to their views for I stood with the men who by their valor and endurance made the name of the Confederate solider immortal. That my humble service then as Private, Sergeant, Lieutenant and Captain cast no stain upon me is shown by the fact that I was near enough the firing line to be wounded four times, once so seriously that I was left upon the field of battle for dead, and that I am now Chairman of the War Committee of the Senate—the second Confederate to occupy that place and probably the last. It should be of interest to those who cherish Southern tradition to know that this Committee, having in case of War the defense of our Republic, is presided over by a Confederate soldier.

When the War was over, I took my place in the ranks of the white people of Alabama and fought their battle to overthrow the rule of the carpet bagger and the negro. I was then in line with my old comrades and my people. I served my party zealously and so much to its satisfaction that when we finally overturned the alien government in Alabama, I was Chairman of the Democratic State Committee. It is certain that I was then in line with my people.

Later the good people of Alabama called on me to be their Governor for two terms. Four years I served them, neglecting all private business and devoting myself with zeal and ardor to enforcing the laws, holding down expenses, extending the terms of our public schools and punishing unfaithful public officials; and it is not to be unexpected that I should have incurred ill-will of some people who do not believe in a strict enforcement of the laws.

That my service was not entirely unsatisfactory to my people is shown by the fact that when they came to choose a successor to the venerable and loved Pettus in the Senate, I was chosen. I must have been in line with them then.

P. #2

I have been in the Senate some six years. I have been in my seat and diligently attending to my duties, serving my people with unfagging zeal and, except when sick, or serving elsewhere under the direction of the Senate, I have not been absent from my post of duty ten day in the entire six years. No one has been found so reckless as to reproach me with neglect of duty. Service is not to be found in the promises of a candidate but in an established record.

I have had no vanity or ambition to promote that made me neglect my duties, my people or my state; I stand for the well established and tried doctrines of my party. I do not swiftly follow untried experiments or unfurl a sail to catch every passing breeze. I believe that the Government should not take from the people one unnecessary dollar or waste it in extravagance; I do not think offices should be multiplied; I have no apprehension that any foreign country will ever invade and conquer our country, and I am opposed to great armies and navies. I believe that in case war should arise we must rely upon the patriotism of our people, who have heretofore never failed to furnish volunteers to maintain our cause. I think that instead of spending seven hundred millions for or on account of War, that we should reduce this vast sum and devote it to purposes of Peace—-to public education, good road, the development of our agricultural, mineral, manufacturing and water power resources.

I have been careful to give my views because I desire to know and to represent faithfully the sentiments of my people. Whilst in the office of Governor and ever since I have been in the Senate, my door has been wide open to all my people, and their letters and requests have received prompt response from me without regard to whether they came from the humble and poor or those in high station.

I am a candidate for reelection to the Senate and am not a quitter; I shall be found at the front when the last shot is fired. It has been the democratic custom to reward faithful servants in this way. My predecessor was so honored when he was over eighty years old. Younger men can await their reward; the Confederate veteran has but a few years now left for earthly rewards.

Yours sincerely,
Jos. F. Johnston

Mr. J. F. Suttles,
Felix, Ala.

DOCUMENT 29:
Letter from Edward Randolph Carter and Dewitt Kelley,
"An Appeal to the Citizens of Atlanta," 1914. Subject File:
Afro-Americans–Civil Rights—Afro-Americans–History
(1877–1964). Folder: Black Community.

Courtesy Kenan Research Center, Atlanta History Center.

This 1914 letter from Reverend Edward Randolph Carter (noted
civil rights leader, pastor of Friendship Baptist Church in Atlanta,
and author of *The Black Side*) and Dewitt Kelley (secretary of an
unnamed civil rights organization) solicits funds from black and
white Atlantans to build a boys and girls reformatory and a home
for "black mammies, that are so well loved by both races."

AN APPEAL TO THE CITIZENS OF ATLANTA

There is a movement on foot by Negroes to secure for the boys and
girls a reformatory, and a home for black mammies, that are so well loved
by both races. We are endeavoring to save Negro boys and girls and to
improve the condition of Negro children generally.

We are asking help from both races and we are endeavoring to make
conditions better. We have bought a farm of (8) acres at a cost of $100.00
per acre. We have accomplished paying for one half of the farm and we
are making an effort now to finish paying for it, and to erect a brick building on the farm.

We have in mind to begin a truck farm in the Spring in order to give
employment to the boys and girls sent to us for keeping. We are asking
each citizen to donate to us not less than 25¢. If every citizen of the city
of Atlanta would give to us 25¢ as a Christmas gift toward the erection
of this building we would have no trouble in raising the desired amount
for its erection.

Find enclosed a self-addressed envelope; in which please place the
donation of 25¢ and mail it to the President, Rev. E. R. Carter, #71
Tatnall Street, who is pastor of Friendship Baptist Church of Atlanta,
Georgia. We are only asking for 25¢ but we would be pleased to have
you give as much as you feel able to donate.

For further information with reference to the reformatory, address Rev. E. R. Carter, Pres., #71 Tatnall Street.

Thanking you in advance, we are,

> Respectfully,
> E. R. Carter, Pres.
> Dewitt Kelley, Secy.

DOCUMENT 30:
Major Innes Randolph, "Unreconstructed Rebel" (also known as "I'm a Good Old Rebel").

This song, popular in the South long after the Civil War, expressed a common sentiment. Originally published in *Collier's Weekly* on April 4, 1914, the lyrics are attributed to Major Innes Randolph, a member of J.E.B. Stuart's staff. It was set to the tune of "Lily of the West" and "Lakes of Ponchartrain." *Collier's Weekly* (later called *Collier's*) was founded in 1888 by Peter Fenelon Collier and was in print until 1957. The song was featured in the 1980 film *The Long Riders,* directed by Walter Hill.

Oh, I'm a good old Rebel soldier, now that's just what I am;
For this "Fair Land of Freedom" I do not give a damn!
I'm glad I fit against it, I only wish we'd won,
And I don't want no pardon for anything I done.

I hates the Constitution, this "Great Republic," too!
I hates the Freedman's Bureau and uniforms of blue!
I hates the nasty eagle with all its brags and fuss,
And the lying, thieving Yankees, I hates 'em wuss and wuss!

I hates the Yankee nation and everything they do,
I hates the Declaration of Independence, too!
I hates the "Glorious Union"—'tis dripping with our blood,
And I hates their striped banner, and I fit it all I could.

I followed old Marse Robert for four years, near about,
Got wounded in three places, and starved at Point Lookout.

I cotched the "roomatism" a'campin' in the snow,
But I killed a chance o' Yankees, and I'd like to kill some mo'!

Three hundred thousand Yankees is stiff in Southern dust!
We got three hundred thousand before they conquered us.
They died of Southern fever and Southern steel and shot,
But I wish we'd got three million instead of what we got.

I can't take up my musket and fight 'em now no more,
But I ain't a'gonna love 'em, now that's for sartain sure!
I do not want no pardon for what I was and am,
And I won't be reconstructed, and I do not care a damn!

DOCUMENT 31:
Jim Crow Laws, Alabama, 1901, Sections 101–103, 1923.

Like all the states of the former Confederacy and many of the border states, Alabama had restrictive laws controlling almost all
aspects of black life and many facets of white life. More subtle,
often unwritten restrictions existed in northern and western states
as well.

Sec. 102. The legislature shall never pass any law to authorize or legal-
ize any marriage between any white person and a negro, or descendant
of a negro.

Sec. 194. The poll tax mentioned this article shall be one dollar and fifty
cents upon each male inhabitant of the state, over the age of twenty-
one years, and under the age of fifty-five years, who would not now be
exempt by law; but the legislature is authorized to increase the maxi-
mum age fixed in this section to not more than sixty years. Such poll tax
shall become due and payable on the first day of October in each year,
and become delinquent on the first day of the next succeeding February,
but no legal process, nor any fee or commission shall be allowed for the
collection thereof. The tax collector shall make returns of poll tax collections separate from other collections.

Sec. 195. Any person who shall pay the poll tax of another, or advance him money for that purpose in order to influence his vote, shall be guilty of bribery, and upon conviction therefor shall be imprisoned in the penitentiary for not less than one nor more than five years.

Sec. 196. If any section or subdivision of this article shall, for any reason, be or be held by any court of competent jurisdiction and of final resort to be invalid, inoperative, or void, the residue of this article shall not be thereby invalidated or affected.

1901
ARTICLE XIV.
EDUCATION
Section 256. The legislature shall establish, organize, and maintain a liberal system of public schools throughout the state for the benefit of the children thereof between the ages of seven and twenty-one years. The public school fund shall be apportioned to the several counties in proportion to the number of school children of school age therein, and shall be so apportioned to the schools in the districts or townships in the counties as to provide, as nearly as practicable, school terms of equal duration in such school districts or townships. Separate schools shall be provided for white and colored children, and no child of either race shall be permitted to attend a school of the other race.

1875
ARTICLE XIII.
EDUCATION.
Section 1. The general assembly shall establish, organize, and maintain a system of public schools throughout the state, for the equal benefit of the children thereof between he ages of seven and twenty-one years; but separate schools shall be provided for the children of citizens of African descent.

DOCUMENT 32:
Letter, Mary Fitzbutler Waring to President Franklin D. Roosevelt, May 11, 1933. General Records of the Department of Commerce (Record Group 40).

Courtesy National Archives.

This 1933 letter to Franklin Delano Roosevelt from physician Mary Fitzbutler Waring (vice president of the National Association of Colored Women) cites injustices directed toward blacks and calls for the end of segregated railroad cars. She explains her request, citing humiliation to blacks and further saying that "it would be a real economy" to the railroad companies if the practice were terminated. Despite assurances by officials that her letter would receive consideration, nothing further was done.

May 11, 1933

Mr. Franklin D. Roosevelt,
President of the United States of America,

Honored Sir:

You have accomplished much, since you have been in office, for the general good of the masses. Politically, you realize that many of us are your friends and supporters. From a humane standpoint you must realize that we deserve to receive the same treatment as other citizens of the United States.

It would be a just act to put an end to discrimination against the millions of American citizens who are of African descent. Laws exist at the present time in the Southern States of this Union which compel the railroads to carry special coaches on all passenger trains. Colored people are forced to ride in these separate coaches. It matters not how cultured or refined members of our race may be, they are subjugated to insult and rough treatment by the white people and railroad employees, because of this segregation, we speak from experience.

Your wise suggestion that railroads conserve by cutting out extra coaches makes this appeal opportune. In your address of May seventh, you spoke of the "Assistance of the government to eliminate the duplication and waste that is resulting in railroad receiverships and continuing operating deficits." We feel that the dropping of the separate coach would make a material difference in expense to the railroad. It would be a real economy.

When the World War broke out, our men answered the call. As loyal Americans, they gave their time, lives, all. Our women served, knit, saved, canteened and gave unstintingly to make a better world in which to live. We came here with emigrants to people this country in 1620. We can not be deported because we have no other country. Since we are loyal, law-abiding citizens; since we desire to instill self-respect and confidence in our youth, we ask that discrimination in public conveyances cease; we pray that discrimination in public places, because of the color of our skin, may end.

We believe that if the people of the white races would learn more about the achievements of the dark races in past ages they would understand that mentally and morally we are not naturally underlings. Continued ill-treatment has made many Negroes have an inferiority complex, and hence they have not measured up to as high a standard as they would have otherwise.

Mr. Roosevelt, we believe in you. You have expedited reconstruction and have given hope to despairing millions. Will you consider us? We appeal to you.

Respectfully yours,
Mary Fitzbutler Waring

DOCUMENT 33:
Photograph, "Waiting Room," c. 1909.

Courtesy Library of Congress.

This undated photograph, c. 1909, shows how much effort and how many resources were required to create and enforce segregation in public facilities. It shows federal employees awaiting treatment at the Public Health Service Dispensary #32.

Document 33

CHAPTER 3

Living Jim Crow

The documents in this section examine the multiple ways in which African Americans and whites lived, worked, and played under the restrictions demanded by Jim Crow.

DOCUMENT 34:
Photograph, "Lynching, 1925."

Courtesy Library of Congress.

Lynching was commonly used as an extralegal form punishment of African Americans during the Jim Crow era. It was condemned by African American leaders such as W.E.B. Du Bois and Ida B. Wells in publications such as *Thirty Years of Lynching in the United States: 1889–1918*, published by the NAACP in 1919. Lynching was not limited to the South, nor were African Americans the only victims, evidenced by the lynching of Leo Frank, a Jewish pencil factory manager in Marietta, Georgia, in 1915.

DOCUMENT 35:
"Negro Lieutenant Ejected from Pullman Was Arrested in Oklahoma and Lodged in Prison Informed Court That He Proposed to Seek Reparation," *Savannah (GA) Tribune,* March 30, 1918.

This article details the experience of Lt. Charles A. Tribbett, a well-educated commissioned officer traveling under military orders, who was arrested for being "'a Negro riding in a Pullman in Oklahoma.'" The *Savannah Tribune* is an African American newspaper that is still in print.

Document 34

NEGRO LIEUTENANT EJECTED FROM PULLMAN
WAS ARRESTED IN OKLAHOMA AND LODGED IN PRISON
INFORMED COURT THAT HE PROPOSED TO SEEK
REPARATION

First Lieut. Charles A Tribbett, 367th, was ejected from the train at
Chickasha, Okla., March 1, on train 411 of the Frisco, J. W. Barlow, conductor. He was placed under arrest by Chief Phillips and placed in the

county jail. An information sworn to by the county attorney charged him with violating the separate coach laws of the state.

Lieut. Tribbett was riding on transportation furnished by the government of the United States and the cause of the difficulty developed out of the fact that "he was a Negro riding in a Pullman in Oklahoma." His checks showed his reservation to be Car 17 Lower 8. E. R. Biggs, 211 Papen street, St. Louis was the porter in charge. The Pullman reservation had been purchased straight through from Camp Upton to Fort Sill.

When the train reached Chickasha, Chief of Police Mitchell proceeded to the coach and informed the army officer that it was against the law of the State of Oklahoma for him to ride where he was.

Tribbett stood silent for a moment and very diplomatically said, "Sir, I have fully decided not to enter your separate coach, but I want you to know that I am entirely at your service." Conductor Barlow then said, "Well, you see, he refuses to go." The Chief said, "Yes," and placed his hand on Lieut. Tribbett's arm; without offering any semblance of resistance Lieutenant Tribbett submitted to arrest and walked down out of the coach.

Editor Roscoe Dunjee and Staff Correspondent J. M. Anderson, of the *Black Dispatch,* who were riding in the separate coach had hurried to the Pullman when the train stopped, now offered their services. They informed the lieutenant that they would secure the immediate services of an attorney and come to the police station, and so it was that when the Chief reached the station, Attorney Robert L. Fortune was waiting.

Chief Mitchell seemed up in the air as to his jurisdiction and visibly showed signs of not knowing what to do. Leaving his prisoner at the office with his race friends he went off to get his bearing. At last after almost an hour he returned and said that his instructions were to deliver Lieut. Tribbett to the sheriff. From the police station the party proceeded across several blocks to the county jail, where a large crown of curiosity seekers stood with Sheriff Hodge F. Bailey to actually see an arrested black officer.

"Well this old boy is who you are looking for," said the Chief. "What is the trouble?" said Bailey, whom no one would ever have taken for a sheriff unless told.

"Well, as near as I could understand it," said the Chief, "this fellow was riding in the Pullman and refused to get out, and the conductor turned him over to me. "Waal," said the sheriff, as he stood and looked a Yale graduate in the face for the first time, "Wa'al, I'd like to have been conductor myself fer about 20 minutes," and the crowd laughed. The army officer was silent and paid no attention to this vicious attempt on the part of the sheriff to intimidate.

On the inside, Editor Dunjee secured telegraph blanks and a message was sent to the Commanding Officer at Fort Sill. As Editor Dunjee was inquiring, over the phone what the charge would be on 60 words to Fort Sill, some of the curiosity seekers behind him said, "He will smell brimstone before he reaches Fort Sill," and some young man who evidently was clothed with authority about the jail, for he had a large gun sticking out from under his coat, proceeded in a loud voice to tell the auditors that the conductor would have lost his job had he "permitted a nigger to ride in a Pullman."

Finally Sheriff Bailey returned and read the information, charging Chas. A. Tribbett with violating the separate coach law of the state and commanding him to appear at once before Justice T. P. Moore, for trial.

There wasn't much formality in Justice Moore's establishment. He read the complaint and said: "Guilty or not guilty." Editor Dunjee protested on the ground that a reasonable amount of time should be given to defendant to secure counsel before he pleaded. Lawyer Fortune was away at the time preparing a writ of habeas corpus. Finally over the protest of the assistant county attorney the justice agreed to wait until the lawyer returned. A plea of not guilty was entered on his return and bond fixed at $50 cash or $200 surety. On agreement, Tribbett went to jail for about an hour so that Grady County might go their limit in their humiliation of an officer of the United States. He was plentifully supplied with funds for such an emergency but preferred letting the record show just what democracy means to a patriotic soldier who has volunteered to fight for his country.

Sheriff Bailey entered and searched Lieut. Tribbett's officer's equipment and when the black officer demanded to know why this was done, the sheriff said he was searching for whiskey. He found none.

In about an hour Lieut. Tribbett put up a cash bond of $50 and spent the night as guest of the Colored Red Cross ladies of Chickasha.

The following morning, on advice of his attorney he pleaded guilty and paid a fine of $5 and cost, totaling $24.00.

According to Lieut. Tribbett's statement, he was kangarooed in the jail and forced to pay the prisoners, who were all white.

Lieut. Tribbett is a native of New Haven, Conn. His family is one of the oldest and most respected of the race in the New England states. He is an electrical engineer. On graduation from the New Haven High school he entered Yale, graduating from the Scientific Research Department. Was never in jail before in his life and through all of the trying ordeal conducted himself as a polished and cultured gentleman. He informed the court that he proposed to seek reparation.

DOCUMENT 36:

Editorial, "Two Advertisements—Two Views—Which Will Win," *New York Age,* January 10, 1920, 4.

In November 1919 in Bogalusa, Louisiana, black and white workers, represented by the International Workers of the World (I.W.W.) went on strike for better wages and conditions. Four (incorrectly listed in the article as three) white men were killed for protecting a "Negro agitator" named Sol Dakus. A month later, thirteen police officers were arrested for the murders but were never indicted or tried. The *New York Age* was an African American newspaper in print from 1887 to 1953.

We have received in the past week two full page advertisements printed in two Southern newspapers. One of these advertisements appears in the Bogalusa *Enterprise,* and was inserted by The Self Preservation and Loyalty League of Bogalusa. The other advertisement appears in the Memphis *Commercial-Appeal,* and was inserted by the Chamber of Commerce of Greenville, Mississippi.

These two advertisements represent the two views of Southern whites on the race question, the two views which are now struggling for ascendancy. One of these views regards the Negro as without any rights that the white man is bound to respect. The other view is the view of that minority in the South which, relatively, may be called liberal. Its main purpose is the establishment of "better relations between the two races."

As an indication of the sentiments expressed by the Bogalusa Loyalty League advertisement, we quote:

Our constitution clearly sets forth the following:
WHITE SUPREMACY

We do not intend to sit supinely by and allow any encroachment on the heritage left us by our fathers, who made the tremendous sacrifices in Reconstruction Days. The Negro in this section
will fare well if agitators will allow him to live in peace and con-
tentment, and such publications as *The Crisis, Menace, Crusader,
Wichita Herald* and other notorious social equality Negro papers
are barred from the mails in the Southland.

In another paragraph the Bogalusa advertisement sets forth as one
of the causes that led to the organization of the Loyalty League the
following:

"The meeting of whites and Blacks together in halls and in private
homes on absolute equality."

We turn now to the Greenville [Miss.] Chamber of Commerce advertisement. The difference between the two advertisements which at once
strikes the eye is that the Bogalusa statement is not vouched for by any
individuals, while the Greenville statement is signed by ninety-one business and professional men and office holders. We quote from the
Greenville statement as follows:

[There follows a lengthy quotation which denounces the I.W.W. and
affirms that the "Industrial Welfare Committee of the Greenville
Chamber of Commerce" will offer "patient and considerate" concern
toward reasonable demands. It ends with this paragraph.]

"With confidence between the races there will be mutual benefit
which suspicion and distrust or dislike would destroy. We wish to pre-
serve the race relations among the present and coming generations
which we see exemplified in the older citizens of the South."

The Greenville statement, despite its reservations, is a step far in
advance of the statement coming out of Bogalusa. . . .

Yet, both of these statements are based upon one common error. It
is the desire and plan in both of these statements to fix a place for the
Negro, to perpetuate a status for him. . . .

In the conquest [misprint for "contest"] for ascendancy between the
Southern sentiments expressed by Bogalusa and those expressed by
Greenville, we want to see Greenville win. At present, Bogalusa is a long
way in the lead. It sometimes seems a hopeless task to get even the sen-
timent of Greenville accepted as the majority sentiment of the South.
And after that is done there is still a long, long way to go.

Both Greenville and Bogalusa have yet to learn that no adjustment of the race situation can be successful or permanent which attempts to place limitations on how far and how high the Negro progresses. The only adjustment that can stand will be one based on the right of every individual to go as far and as high as his powers and ability enable him to go. . . .

We may all of us show due appreciation for what the Greenvilles say and do, but we must not forget that it is our primary business just now to have the police on the Bogalusas.

DOCUMENT 37:

Constance Fisher, "The Negro Social Worker Evaluates Birth Control," *Birth Control Review* 16 (June 1932): 174–175.

Fisher, an African American social worker and district supervisor of the Associated Charities organization in Cleveland, Ohio, wrote this article to counter the idea that birth control was a form of genocide advocated by racists. *Birth Control Review* was started by Margaret Sanger in 1917. By 1922, the monthly magazine had a circulation of ten thousand. It remained in print until 1940.

With the general tendency of more tolerance on birth control clinics and information, and with the increasing freedom in asking for direction in matters concerning birth control, attention is drawn to cross sections of people as well as to the general group. We are naturally interested to know what this new trend means in terms of social conditions or solutions of problems.

The Negro has been emerging from an agricultural to an industrial state of existence in the past fifteen years, more or less. Just before and after the World War the transition seemed to take place speedily. In earlier years, in the more predominately agricultural state, each child born to a family became an economic asset; all life was a struggle with nature and the more children there were to fight, the easier and better it was. Moreover, the large family was supposed to be the happy family and the more children a man had the more he won the respect and regard of his community. Then, too, there was the sense of security in old age, which parents felt because of the children who would always take them in and care for them. But when the pendulum began to swing in the direction of an industrial existence, it seemed that a wage Utopia had come and it was no longer necessary to have such large families to insure the bare necessities of life; still every additional person was of value in bringing in extra money and security to the home.

With the present period of economic depression the story has begun to change. When a plant closes down for lack of work or when Negro labor or help is being replaced by others, the larger family does not help matters. When landlords refuse to accept a family because of too many children, and force it to go from house to house hunting a place to stay, the children become liabilities rather than assets. Despite the fact that many say "the Lord will provide," each new baby seems, inevitably, more of a burden than the last. Negroes are usually the first to feel any cuts in jobs or wages or any general lay-off. What their future in industry is no one knows. Suffice to say that in the present situation the smaller family is an asset.

Family case workers frequently hear what might be called the song of regret from their clients who are finding their other problems intensified because of the narrow economic margin on which they are forced to exist; they want no more children now and they ask often where they may obtain *bona fide* and scientific information concerning this. Not only is the question coming from those concerned chiefly over their economic situation, but also from those homes in which the social worker finds domestic compatibility, alcoholism, and many other social ailments. In many instances the case worker sees the need for birth control where and when the couple involved do not. Where there is low mentality, a serious health impairment, or other very obvious complications, it is very easy to see the need for information of this sort.

In making a study of desertion a few years ago, the writer was impressed with the fact that in even the small sample studied at the time, the factor at the bottom of the difficulties in well over half the situations was sex maladjustment. This frequently bred feelings of inadequacy, insecurities of every sort, alcoholism, infidelity, desertion, and generally broken homes. And in most of the families the objections to constant pregnancy came from the mother, though the father was often greatly discouraged over the situation too.

Obviously the family case worker must play some role in this new trend in public opinion, whether it is active or passive. When her clients come to her with their questions and problems, she must make some effort to help them find solutions, and when she goes into their homes she needs to be alert for causative factors as well as symptoms of difficulties. Her job is not to proselytize, but to administer her treatment of the case on as sound and thoughtful a basis as possible. If the family recognizes the need for birth control as either one of or the chief factor in working out its problems, and asks the worker for advice on the matter, she must meet her responsibility adequately. In instances where she sees a definite need for advice of this sort, the writer feels that she owes it to the community, as well as to the family, to use the birth control clinic as a tool for preventative social therapy as well as remedial and palliative treatment.

The trend toward greater use of birth control clinics is one which must be recognized and reckoned with. Not every worker is qualified to suggest or advice procedures to families on this level of treatment, any more than every medical doctor is capable of diagnosing a psychosis or neurosis, but in the hands of an alert and capable worker, there is little danger. The Negro client is feeling less and less guilty about asking for and receiving information on birth control and is expressing himself freely as having wanted such guidance for a long time without knowing where to get it. There are still a great many who have not lost their sense of sinning in seeking such help, or who have superstitions concerning it, or who fear that it will only breed greater difficulties in the home. Yet, there are increasing numbers who seek birth control information because they feel that if they go on resenting themselves and their mates for physical, economic, and emotional reasons, greater problems are certain to arise, and the existing tensions in their family life are bound to be stretched to their logical ends—the breaking point.

DOCUMENT 38:

Speech, Oscar Stanton De Priest, "Jim Crow and Eating: Washington, D.C." *Congressional Record,* March 21, 1934, 73rd Congress, 2nd session, LXXVII, 5047–5049.

This speech, an excerpt of which is included here, was prompted by an incident in which Congressman Oscar Stanton De Priest's

secretary, Morris Lewis, was refused service in the restaurant operated inside the Capitol building. On April 25, 1934, by a vote of 237
to 114 in the House of Representatives, a committee was formed
to "investigate the matter," which effectively ended the possibility
of an effective and swift resolution. De Priest, in 1928 in Illinois,
became the first African American congressman elected in the
twentieth century.

Mr. De Priest. Mr. Chairman and members of the Committee, I came
to Washington as a Representative in Congress on the 15th of April 1929.
Up until the 23d day of last January I never heard this question raised
which has now been raised by the Chairman of the Committee on
Accounts this year. On that day when my secretary went into the grillroom downstairs he was told by Mr. Johnson that by the orders of the
Chairman of the Committee on Accounts he could not be served in that
restaurant.

I read in the newspapers an interview where the Chairman of the
Committee on Accounts said that no Negro had been served there and
would not while he was here. I hope he was not quoted correctly.

I want to say that if the chairman was quoted correctly in that
article "that Negroes had not been served there before" he was mistaken. I have seen them there in the grillroom several times. In the last
5 years I think I have seen them there 50 times.

I want to say further, after talking with some Members of the
Committee on Accounts, that this question has never been raised in the
committee before, and never was raised officially in the committee, if I
am correctly informed.

It seems to be an arbitrary ruling on that question.

The restaurant of the Capitol is run for the benefit of the American
people, and every American, whether he be black or white, Jew or gentile, Protestant or Catholic, under our constitutional form of Government, is entitled to equal opportunities.

I introduced a resolution on the 24th of January, asking for an investigation of this ruling by the chairman of the committee. That resolution went to the Committee on Rules. The Committee on Rules has not
acted as yet. I waited 30 legislative days, and then I filed a petition with
the Clerk of this House to discharge the Committee on Rules and to
bring the resolution to the floor of the House.

That resolution calls for an investigation only. If the Chairman of the Committee on Accounts has that power, I should like to know it. If the Chairman of the Committee on Accounts has that power, the American people are entitled to know it.

I am going to ask every justice-loving Member in this House to sign that petition, as that seems to be the only way it can be threshed out on the floor of the House.

I come from a group of people—and I am proud of it and make no apology for being a Negro—who have demonstrated their loyalty to the American Government in every respect, making no exception. They have always proved to be good American citizens and have supported the Constitution. I challenge any man to contradict that assertion. If you are going to keep them good American citizens, like I pray they shall always be, it must be done by defending their rights as American citizens.

If we allow segregation and the denial of constitutional rights under the dome of the Capitol, where in God's name will we get them?

I appreciate the conditions that pertain in the territory where the gentleman comes from, and nobody knows that better than I do.

But North Carolina is not the United States of America; it is but a part of it, a one forty-eighth part. Then I expect, too, as long as I am a Member of this House, to contend for every right and every privilege every other American citizen enjoys; and if I did not, I would not be worthy of the trust reposed in me by constituents who have sent me here. [Applause.]

This is not a political problem. Someone said that I was trying to play politics. I did not instigate this; I did not start it; but, so help me God, I am going to stay to see the finish of it.

Mr. Blanton. Mr. Chairman, will our colleague yield to me for a question?

Mr. De Priest. Not now, Mr. Blanton; and I consider you one of the best friends I have on the Democratic side.

Mr. Blanton. I thought therefore you would yield for a question.

Mr. De Priest. I shall later on, but not now.

The Chairman. The gentleman declines to yield.

Mr. De Priest. I say to the Members of this House—and I have no feeling in the matter—this is the most dangerous precedent that could be established in the American Government. If we allow this challenge to go without correcting it, it will set an example where people will say

Congress itself approves of segregation; Congress itself approves of denying 0.1 of our population equal rights and opportunity; why should not
the rest of the American people do likewise? I have been informed that if
I insisted on pressing this question it might hurt my usefulness down here.
If I did not press it, I would not stay here very long. The people who sent
me here would retire me next November, and they would rightly retire
me because I should not be here if I did not stand up for a group of
people who have always been on the square with this Government. I did
not come here from a group of people who have committed treason
against the Government; I did not come here from a group of people who
are Communists or Socialists; I come here from the most loyal American
citizens that we have.

During the World War when emissaries of the enemy were scatter-
ing pamphlets over the battlefields of Europe asking the colored people
to desert the colors because they received inhuman treatment in America,
no colored man deserted, and no man can say and history does not record
when a Negro deserted the colors—not one. How do you expect them
to go on giving loyal service to America, at a time when there is unrest
over the whole world, when the Reds are trying to make inroads amongst
my group because they are the lowest in the scale of society, from an economic standpoint, unless we give them something like a square deal in
this country? I appreciate all that has been done so far, but the work has
not been completed yet. And I say further, ladies and gentlemen of the
Congress, that America never will be what it was intended to be until
every citizen in America has his just rights under the Constitution.
[Applause.] I would not have filed this petition if I could have gotten a
hearing before the Committee on Rules. I asked for it. I was not even given
the courtesy of a hearing before that committee.

Mr. Lundeen. Mr. Chairman, will the gentleman yield?

Mr. De Priest. Yes.

Mr. Lundeen. Will the gentleman tell us how many names are on
that petition now?

Mr. De Priest. There were 93 names on it an hour ago.

Mr. Blanton. Mr. Chairman, will our colleague yield to me now?

Mr. De Priest. Yes; I yield with pleasure to the gentleman from
Texas.

Mr. Blanton. The restaurant is for the benefit of the Members of
the Congress because we have to be here at meal-time.

Mr. De Priest. I agree with the gentleman.

Mr. Blanton. Has not our colleague been allowed to go in there every time he wanted to? He can go in there right now and take anybody with him that he wishes to take.

Mr. De Priest. That is all true.

Mr. Blanton. What more do you ask? You go there at will and are allowed to take your friends with you at will. Is not that equal justice and right to you, the same as to the rest of us?

Mr. De Priest. I am asking for the same rights for my constituents that the gentleman from Texas wants for his, and that is all. . . .

DOCUMENT 39:

Richard Wright, "I Have Seen Black Hands," *New Masses* 11, no. 13 (June 26, 1934): 16.

A native of Mississippi, Richard Wright (1908–1960) wrote this dramatic poem to celebrate the labor of black America in the Jim Crow era. In print from 1926 to 1948, the *New Masses* was a prominent Marxist magazine that was edited by Michael Gold and, briefly, by Whittaker Chambers. Well-known writers such as Dorothy Parker, Langston Hughes, and Ernest Hemingway were contributors.

I

I am black and I have seen black hands, millions and millions of them—
Out of millions of bundles of wool and flannel tiny black fingers have
      reached restlessly and hungrily for life.
Reached out for the black nipples at the black breasts of black mothers,
And they've held red, green, blue, yellow, orange, white, and purple
      toys in the childish grips of possession.
And chocolate drops, peppermint sticks, lollypops, wineballs, ice cream
      cones, and sugared cookies in fingers sticky and gummy,
And they've held balls and bats and gloves and marbles and jack-knives
      and sling-shots and spinning tops in the thrill of sport and
      play,

And pennies and nickels and dimes and quarters and sometimes on
New Year's, Easter, Lincoln's Birthday, May Day, a brand
new green dollar bill,
They've held pens and rulers and maps and tablets and books in palms
spotted and smeared with ink,
And they've held dice and cards and half-pint flasks and cue sticks and
cigars and cigarettes in the pride of new maturity . . .

II

I am black and I have seen black hands, millions and millions of them—
They were tired and awkward and calloused and grimy and covered
with hangnails,
And they were caught in the fast-moving belts of machines and
snagged and smashed and crushed,
And they jerked up and down at the throbbing machines massing
taller and taller the heaps of gold in the banks of bosses,
And they piled higher and higher the steel, iron, the lumber, wheat,
rye, the oats, corn, the cotton, the wool, the oil, the coal,
the meat, the fruit, the glass, and the stone until there was
too much to be used,
And they grabbed guns and slung them on their shoulders and
marched and groped in trenches and fought and killed and
conquered nations who were customers for the goods
black hands had made,
And again black hands stacked goods higher and higher until there
was too much to be used,
And then the black hands held trembling at the factory gates the
dreaded lay-off slip,
And the black hands hung idle and swung empty and grew soft and
got weak and bony from unemployment and starvation.
And they grow nervous and sweaty, and opened and shut in anguish
and doubt and hesitation and irresolution . . .

III

I am black and I have seen black hands, millions and millions of them—
Reaching hesitantly out of days of slow death for the goods they had
            made, but the bosses warned that the goods were private
            and did not belong to them,
And the black hands struck desperately out in defence of life and
            there was blood, but the enraged bosses decreed that this
            too was wrong,
And the black hands felt the cold steel bars of the prison they had
            made, in despair tested their strength and found that they
            could neither bend nor break them,
And the black hands fought and scratched and held back but a thou-
            sand white hands took them and tied them,
And the black hands lifted palms in mute and futile supplication to the
            sodden faces of mobs wild in the revelries of sadism,
And the black hands strained and clawed and struggled in vain at the
            noose that tightened about the black throat,
And the black hands waved and beat fearfully at the tall flames that
            cooked and charred the black flesh . . .

IV

I am black and I have seen black hands
Raised in fists of revolt, side by side with the white fists of white
            workers,
And some day—and it is only this which sustains me—
Some day there shall be millions and millions of them,
On some red day in a burst of fists on a new horizon!

DOCUMENT 40:

William Edward Burghardt (W.E.B.) Du Bois, "Segregation in the North," *The Crisis* 41 (August 1934): 115–116.

In this article, W.E.B. Du Bois compares segregation in northern cities during the Great Depression to the decade before World War I, suggesting the fluidity and arbitrary nature of Jim Crow laws. He raises the quandary of separation and integration, which articulates his differences with the NAACP. Du Bois founded *The Crisis* in 1910, which became one of the most outspoken periodicals devoted to civil rights. After the publication of this article, Du Bois resigned from the NAACP.

I have read with interest the various criticisms on my recent discussions of segregation. Those like that of Mr. Pierce of Cleveland, do impress me. I am not worried about being inconsistent. What worries me is the Truth. I am talking about conditions in 1934 and not in 1910. I do not care what I said in 1910 or 1810 or in B.C. 700.

The arguments of Walter White, George Schuyler and Kelly Miller have logic, but they seem to me quite beside the point. In the first place, Walter White is white. He has more white companions and friends than colored. He goes where he will in New York City and naturally meets no Color Line, for the simple and sufficient reason that he isn't "colored"; he feels his new freedom in bitter contrast to what he was born to in Georgia. This is perfectly natural and he does what anyone else of his complexion would do.

But it is fantastic to assume that this has anything to do with the color problem in the United States. It naturally makes Mr. White an extreme opponent of any segregation based on a myth of race. But this argument does not apply to Schuyler or Miller or me. Moreover, Mr. White knows this. He moved once into a white apartment house and it went black on him. He now lives in a colored apartment house with attendant limitations. He once took a friend to dine with him at the celebrated café of the Lafayette Hotel, where he had often been welcomed. The management humiliated him by refusing to serve Roland Hayes.

The attitudes of Schuyler and Kelly Miller are historically based on the amiable assumption that there is little or no segregation in the

North, and that agitation and a firm stand are making this disappear; that obvious desert and accomplishment by Negroes can break down prejudice. This is a fable. I once believed it passionately. It may become true in 250 or 1000 years. Now it is not true. No black man whatever his culture or ability is today in America regarded as a man by any considerable number of white Americans. The difference between North and South in the matter of segregation is largely a difference of degree; of wide degree certainly, but still of degree.

In the North, neither Schuyler nor Kelly Miller nor anyone with a visible admixture of Negro blood can frequent hotels or restaurants. They have difficulty in finding dwelling places in better class neighborhoods. They occupy "Lower 13" on Pullmans, and if they are wise, they do not go into dining cars when any large number of white people is there. Their children either go to colored schools or to schools nominally for both races, but actually attended almost exclusively by colored children. In other words, they are confined by unyielding public opinion to a Negro world. They earn a living on colored newspapers or in colored colleges, or other social institutions. They treat colored patients and preach to colored pews. Not one of the 12 colored Ph.D.'s of last year, trained by highest American and European standards, is going to get a job in any white university. Even when Negroes in the North work side by side with whites, they are segregated, like the postal clerks, or refused by white unions or denied merited promotion.

No matter how much we may fulminate about "No segregation," there stand the flat facts. Moreover, this situation has in the last quarter century been steadily growing worse. Mr. Spingarn may ask judicially as to whether or not the N.A.A.C.P. should change its attitude toward segregation. The point that he does not realize is that segregation has changed its attitude toward the N.A.A.C.P. The higher the Negro climbs or tries to climb, the more pitiless and unyielding the color ban. Segregation may be just as evil today as it was in 1910, but it is more insistent, more prevalent and more unassailable by appeal or argument. The pressing problem is: What are we going to do about it?

In 1910, colored men could be entertained in the best hotels in Cleveland, Detroit and Chicago. Today, there is not a single Northern city, except New York, where a Negro can be a guest at a first-class hotel. Not even in Boston is he welcome; and in New York, the number of hotels where he can go is very small. Roland Hayes was unable to get regular hotel accommodations, and Dr. Moton only succeeds by powerful white influence and by refraining from use of the public dining room or the public lobbies.

If as Spingarn asserts, the N.A.A.C.P. has conducted a quarter-century campaign against segregation, the net result has been a little less than nothing. We have by legal action steadied the foundation so that in the future, segregation must be by wish and will and not law, but beyond that we have not made the slightest impress on the determination of the overwhelming mass of white Americans not to treat Negroes as men.

These are unpleasant facts. We do not like to voice them. The theory is that by maintaining certain fictions of law and administration, by whistling and keeping our courage up, we can stand on the "principle" of no segregation and wait until public opinion meets our position. But can we do this? When we were living in times of prosperity; when we were making post-war incomes; when our labor was in demand, we perhaps could afford to wait. But today, faced by starvation and economic upheaval, and by the question of being able to survive at all in this land in the reconstruction that is upon us, it is ridiculous not to see, and criminal not to tell, the colored people that they can not base their salvation upon the empty reiteration of a slogan.

What then can we do? The only thing that we not only can, but must do, is voluntarily and insistently to organize our economic and social power, no matter how much segregation it involves. Learn to associate with ourselves and to train ourselves for effective association. Organize our strength as consumers; learn to co-operate and use machines and power as producers; train ourselves in methods of democratic control within our own group. Run and support our own institutions.

We are doing this partially now, only we are doing it under a peculiar attitude of protest, and with only transient and distracted interest. A number of excellent young gentlemen in Washington, having formed a Negro Alliance, proceed to read me out of the congregation of the righteous because I dare even discuss segregation. But who are these young men? The products of a segregated school system; the talent selected by Negro teachers; the persons who can today, in nine cases out of ten, earn only a living through segregated Negro social institutions. These are the men who are yelling against segregation. If most of them had been educated in the mixed schools in New York instead of the segregated schools of Washington, they never would have seen college, because Washington picks out and sends ten times as many Negroes to college as New York does.

It would, of course, be full easy to deny that this voluntary association for great social and economic ends in segregation; and if I had done this in the beginning of this debate, many people would have been easily deceived, and would have yelled "No segregation" with one side of their mouths and "Race pride and Race initiative" with the other side. No such distinction can possibly be drawn. Segregation may be compulsory by law or it may be compulsory by economic or social condition, or it may be a matter of free choice. At any rate, it is the separation of human beings and separation despite the will to humanity. Such separation is evil; it leads to jealousy, greed, nationalism and war; and yet it is today and in this world inevitable; inevitable to Jews because of Hitler; inevitable to Japanese because of white Europe; inevitable to Russia because of organized greed over all the white world; inevitable to Ethiopia because of white armies and navies; inevitable, because without it, the American Negro will suffer evils greater than any possible evil of separation: we would suffer the loss of self-respect, the lack of faith in ourselves, the lack of knowledge about ourselves, the lack of ability to make a decent living by our own efforts and not by philanthropy.

This situation has been plunged into crisis and precipitated to an open demand for thought and action by the Depression and the New Deal. The government, national and state, is helping and guiding the individual. It has entered and entered for good into the social and economic organization of life. We could wish, we could pray, that this entrance could absolutely ignore lines of race and color, but we know perfectly well it does not and will not, and with the present American opinion, it cannot. The question is then, are we going to stand out and refuse the inevitable and inescapable government aid because we first wish to abolish the Color Line? This is not simply tilting at windmills; it is, if we are not careful, committing race suicide.

Back of all slogans lies the difficulty that the meanings may change without changing the words. For instance, "no segregation" may mean two very different things:

1. A chance for the Negro to advance without the hindrances which arise when he is segregated from the main group, and the main social

institutions upon which society depends. He becomes, thus, an outsider, a hanger on, with no chance to function properly as a man.

2. It may mean utter lack of faith of Negroes in Negroes, and the desire to escape into another group, shirking, on the other hand, all responsibility for ignorance, degradation and lack of experience among Negroes, while asking admission into the other group on terms of full equality and with full chance for individual development.

It is in the first sense that I have always believed and used the slogan: "No Segregation." On the other hand, in the second sense, I have no desire or right to hinder or stop those persons who do not want to be Negroes. But I am compelled to ask the very plain and pertinent question: Assuming for the moment that the group into which you demand admission does not want you, what are you going to do about it? Can you demand that they want you? Can you make them by law or public opinion admit you when they are supreme over this same public opinion and make these laws? Manifestly, you cannot. Manifestly, your admission to the other group on the basis of your individual desert and wish, can only be accomplished if they, too, join in the wish to have you. If they do so join, all problems based mostly on race and color disappear, and there remains only the human problems of social uplift and intelligence and group action. But there is in the United States today no sign that this objection to the social and even civic recognition of persons of Negro blood is going to occur during the life of persons now living. In which case there can be only one meaning to the slogan "No Segregation"; and that is, no hindrance to my effort to be a man. If you do not wish to associate with me, I am more than willing to associate with myself. Indeed, I deem it a privilege to work with and for Negroes, only asking that my hands be not tied nor my feet hobbled.

What is the object of those persons who insist by law, custom and propaganda to keep the American Negro separate in rights and privileges from other citizens of the United States? The real object, confessed or semiconscious, is to so isolate the Negro that he will be spiritually bankrupt, physically degenerate, and economically dependent.

Against this it is the bounden duty of every Negro and every enlightened American to protest; to oppose the policy so far as it is manifest by laws; to agitate against customs by revealing facts; and to appeal to the sense of decency and justice in all American citizens.

I have never known an American Negro who did not agree that this was a proper program. Some have disagreed as to the emphasis to be put on this and that method of protest; on the efficacy of any appeal against American prejudice; but all Negroes have agreed that segregation is bad and should be opposed.

Suppose, however, that this appeal is ineffective or nearly so? What is the Negro going to do? There is one thing that he can or must do, and that is to see to it that segregation does *not* undermine his health; does *not* leave him spiritually bankrupt; and does not make him an economic slave; and he must do this at any cost.

If he cannot live in sanitary and decent sections of a city, he must build his own residential quarters, and raise and keep them on a plane fit for living. If he cannot educate his children in decent schools with other children, he must, nevertheless, educate his children in decent Negro schools and arrange and conduct and oversee such schools. If he cannot enter American industry at a living wage, or find work suited to his education and talent, or receive promotion and advancement according to his deserts, he must organize his own economic life so that just as far as possible these discriminations will not reduce him to abject exploitation.

Everyone of these movements on the part of colored people are not only necessary, but inevitable. And at the same time, they involve more or less active segregation and acquiescence in segregation.

Here again, if there be any number of American Negroes who have not in practical life made this fight of self-segregation and self-association against the compulsory segregation forced upon them, I am unacquainted with such persons. They may, of course, explain their compulsory retreat from a great ideal, by calling segregation by some other name. They may affirm with fierce insistency that they will never, no never, under any circumstances, acquiesce in segregation. But if they live in the United States in the year of our Lord 1934, or in any previous year since the foundation of the government, they are segregated; they accept segregation, and they segregate themselves, because they must. From this dilemma I see no issue.

DOCUMENT 41:

W. Rollo Wilson, "They Could Make the Big Leagues," *The Crisis* 41 (October 1934): 305–306.

A sports columnist for the *Pittsburgh Courier* and commissioner for the Negro National Association for Professional Baseball Clubs, W. Rollo Wilson laments the racial prejudice that prevents the integration of baseball.

A few weeks ago I sat in the lofty press box in the White Sox park, Chicago, covering the second annual "East-West" baseball game. The opponents were picked, all star teams of Negro players, coming mostly from the National Association of Negro Baseball clubs.

Almost twenty-five thousand fans paid from fifty cents to one and a half dollars to sit in on the spectacle. It marked the "high" of attendance for a Negro sports event

On Memorial Day, in Pittsburgh, more than 12,000 saw two baseball games between the Pittsburgh Crawfords and the Homestead Grays, both members of the league.

Not all of the fans who go to these games are colored; in Chicago it was estimated that at least 10% of the crowd was white. In Philadelphia and other cities sundown clubs attract large numbers of whites in their home parks and when they play white teams in white parks the attendance is largely white. Indeed, the best drawing cards on the sandlots are the high class Negro nines.

All of which leads up to the questions—why are there no colored players in Organized Baseball and will there ever be any colored players, as such, in Organized Baseball?

In recent years a symposium on the subject conducted by this writer and his associates on several weekly newspapers revealed the answer to the first question through the typewriters of many nationally known white sportswriters.

Racial prejudice which, according to Bill Dooly, of the Philadelphia *Record,* is harder to change than a lead quarter, precludes the possibility of a Negro team or Negro players in the major leagues.

Organized Baseball is built on a system of leagues of graduated ability. It is nation-wide. Not all Negro players would be eligible for the "big time" and would have to prove themselves in loops of less rating. Except in some northern spots they could never play on mixed teams. Big league teams must go South for their preliminary training and tell me a city in the South where colored athletes could live and work with their white companions.

Briefly, you have the reasons; now, whether there ever will be Negro players in the big leagues, I cannot answer. The economic conditions of the game, desperate efforts some time in the future to give it new color and added stars, may pave the way. I am hopeful—and fearful.

Denied their place in the baseball sun because of racial prejudice Negro players have gone along, playing for little or nothing and have made reputations which have endured. Here in Philadelphia you will find hundreds of white fans who will tell you that they prefer seeing colored league games to going out to watch either the A's or Phils. We have educated them to high grade baseball by colored athletes.

Many of the men I have seen playing the game in the years agone and during the current season might have been big league stars had they been given the chance.

Out in Chicago on that eventful Sunday a few weeks past was one hurler who stood head and shoulders—literally and figuratively—above his fellows. After the game the fans were full of praise for Leroy Paige, ace pitcher of the East who had turned back the West menace in critical times.

They didn't refer to him as "Paige"; to each and everyone he was "Satchell," so yclept because of his long feet. Satchell Paige is the Dizzy Dean, the Rube Waddell (except that he is a right-hander) of colored baseball. Today you have him pitching a low-hit game for you; when you want him again he is on his way to the Dakotas or Dahomey. Satchell has wandering feet—maybe that's why they are so large—and he is a real problem to his owner and manager.

Jim Bell of the Pittsburgh Crawfords, scored the only run of that game and his fleetness of foot did it. He walked and stole second and tallied on a little hit which rolled across second base. A great outfielder, major league stars have said that he is the fastest man in baseball. They ought to know for many of them play with or against him during the off seasons. (In Cuba, Porto Rico or on the Coast playing with Negro stars does not brand white players with the bar sinister, it seems.)

Even Babe Ruth, himself, has driven no baseball farther in the

Yankee Stadium than I have seen Josh Gibson, catcher, hit them. During a series several years ago between the Homestead Grays and the Lincoln Giants, Josh, then serving his first year in tophole Negro baseball, hit one homer over the extreme left wing of the grandstand in the "House That Ruth Built."

"Ted" Trent of the Chicago American Giants, is another pitcher who ought to be in the big leagues. He has everything which any big league club needs in the way of a hurler. Recently he held the hard-hitting Philadelphia Stars to two hits and lost a 3–2 game. Unfortunately for him both of the hits were home runs and one came after a runner had been put on the sacks by a teammate's error.

I have not seen a first baseman anywhere who has impressed me as much as "Buck" Leonard, of the Homestead Grays. He is a certain fielder and a hard, steady hitter who would mace as many four-masters in the big circuits as Jimmy Foxx and Lou Gehrig.

I could fill this magazine with tales of players who might have been in the big leagues but space is too limited.

For instance, there was Joe Mendez, the Cuban, nicknamed by John McGraw "the black Christy Matthewson" and Mac's statement that he would sign him for the Giants if it were possible.

Oscar Charleston fifteen or more years ago was hailed as a greater fielder and faster base runner than Max Carey, then the idol of the Pittsburgh Pirates. That praise from a white baseball writer caused Barney Dreyfuss, late president of the Pittsburgh National league club, to refuse the use of his park to Negro teams for many years.

Without any reasons I'll give the names of some of the stars of our game who might have been in the big leagues and maybe I'll get the space to explain later on. Here goes: John Henry Lloyd, Louis Santop, Dick Redding, Dave Brown, Nip Winters, Phil Cockrell, Joe Williams, Dan McClelland, Rube Foster, Willie Foster, "Chet" Brewer, Dick Lundy, Bill Monroe, Bullet Rogan, Willie Wells, Vic Harris, Clarence Williams, Pete Hill, Jess Barbour, Bill Holland, Walter Cannady and many others. Most of these lads, if given the chance—and if prejudice were not the powerful agent we know it to be—would be valuable decorations in any American or National league ballyard.

DOCUMENT 42:
Interview, Paul Robeson, "I Breathe Freely," *New Theater*
2, no. 7 (July 1935): 5.

Actor and singer Paul Robeson (1898–1976) gave this interview to
Julia Dorn while in Moscow during the Great Depression. A tireless advocate for civil rights and oppressed peoples, Robeson was
never a communist, but was sympathetic to the Soviet Union and
a defender of Joseph Stalin. Fluent in Russian, he claimed that,
while there, he "was rested and buoyed up by the lovely, honest,
wondering looks which did not see a 'negro.'"

Paul Robeson, looking for a medium and a starting-point from which
to determine the true African culture, has found in Soviet Russia the
closest and most friendly attitudes to his own. The internationally
known Negro singer and actor, at the end of his first visit to the Soviet
Union early this year, said, "In Soviet Russia I breathe freely for the first
time in my life. It is clear, whether a Negro is politically a Communist
or not, that of all the nations in the world, the modern Russians are our
best friends."

Since he speaks Russian, Robeson was able to talk directly with children, peasants and workers. Everywhere, in tramways, buses, streets and
parks, he met with the same reaction from the people, he told this interviewer. "I was rested and buoyed up by the lovely, honest, wondering
looks which did not see a 'negro,'" he said. "When these people looked
at me, they were just happy, and interested. There were no 'double looks,'
no venom, no superiority. . . ."

Looking for roles and songs, he has reached the same conclusion as
Professor Kislitsan, the Russian sociologist, who has announced facts to
prove that all races are related in culture, differing in the degree of their
development only so far as they are affected by natural resources or the
hindrances of exploitation.

"I find," declared Paul Robeson, "that the handicraft of certain periods of the Chinese and African cultures are almost identical; and that
the Negro is more like the Russian in temperament and character."

Robeson has taken a keen interest in the Soviet minorities, their culture and the policy on national minorities. During his short stay in

Moscow, he talked with representatives of the Commissariat of Public Education, and saw the policy in action. He plans to return to the Soviet Union to make a serious study of minority groups, which is to be linked with his intensive researches into Asiatic and African culture. He has insisted, in answer to press comments labelling his interest in Africa "jingoistic," that he is not trying to "escape" race oppression in America and Europe by taking a nationalist attitude.

"I came here," he says, "because the Soviet Union is the only place where ethnology is seriously considered and applied. . . . Africa does not realize that it has something to contribute, that it has a culture as clear as the European. The Africans, instead of preserving their own culture, are fighting the idea of 'be what you are,' and go European as soon as they can. . . . The African and American Negro problem is not purely racial. These cultures must be freed, formulated, and developed, and this cannot be done without a change in the present system. The Negro cannot develop his culture until he is free."

Africa must be taught to be proud of its contributions. "Stalin speaks of the cultures of the different nationalities of the Soviet Union as 'socialist in content and national in form.' . ."

Mr. Robeson was interested in the Eastern and Russian music, which he believes African music strongly resembles.

"The Negro folk songs and African music strongly resemble Eastern and Russian music. When I approached Russia, I found that I was interested in the Eastern part. I can't read Turgeniev, whose language is influenced by France and the West," said Mr. Robeson, who reads and speaks Russian fluently, "but I am interested in Gogol and Pushkin, who show more Eastern and Tartar influence. . . ."

Paul Robeson is vitally interested in the efforts of the Western Negroes to free themselves. He stated, "I believe there is no such thing in England and America as inter-racial *cooperation* from the NAACP point of view. Our freedom is going to cost so many lives that we mustn't talk about the Scottsboro case as one of sacrifice. When we talk of freedom, we don't discuss lives. Before the Negro is free, there will be many Scottsboros. The Communist emphasis in that case is right."

Becoming more personal, Mr. Robeson spoke of needing something to sing outside of Negro and English folk songs, and Western peasant folk material, and of discovering, about four years ago, the Hebrew and Russian songs. He learned the two languages, finding that they were both quite easy for him.

"There is little audience in England and America for the things I feel like singing or playing. They want Negro religious songs from which they take, not the suffering, but the comfort of the resignation they express (not heeding that the song's cry for heaven is only a reflex from the Negro's having suffered hell on earth). . . ."

Although he did not give any concerts during this visit, Mr. Robeson sang some of his most popular songs to the workers of the Kaganovitch Ball Bearing Plant, where he was applauded by a group including a great many foreign and American workers. He also broadcast; and on his return, he plans a concert tour of folk songs, and there is talk of a film with Eisenstein. He said, "The most important development in Soviet culture I have seen is in the moving picture field."

Among the theatres he visited, Mr. Robeson was most interested in the Moscow Children's Theatre, and the Realistic Theatre. At the former, he was pleased by *The Negro Boy and the Monkey,* a popular play about a little African who comes to the Soviet Union and is guided by his Pioneer comrades. The production method of Oxlopkhov (regisseur of the Realistic Theatre) impressed him with its similarity to motion picture technique, which he feels is best adapted to the tempo of life in the Soviet Union. Its plan, with the audience surrounding the stage platform, and participating in the performance, agrees with his own feeling that the artist should be in close contact with his audience.

Paul Robeson's activities have been put, with the enlargement of his interests, on an international scale, including studies and experiments in Eastern cultures along with his participation in African and American affairs. In correlating racial cultures, he sets a standard of awareness, saying, "The Negro must be conscious of himself and yet international, linked with the nations which are culturally akin to him."

DOCUMENT 43:
Albert Jackson, "Alabama's Blood-Smeared Cotton," *New Masses* 16, no. 13 (September 24, 1935): 13.

This report was from the secretary of the Share Croppers Union. It was a communist organization that sought to organize agricultural workers in the South. This document examines rural life in Alabama during the Great Depression for African Americans.

"Your time has come, you black————!" screeched through the woods surrounding Ed Bracy's home. A few seconds later the gang of vigilantes broke into the house and shot him nineteen times in the neck and head. This was the second killing during the Cotton Pickers Strike. It happened on Labor Day.

Ed Bracy, militant Negro leader of the Share Croppers Union, around Hope Hill, had continued to lead the masses of strikers in spite of terror and murder threats. Sheriff R. E. Woodruff's vigilante gang sneaked in at night, like the cowards they are, to murder another leader. The masses have already answered this attack on leaders—"We are all leaders and we will fight on to victory," they say. Since August 19, through the most vicious terror the landlords could unleash, the strikers have held their ranks solid. Such determination can only be born of dire poverty, starvation and oppression.

The terror drive continues. As I write this, there is a look-out to warn me of the approach of lynchers. Constant vigil is kept at all times. Sleep is tortured with nightmares of lynching, terror and murder. Food settles in lumps in your stomach. But the struggle must go on! The attack of the lynchers must be answered!

On August 22 they murdered Jim Press Meriwether, a Negro strike leader near Sandy Ridge. He walked by the home of Bennie Calloway, another striker, where Sheriff Woodruff's gang was beating the women. John Frank Bates, a Fort Deposit landlord, shot him down without a word. They found Jim's wife, beat her and hanged her from the rafters of the house for awhile before releasing her. Then they carried Jim to C. C. Ryles' plantation to question him. Getting no information from the dying man, they carried him out on a hillside and riddled his body with bullets.

Night riders, carrying Negro strikers out from their beds to beat them almost to death and throw them in the swamps. No sleep, no rest, but always watching for the terror gang. More than six strikers were carried out to be beaten. Some of them were unable to wear clothes on their back because of their wounds.

The search is hottest for me. Charles Tasker and James Jackson, Negro workers of Montgomery, were arrested on August 30. They were questioned continually about where I am. Later an I.L.D. lawyer secured their release. Detective Moseley carried them to the county line and told them to "Keep going and never come back!" They are forced to leave their homes and families.

The strike spreads. Montgomery, Talapoosa, Chambers, Lee and Randolph Counties are out solid now. The masses are willing to struggle, willing to sacrifice.

The small demands of the strike—$1 a hundred for picking cotton, $1 for 10 hours' work for wage hands, 20 cents an hour, 40 hours a week with pay in cash for relief workers—are more than 100 percent above the present rates, a grim testimony to the starvation conditions existing in the farming sections of the South. To maintain these conditions the landlords murder, terrorize and beat the strikers. The ugly head of fascism is rearing up in Dixie, in the "Cradle of the Confederacy."

Strikers hide out in swamps in the daytime to avoid attacks of the vigilante gangs. The night Jim Meriwether was killed the strikers got their guns and waited for another vigilante attack. When the lynchers arrived the strikers sounded the battle cry, it was to be steel for steel on even terms. The lynchers, cowards at heart, turned and ran before a shot was fired.

In the meantime, the landlords are beginning to crack. In lower Montgomery County a landlord is paying his hands $1 a day. In Reeltown, scene of the heroic Reeltown struggle of 1932, the landlords agreed to pay 75 cents a hundred and two meals for picking cotton. Around Dadeville and other parts of Talapoosa County the price is rising, but the masses refuse to pick for less than their demands. Only the small farmers, tenants and croppers who pick their own cotton are carrying anything to the gin. The landlords' fields are heavy with cotton that has been ready to pick for three weeks. On J. R. Bell's plantation in Lowndes County, the strikers say "$1 a hundred or let the cows eat it."

In the meantime, the Share Croppers Union waits word from the Southern Tenant Farmers Union on the question of amalgamation.

Now more than ever before the necessity for one powerful union in the cotton fields rings out. The murder and terror drive of the landlords is a clarion call for unity, for a powerful united struggle against the fascist attacks of the landlords and for raising the miserably low living standards of the southern rural masses.

In spite of all the odds, the strike goes on. It is historic, it is the greatest strike movement the landlords have ever witnessed. It is significant to all labor, it is raising the miserably low-wage standard on which Roosevelt based his wage-smashing Relief Wage Scale. It loosens the spirit of the Negro masses; they are struggling to the bitter end for their rights. It is imperative to America, it is battering down the ugly head of fascism in the "Cradle of American Fascism."

DOCUMENT 44:
Photograph, Sharecroppers' Families, July 1936.

Courtesy Library of Congress.

This image, taken by noted photographer Dorothea Lange, shows sharecropping families from Hill House, Mississippi, gathered for a Fourth of July celebration during the Great Depression. Sharecropping, a system by which tenants were allowed to live on and work a piece of land in exchange for a share of the crop produced, was available to poor blacks and whites and was often an abusive system that kept workers in debt.

DOCUMENT 45:
Photograph, Halifax, North Carolina, 1938.

Courtesy Library of Congress.

Taken by the Farm Security Administration (FSA), this photograph depicts an African American child in Halifax, North Carolina, at a segregated water fountain in April 1938. Part of the New Deal, the FSA was originally created as part of the Resettlement Administration in 1935. It promoted "rural rehabilitation" to bring sharecroppers, tenant farmers, and poor laborers together to work on collective farms that were subsidized by the government and used the newest technologies. The program was eventually reorganized to help farmers buy land.

Document 44

Document 45

DOCUMENT 46:

Cecelia Eggleston, "What a Negro Mother Faces," *The Forum and Century* (August 1938): 59-62.

A graduate of Howard University and a devoted Roman Catholic, Cecelia Eggleston was a social worker in New York City. This article is unique in that it addresses whether African American women should have children in the era of Jim Crow for a periodical that enjoyed a mainly white readership. The *Forum and Century* was published from 1886 to 1941.

The Negro wife of today who is a thinking woman pauses and ponders deeply before she decides to assume what is to any woman the gravest of responsibilities—motherhood. Why?

Not because of the specter of poverty; for, although economic insecurity is widespread, it is the woman in fairly comfortable circumstances who hesitates most to have a child. Nor does the fear of hereditary taints trouble her more than any other intelligent layman of good education. Certainly she possesses the common instinct of motherhood. She must, or else, in these days of contraceptives, she would have no problem.

The Negro woman hesitates because she is faced most cruelly with the responsibility of bringing into the world a child victimized not by disease or extreme poverty but by that over which neither he nor his parents have any control—the color of his skin.

In fact white people are prone to regard the problems of Negroes in general very much as they do the grievances of children—disturbances of the moment, easily quieted, quickly forgotten. They know that Negroes may be blue or low-spirited or miserable, but it just does not occur to them that they are *people,* adults, capable of being deeply unhappy, torn by conflicting emotions, or weighted with problems that cannot be laid down by the river side.

A woman writer widely known for syndicated articles of opinion once wrote what she thought about the Negro woman.

The gist was that the Negro woman in what was described as her native habitat was a fine specimen of womanhood. It was only when she moved into the city and aped her white sisters that she became unworthy of anyone's interest or respect. Her native habitat was a cabin in which she was surrounded by the white folk's clothes and her own brood of seven or eight—of divers fathers. There she was a happy and an admirable character.

One might forgive this writer for her callous and superficial designation of her Negro woman as happy, because a certain sort of passive adjustment is mistaken for happiness in many situations. But to refer to her as admirable was not only unforgivable but absolutely disastrous to the ideals Negroes have been fighting for, all these years.

If this writer were to be honest with herself, she would admit that she would not dare to label as admirable that type of woman representing any other race of people under the sun. Indeed, if she were mentioned at all, she would be described as lazy, loose, unambitious, shiftless, and downright immoral. The question would be why did she not emulate her sisters, instead of being content to remain in her old environment. But, when the *Negro* woman attempts to better herself, then she is aping her white sisters and loses her charm.

Loses it for whom? Why, for white people who cannot relinquish this mental stereotype of the Negro woman, a relic of the days when no consideration was given the Negro woman's morality and her home ties were broken at the whim of the master.

This is a part of the slave heritage which my child, no matter what its sex, could not escape. Contrast it with our attitude toward foreigners who come there totally unacquainted with American ways and standards. They are encouraged by every means to adapt themselves to our life. The quicker their adjustment, the more desirable they are thought to be as citizens. Their assimilation is regarded as a promising sign of their versatility. But in an American Negro this is aping.

In considering whether I shall have a baby, my first thought is naturally of the child's health and physical well-being. Fortunately I live in a city where excellent medical attention is available and I feel sure that I should have prenatal care as fine as the nation affords for its great mass of citizens. But, were I in the deep South, my situation would be entirely different.

A Negro sorority I am familiar with has recently been operating a health project there. The women fled at the sight of doctors and nurses. A doctor at childbirth was unheard-of; prenatal attention was not even a myth. These mothers die in childbirth at the rate of three out of ten. The infant mortality is even higher.

Now I realize it is not because they are Negroes that these women and their offspring die, I know that their deaths are due to extreme poverty, ignorance, and neglect. Yet, when I read the cold, bare statistics, that the mortality rate for Negro women in childbirth is eight times that for whites, I am a bit panicky in spite of my personally favorable circumstance.

We Negroes teach our youth that the salvation of the Negro lies within the race itself; that, as soon as we become economically independent, educated, cultured, and skillful, we shall arrive. But wealth, education, culture, and technological advancement did not save the Jew in Germany.

Although Americans entertain no fears that the Negro in America will ever threaten a civilization which he lacks the inherent power, according to them, to sustain, they are nevertheless extremely careful to block all roads from the start.

The Negro child of today, then, must be imbued with more than a normal share of courage, for he has to clear the road before he starts on the journey. It is difficult to see from what source he can draw this courage.

Suppose I ask myself just what I have done as an individual to make this a better world into which to bring a child.

I have thought that one way of opening for my child doors that have been closed to me is via the interracial committee. The trouble is, I believed, that we do not know each other. If only we did, these mutual prejudices would melt away.

And indeed we do grow to know each other. The whites learn that all Negroes do not wait until Saturday to take a bath and that a high percentage of Negro women have a wholesome respect for their marital vows. The Negroes find that the white people on the committee are agreeable, well-meaning persons who feel that white people have a responsibility and that something must be done. So we chat pleasantly over the cups of tea and pass resolutions. But we get little further than the teacups.

Few, if any, lasting personal friendships develop from the association of the races on these committees. The white members are all friends of the Negro in a vague, impersonal sort of way. . But real friendship in the sense that involves exchanging visits outside of meeting nights, showers for the bride, bridge, picnics, trips together, informal occasions where people really get to know each other—that is out of the question. After all, someone invariably protests, the purpose of the Committee is not to foster personal relationships and individual friendships. It is something much bigger than that—to create good will between two races, to break down prejudice and misunderstanding. Do not confuse the two interpretations of the term *social*. This is its more restricted use.

But, in spite of all resolutions passed for the social (in the larger sense) advancement of the Negro, I still cannot buy a house where I might wish to do so and I still would have to take my baby to the clinic on the special days for Negroes. And thus, before he left my arms, he would begin to live a lie, to learn day by day in a hundred subtle but nonetheless definite ways that he was different—somehow inferior. Thus he would grow to a manhood that could not make him a man, led on by first one mirage, then another, until at last the barrenness of the life about him met the nakedness of his own soul.

Why not try God? Surely, if anywhere, in the folds of Christianity I would find an approach to my problem.

Problem? I had no problem, only a duty clear and undivided. A married woman has no choice, according to the Roman Catholic Church, in which I was reared. I must bring my child, then, into the same kind of church world in which I grew up.

Should his baby feet stray in the house of God beyond the last three rows, frantic ushers would seize him and return him to his proper place—the last three rows or, it might be, the dusty gallery above the choir loft.

His baby ears would hear the same sermons that mine had listened to. He would learn how Christ had died to save all, rich and poor, high and low, black and white. He would swallow it all as I had swallowed it before him, until he, too, discovered that the Fatherhood of God and the brotherhood of man is a beautiful theory, harmless to believe in, dynamite to practice.

The parish priest inquires why you do not attend your duties. "That's the trouble with you people," he says. "As soon as you get a bit of education, you forget God."

As if God and the church were synonymous. I should not say that education makes us forget God but I do hold that it does for us what it is supposed to do for all exposed to its influence. It makes us think for ourselves and heightens our realization of the travesty that is carried on in the name of Christ.

From my last attendance at mass some years ago I have retained an indelible picture in my mind. I can still see the Negro communicants kneeling at the back of the church, waiting for the white faithful to leave the altar rail. A nausea came over me then, a nausea which now replaces the pious genuflection I used to make every time I passed a Catholic church.

Some loyal and devout Negro Catholics maintain that Holy Mother Church is much more liberal than the Protestant churches (at least in the South), for she does admit us within her doors—to the last three rows—and she will serve us communion—after the whites are served. Alas, the distinction is too fine for me to appreciate.

Some people may feel that it would not be fair for me to transmit to my child the discouragement and disillusionment my experiences with religion, as it is practiced in the Christian churches of America, have brought me. But I believe it might be kinder to prepare him for it in advance. Blessed are they who expect nothing, for they shall not be disappointed.

Since I find no encouragement in the faith of our fathers, I turn to other fields more practical and tangible. What are the prospects for my Negro child in industry, science, business, or the arts?

From latent ability on both sides of the family, this child, unborn, unconceived even, might develop marked dramatic ability. What would this mean for him?

If the child is a boy, it would mean, by present reckoning, buffooning, clowning. It might mean a variation of a character from *The Emperor Jones* or *Porgy* or a *Green Pastures* of a brighter hue but it most assuredly would not mean the rest of O'Neill—or Ibsen or Shakespeare.

If, still less happily, this Negro child should be a girl with dramatic ability, she might as well start learning her dialect in the cradle; for, in the years to come, Mammy will go marching on. Scarlett O'Hara may be gone with the wind, but good old Mammy—primitive, ignorant, stupid in every way save in her instinct to protect her li'l white lamb— Mammy will be the last of the stereotypes to go.

Here I interrupt with a timid song, "I Didn't Raise My Girl to Be a Mammy."

Sacrilege! screams the South. How dare you? She couldn't represent anything finer, more beautiful, more—.

Yes, yes. I know the rest.

In the business and scientific world the situation is different. It is much worse.

The chances of a Negro's getting proper preparation and training are growing slimmer and slimmer. Not only are increased costs in the great technical schools prohibitive, but the opportunities for Negroes to learn the practical side of this kind of work are extremely limited.

It is the same story in the matter of preparation for the professions. The colleges and universities pass the buck to the public. We are willing to accept you as students, they say to the Negroes, but we cannot force you on the public for practice.

It is interesting to note that these same educational centers feel duty-bound to take the initiative in guiding the public in its democratic duty in other situations. But, in a matter involving racial injustice, the cause of social reconstruction is politely laid aside, and the less provocative cloak of realism is assumed.

Even when the Negro youth manages somehow to acquire the necessary preliminary training for a career, he is not much better off. Several young men of my acquaintance who hold degrees from the business schools of leading universities are working on P.W.A. projects scarcely requiring an eighth-grade education. Furthermore, as the little businessman in all other groups yields steadily to the pressure of big business, the Negro businessman disappears altogether. In Negro shops of personal service, white syndicates are pushing out the few Negro owners and proprietors left. For the purpose of attracting the Negro trade they put in a Negro *front* in the persons of a few low-salaried Negro attendants.

In my frantic search for a desirable future for this child whose birth I debate so fearfully, I turn at last to the United States Government.

Is my answer to be found in longer relief rolls? Well, if Negroes are constantly denied admission to the openings compatible with their abilities, in all capacities from the lowest to the highest, they will have no choice but to become helots of the government.

The civil service offers no protection. With its photo requirement and the patronage dispenser's prerogative of choosing among the first three on the list, a Negro with a Sigma Chi Rho in chemistry is wasting his time taking an examination to qualify as even a laboratory assistant at $1,200 a year. When a few fortunate Negroes eventually succeed in receiving minor appointments as messengers or skilled laborers, they remain such, with no hope of promotion.

A few Negro lawyers in the North and Midwest, realizing how limited is their field in practicing in white courts, turn to politics as an outlet for their ambitions and energies. The returns are hardly worth the time and effort. It is lamentable that there is only one Negro congressman for 10,000,000 people. And Negroes really hold fewer important government positions than they did in the early part of the century. The so-called special assistant appointments made in the various departments and bureaus are merely sops to the Negro voters.

A white woman whom I met recently feels that I am unduly pessimistic. "For instance," she says, "I could just sit and worry about the things that could happen to my own child, natural catastrophes or a disastrous change in government. In such events my child would be no better off than yours."

I might have answered that, in the light of recent experiences of Negroes in flood and drought relief, sufficient evidence could be furnished to prove that, though nature was undeniably color-blind in delivering the blow, democracy was far from it in giving succor.

If, as some students of social and political trends maintain, we are drifting toward a fascist state, then indeed is the doom of the Negro sealed. Then what is now chronic would become acute, as Sinclair Lewis points out in *It Can't Happen Here.*

A change toward communism, on the other hand, appears to offer more hope of equal opportunity and protection under the law. But aren't *these same rights* guaranteed by our most sacred Constitution? Can we believe that another system will change the hearts of men?

Most Negroes are willing to struggle along under the palliative measures of the New Deal, which they believe will lead ultimately to a new day for themselves and their progeny. They naïvely trust that *new day* means *better day.*

Those Negroes who really wish to take an intelligent and active part in social reconstruction are looked on with suspicion by both Negroes and whites—by whites, because the thinking Negro does not conform to their stereotype of the happy, carefree Negro; by Negroes, because they feel that such individuals may jeopardize the slight gains already made.

There was a time when colored people living in some degree of comfort compensated for the limitation of their opportunities to get on in the world by saying that they would rather be high-class Negroes than poor whites. That time recedes further into the past, for Negroes now realize that nothing—education, wealth, culture, travel—can compensate for the lack of a white face. Any white person who believes that Negroes are oversensitive in this attitude need only black his face for a time. The Negroes, knowing they cannot, do not ask to be white. They do ask, however, to be *people.*

The Negro woman who asks her inner self, *Should I have a baby?* will find no ready-made answer. Before she responds to the question irrevocably, she might put it in another way: *Will my child rise up to call me blessed or curse the day that he was born?*

DOCUMENT 47:
Eric Williams, "Race Relations in Puerto Rico and the Virgin Islands," *Foreign Affairs* 23 (January 1945): 308–317.

Courtesy Foreign Affairs.

This essay was published when Eric Williams (1911–1981) was an assistant professor at Howard University and research member of the Anglo-American Caribbean Commission. The commission was founded in 1941 to supervise economic and social programs in the region. Williams would later lead Trinidad and Tobago to independence and become prime minister. This essay provides a useful comparison to race relations in the American South.

I

The islands of the Caribbean differ in size, political affiliation, religious beliefs and language; but the basic difference is ethnic. Racially, the Caribbean falls into two distinct groups: the territories with a comparatively large white population, and the territories with a predominantly black or colored population.

In the 1940 United States census, the population of Puerto Rico was given as 76.55 percent white; the corresponding figure for the Virgin Islands was 9 percent. There are further divergencies within the Virgin Islands group. Only 3.2 percent of the population of the island of St. Croix was given as white, as compared with 15.8 percent for the island of St. Thomas. Charlotte Amalie, the chief city of St. Thomas, had a white population of 12.1 percent; the two chief cities of St. Croix had white populations of 2.2 and 4.3 percent respectively. This ethnic difference is the consequence of the particular economy developed in the various regions. Where the plantation economy based on sugar predominated, Negro slavery was essential and the territory automatically became black. The Virgin Islands fell in this category, together with Haiti and the British, French and Netherlands possessions. Where the small farmer survived, in a coffee or tobacco or livestock economy, white labor was predominant. Puerto Rico, Cuba and, to a lesser extent, The Dominican Republic were in this group . . .

In Puerto Rico today a population of close to two million people is crowded on a small island of slightly more than two million acres, less than half of which are arable. The population has doubled twice in the last century and is increasing at a net rate of 30,000 a year. The chief means of subsistence is the land, and the principal crop sugar. The sugar industry accounts for 60 percent of the total export trade, occupies 40 percent of all farm lands, employs 40 percent of the working population, and accounts for 90 percent of the freight hauled by the public railways. The industry achieved this supremacy by reason of tariff protection in the United States market, and without this tariff protection the crop would be almost eliminated. Its further expansion is prohibited by the quota system. Sugar has brought to the island a phenomenal increase in wealth, but the average Puerto Rican is today a landless wage earner, ill-fed, ill-housed and ill-clothed, living on an income of $341 a year. Puerto Rico today has a subsidized economy. Federal contributions, direct and indirect, amounted to $57,000,000 in 1942, or approximately $30 per capita.

In the Virgin Islands a population of 25,000 people live on 85,000 acres, of which less than one-sixth is crop land. With 11,600 acres of cropland and 8,000 acres in cultivation, St. Croix, the agricultural center of the group, supports a population of nearly 13,000. Yet the population has declined by more than 50 percent in the last century; the decline in St. John is more than 70 percent, while for the group as a whole it is more than 40 percent. Large-scale emigration represented an unconscious effort to achieve some equilibrium between population and means of subsistence. In spite of such emigration, the Administrator of St. Croix estimates that the present population of that island is 25 percent greater than the island can support. The National Resources Planning Board is even more pessimistic. In its "Development Plan for the Virgin Islands,'" the Board frankly confesses its inability to see a way of providing for more than 60 percent of the population of the area. Sugar, the main crop of St. Croix, yields 10 tons per acre as compared with 30 in Puerto Rico. Without tariff protection the industry would collapse overnight. Before the war, tourist expenditures were the chief supplementary source of revenue. National defense projects have taken their place during the war. The average income in St. Croix is $400 per year; the income of the working classes is much lower. Even this standard of living is achieved only by subsidies. Federal contributions in 1942 amounted to nearly $1,000,000, or $39 per capita.

It is in this concrete economic setting that we must view the question of race relations. The struggle for survival, by the community and by the individual, is a grim one.

II

Legal discrimination in the two countries is unknown. Children of all colors meet on equal terms in the public schools, though discrimination is prevalent in private schools, even those which receive government grants. There are no segregated housing areas. Whites, blacks and mulattoes sit side by side in theaters, churches and public vehicles, and lie side by side in the cemeteries. The law recognizes no differences based on race, color, creed, national origin or previous condition. Lynchings are unheard of.

This absence of legal discrimination against the Negro arises from the fact that racial differences are subordinate to those of class. Muñoz Marín, Puerto Rico's distinguished statesman and popular leader, tells the story of the white voter who was asked by a colored lawyer to vote for a certain candidate. The white voter replied: "You *blanquitos* ["little whites," not to be confused with the American term "poor whites"] have too much." The story is very revealing. "White" denotes class and status rather than color and race. In the Caribbean generally a man is not only as white as he looks. If by virtue of his position or his wealth he moves about in white society, he automatically becomes "white." An American student, Dr. Charles C. Rogler, has made an intensive study of a small Puerto Rican town, Comerío. He found that social distinctions were based on class and not race, and that the two coalesced merely because the Negro is never found in the upper class. "However," he adds, "if, to take a hypothetical case, a dark mulatto were to belong to the upper class, he would be socially defined as a white person." There is no unanimity as to who are Negroes and who are not. Some Puerto Rican families may have one child classified in the census as white, another as colored. It is well known that, in order not to antagonize some prominent family which does not wish to be identified with Negroes, the census officer would classify its members as white, and perhaps change the classification later. For this reason some observers believe that the percentage of colored people in the Puerto Rican census has been grossly underestimated. It is a notorious fact that these "white-minded Negroes," as they are called in St. Thomas, have colored ancestors. The mulatto in the United States Caribbean possessions thus has a much greater social mobility than his kinsfolk in the United States. It must be emphasized that this mobility is very largely a result of historical causes.

The mulatto's concern with color is understandable in a society where his handicaps increase more and more drastically as the pigmentation deepens. But the consciousness of legal equality tends to give the colored people confidence in social relationships. For example, within the last 70 years numbers of French people have migrated to St. Thomas from the French island of St. Barthélemy. Today this French colony has more than a thousand members, concentrated in a fishing village three miles west of Charlotte Amalie and in a community of farmers on the northern side of the island. They keep very largely to themselves, speak a French patois though they understand and speak English, and are easily identified by the obvious signs of malnutrition they reveal. The islanders derisively call them *Chachas*. The attitude of the colored people to this French community is, indeed, one of unveiled contempt. Some of the French people send their children to the schools, wearing shoes. Some of the adults have taken to trade, and own grocery stores and liquor bars in the French district. But the prejudice against them remains, and the marriage of a colored girl to one of these Frenchmen is an occasion for endless gossip. The children, it is said, will always have "the Chacha look." The feeling is unmistakable in St. Thomas that "the Chachas are all right in their place." It is a complete reversal of the relationship that would prevail in other countries.

The Negro enjoys equality with the white man politically as well as legally. Negroes in Puerto Rico vote not as Negroes but as Puerto Ricans identified with one of the major parties. The Republican Party was founded by a colored Puerto Rican, Dr. José Celso Barbosa, one of the great names in Puerto Rico's history. Today colored Puerto Ricans are found in the Insular Congress and in municipal government, as well as in high administrative positions. Ramos Antonini, the colored deputy leader of the Populares Party, was elected as representative-at-large in the 1942 elections and polled the largest vote. In other words, he does not represent a Negro constituency nor are his supporters Negroes only. His color debarred him from becoming Speaker of the House of Representatives, however. Dr. Leopoldo Figueroa, another colored Puerto Rican, head of the maternity section of the Municipal Hospital, is one of the chief stalwarts of the Coalition Party. Until recently a prominent Negro lawyer sat on the Public Service Commission; another is Chief Examiner of the Civil Service Commission. In the Virgin Islands in recent years, very dark men have taken positions that were reserved, under the Danes, for Europeans or light colored people.

Thus it is that, by virtue of the absence of legal discrimination, the high degree of social mobility, the emphasis on class, and the political equality that prevails, unity among Negroes on the race question does not exist in Puerto Rico and the Virgin Islands. The word "Negro" is seldom used in the Caribbean, and, when used, is not a "fighting" word. All over the Caribbean it is either synonymous with "slave," or is a term of endearment, used colloquially by both whites and Negroes. The Spanish word for slaveship is, significantly, *negrero,* but there is no Spanish equivalent for "nigger" or "damned nigger." The militancy of American Negroes has no counterpart in Puerto Rico and St. Thomas. To repeat—the issue in the Caribbean is not one of race but one of class. Puerto Ricans talk not so much of "the colored race" as of "the colored class." The conflict is not between white and black but, as in St. Thomas, between those who live on one of the three hills on which the town is built and those who do not. Muñoz Marín puts the same idea in different words: there are in

Puerto Rico only two classes, those who wear neckties and those who don't. The situation is the same in the British West Indies, where the mark of differentiation is the wearing of shoes rather than of neckties. It is to be noted that similar conditions prevail in Haiti where there is no considerable number of white people.

III

Legally, the Negro is on a footing of equality with the white man. On the social level, however, race prejudice antedated the American occupation, exists today, and is increasing. It will be readily appreciated, however, that in the nature of things social discrimination does not affect the large majority of colored people. The entry of foreign capital has brought the practices associated with the countries of origin. It is not the influx of Americans as individuals but of American capital that has resulted in the recrudescence of the race problem. Social discrimination is most obvious in private employment in the upper brackets. Conventionally, none but white people or the fairest-skinned among the colored are employed by banks, sugar corporations, airlines and shipping companies, and the large department stores.

Discrimination is common in all the better hotels and restaurants. A few years ago a well-known restaurant in San Juan, then under non-local management, refused to serve people of color. The issue was taken to the District Court, where a decision in favor of the management was given. The Supreme Court upheld the verdict, and the practice continued until the establishment passed into Puerto Rican hands. In the leading hotel in Puerto Rico the patronage is almost wholly composed of whites from the United States. Colored people are never seen in the dining room or at the bar unless they are foreigners traveling on government missions. The outstanding hotel in St. Thomas, government-owned, and leased on a contract which specifically prohibited racial discrimination, refused to admit colored people until recently, when it was turned over to a new manager who is colored. There is, however, another hotel which still refuses to serve colored people, on the plea that it is reserved for service men. Clubs in Puerto Rico are customarily classified as "first class" and "second class." Whites belong to both types of club, but Negroes belong only to "second class" ones. Cases have arisen in recent years of refusal by night clubs to serve colored people; in one instance the establishment was fined $25.

Such small fines are locally considered a joke. In the University of Puerto Rico, colored students, the majority destined to be schoolteachers, are freely admitted. Yet two members of the faculty, in a special study of the Negro in Puerto Rico, have brought to light a number of sayings about the Negro common to university students. The saying, "God made the Negro so that animals can rest," is an example.

Social discrimination has increased in Puerto Rico to such an extent that the legislature passed a Civil Rights Act in 1943 guaranteeing the right of all persons irrespective of differences of race, creed or political affiliation to enjoy the facilities afforded by public places, businesses and any agency of the Insular Government. The penalties decreed are a fine of from $25 to $100, or a jail term of from ten to a hundred days. Despite this law, however, colored people in Puerto Rico are very reluctant to visit certain hotels or night clubs.

IV

The lower classes of Caribbean society look to America as the land of opportunity. They are the underdogs now, since they are black, and the left-handed racial egalitarianism of the United States, where one drop of colored blood makes one a Negro, gives them that feeling of equality with the colored aristocracy which is ruled out at home by the emphasis on status. To these people contact with the United States means material benefits, the opportunity of education and the monthly remittances from emigrants who have made good.

But the islanders are even more aware of racial distinctions than they were before American rule. This is not to say that the presence of large numbers of American troops, mostly colored, in the area has produced any serious change in the racial situation, as far as the masses are concerned. The rank and file of American troops have fitted into local society. Barred from officers' clubs, looked down upon by white and colored aristocracy, the enlisted men have gravitated toward the people of their own social milieu, the colored middle and lower classes. Left alone, white soldiers and colored population can and will work out an adjustment of their own. It is particularly important that they should do so. One instance taken from Jamaica suggests the problem. On December 8, 1943, an advertisement appeared in *The Gleaner* of Jamaica for "help" at the American base. The advertisement specified: "White, Male and

Female." The next day the same advertisement appeared, minus one word: "White." But Kingston was in an uproar. Letters and protests poured in, the Corporation met and passed a resolution vigorously condemning the "insult," and voted that a copy of the resolution be sent to President Roosevelt. The United States Base Commander made a public apology, but the tension continued. Discriminatory notices are, in fact, a common feature of the West Indian press. But the incident is a reminder of Caribbean sensitiveness on the race question and of the perils inherent in the situation.

The constituents of the race problem in Puerto Rico and the Virgin Islands are, in short, a historical background that emphasizes class rather than race; an economic setting in which the problem of the Negro is merged in the larger problem of the community; the absence of legal discrimination against the black masses; and the pressure of social discrimination on the lighter-skinned middle class minority. There is no "solution" to such a problem. With the economic and social forces as they are it is difficult to see how there can be any substantial changes in race relations in the two communities. Ultimately, the shape of race relations in the United States will be the decisive factor in the relations between races in these colonies.

Some Puerto Rican sociologists advance as a solution the long tradition of interbreeding, which will, they believe, "whiten" the Puerto Rican Negroes in 75 to 100 years. But this is quite ridiculous, since the essential character of the present relations would prevent this "whitening" even if it were desirable and, within reasonable human expectation, possible. On the occasion of the Jamaican incident referred to above, a publicist advanced a more serious proposal. Americans, he said, must learn West Indian psychology. "It will not be enough for the Americans to say they followed the local custom."

There are many Americans in the islands who take these questions seriously. They must seek to understand that conditions in the West Indies are not like conditions at home. President Roosevelt's directive to United States forces in the Caribbean to respect local customs has had good results, in this regard. All Americans in the area must recognize the particular racial background and historical development of the islands. The Administration must try to formulate policy and practice in accordance with the history and patterns of the area, and not allow itself to be influenced by the national traditions of the interests which it represents. Given the history and social sentiments of the island, it is not at all impossible for the United States Administration in Puerto Rico to strike blows at race prejudice and to try to develop an official attitude toward race relations in harmony with the aspirations and practice of the colonial areas. There are already signs that the American and British authorities recognize the necessity of action on this question. It is interesting to note that a special correspondent of the London *Times,* in two articles on the West Indies published on October 29 and 30, 1943, said that "it is time to consider whether Colonial Office officials should not in future be forbidden to belong to clubs which impose a color bar . . . sooner or later, the color bar which at present surrounds the higher administrative posts must be broken down."

Asked his views on the subject, Muñoz Marín replied simply: "More democracy." Even the colored opponents of this Puerto Rican leader agree that he and his party have given Negroes a square deal and opened positions to them, especially in the teaching profession and the higher ranks of the police force, from which they were conventionally debarred. The popular movement in these island possessions of the United States stands for "no discrimination," as opposed to what it considers the American trend toward greater discrimination. Similarly the Communist Party has consistently opposed racial discrimination. Recent events in Europe have shown that even liberty and racial rights which have been exercised for centuries are not safe except in a fully democratic order. In trying to base the struggle against racial discrimination upon the democratic aspirations of the people, Muñoz Marín is in harmony with the best thought and increasing practice of the age.

DOCUMENT 48:
Pamphlet, Welborn Victor Jenkins, *Who Are the Thespians?* Subject File: Afro-Americans—History—1964. Folder: Afro-Americans—Georgia—Social Life and Customs.

Courtesy Kenan Research Center, Atlanta History Center.

This undated pamphlet, written by Welborn Victor Jenkins, the founder of the Thespian Literary Association, criticizes African Americans who give their children white dolls, read books or buy art by white authors and artists, and fail to support African American newspapers. The Thespian Literary Society was optimistically organized to uplift the race "thru literary exercises, inspiring speakers, newspapers, pamphlets, books, and magazines."

A few years ago I was the silent observer of a little drama—nay, it was a little tragedy—which came nearer discouraging me, so far as my race is concerned, than anything I ever witnessed. It was Christmas in a small town and the "farmer folk" were crowding into the store to buy presents for the children. I noticed an especially handsome couple looking over the doll counter evidently intending to buy a doll for their little girl, a dark brown cherub about six years old. They seemed to be very much taken up with a pretty colored doll which for some strange reason happened to be in the collection. Negro dolls are often found in the toy-stores and are much in demand as cooks and maids in the playhouses of little white children. But always they are the ugliest dolls that can be made. However, this especial colored doll had been left on hand for several seasons and had found no white buyers for the reason, no doubt, that it was as pretty a doll as can ever have been made. Also there was an unusual coincident touching the matter at hand for never before have I seen a doll look so much like a child as this same doll looked like the child in question.

The clerk had made a bargain price to the parents and was on the verge of delivering the doll when the little girl happened to get a glimpse of it. Throwing down her candy, she screamed like one who might have fallen into the fire. She stamped her foot and went into a rage, entreating her mother not to buy for her "an ugly old doll like that."

• • • •

The store was crowded. Everybody turned to see what had made the little girl so angry. In order to quiet her, the friendly white clerk gave her several white dolls to choose from. Immediately she picked out one that struck her fancy and seeing it wrapped up for her, grew quite satisfied and happy.

The clerk laughed. The fond, foolish parents knew no better than to laugh. The child laughed. Everybody laughed.

But I didn't laugh. Instead, a pain sprang into my heart which nothing since has been able to move. I did not laugh. To me, the scene was a direful tragedy. I have never felt so humiliated in all my life.

• • • •

What was the cause? What was wrong?

For years and years our children have been given nothing but white dolls to play with. They have developed a decided dislike for dolls that look like themselves. Few colored people realize what a colossal blunder has been made by our parents in this simple matter of dolls. Heretofore nearly all dolls made were white dolls. But God be praised for the fact that certain factories are now turning out thousands of beautiful colored dolls; and within twenty years there will be colored dolls in every home. However, it will be fully three hundred years before we shall be able to undo the harm already done.

And just as it has been with dolls so it has been with pictures. Go into almost any colored home. What sort of pictures do you see on our walls? Only now and then in ever so many hundred homes do you see any decent, inspiring pictures of our own people on the walls of our homes. I do not mean the dollar-ninety-eight-cent enlargements with which white agents have grown rich off of our people. I mean pictures of great and noble Negro characters like Dumas and Fred Douglas, Maceo and. Toussaint L'Ouverture. We cannot condemn too strongly the habit of our people of putting pictures on their walls with no thought whatever of the effect they will have on the children growing up in the home.

We may say indeed that decent Negro pictures are not made. But suppose they were made? Is it not a fact that we are creating a distaste for them by worshipping the pictures of another race rather than our own exclusively?

Then take books for instance.

The world is full of books. The book-stores groan with loads and loads of them. Every house you see has a library or a book case full of books. But they are all books written by the white race, printed by the white race and published by the white race.

The next time you see a pile of books, look for one that was written by a Negro. That kind is very scarce. Then look for one that was printed and published by our people. There isn't one in a thousand.

Do you know why?

It is not that we have no writers. There is an army of young Negro writers springing up in this country. It is not because we have no thinkers. The Negro race is beginning to think. We have the writers and we have the thinkers. But we have no great publishing house to publish what these writers write and what these thinkers think. So we are in great danger of developing a distaste for Negro books and literature just as we have for Negro dolls and pictures for the simple reason that the books which white people write about us are very often just as ugly as the dolls they have made to look like us and the pictures they have made to represent us. White publishing houses will not print and publish of their own accord the kind of books which our people ought to read and need to read. When the average colored writer appears before a white publisher, he is requested to put up the total cost of the entire edition of his book in advance and assume all the risks of publication. For this reason there are practically no Negro books published. There is but one way our people shall ever have a literature that does us justice. We've got to write it ourselves, print it ourselves and publish it ourselves.

• • • •

Take our newspapers for an instance.

Do you know that in the great State of Georgia only one newspaper is printed out and out by colored people and that is Sol Johnson's Tribune of Savannah? Who prints the others? White people print them. White people print the Atlanta Independent. White people print the Atlanta Post. And the others that are not printed by white people are set up by them. How then can we ever develop race pride, race loyalty, racial power and efficiency or racial independence and confidence so long as our literature, which is the very bread our souls must live and grow upon, must be ground in the white man's mills, sifted thru the white man's hoppers, baked and served to us from the white man's factories?

Wake up people!

We've got to make a long hard fight to gain a foothold in this country. We've got to fight, not with guns but with brains and co-operation. Co-operation (that's the magic word) backed up by brains. That indeed is our last resort. Co-operation is the steam drill with which we must bore into the rock of our racial resources; it is the steam-shovel with which we must plough thru the mountains of competition and opposition; it is the steam-hammer with which we must tamp down a foundation to stand upon; it is the machine gun with which we must fight our way inch by inch to victory; it is the dynamite with which we must blast our way to economic freedom.

From this day on it shall be necessary for the Negro to play the shrewdest, most carefully planned, the cleanest and fairest yet most strategic game ever played by any nation in the history of the world. For while remaining perfectly friendly as far as possible with the white people North and South, we must be able to look them in the eye and frankly tell them that we want our rights, and that altho we are anxious for their friendship, we are fighting for our rights, fighting for room to live and breathe, fighting not with bombs but with co-operation, unity and singleness of purpose.

. . . .

The first step is to establish an Intelligence Plant right here in the heart of the South. We want a literary factory that will grind out corn at a price in reach of all. Our people need to be reading thousands of books they cannot now get. They need to be reading newspapers and magazines that they print themselves. Hundreds of our girls ought to be put to setting type and printing the books that our people ought to be reading.

What then shall we do?

We shall build in Atlanta, Ga., the **World's Largest Negro Publishing House.** We shall call it the **Voice Publishing Company.** We shall publish in Atlanta the **World's Greatest Negro Newspaper.** We shall call it the **Atlanta Voice.**

In order to do this we are now organizing a literary league to be known as the **Thespian Literary Association.** There shall be in the State of Georgia three hundred branches of this association, each branch headed by a president. And we shall choose the most progressive lady in each community as the Thespian president of the branch in that community.

HOW WE SHALL ORGANIZE.

After presidents shall have been appointed in the three hundred communities of our state then each president shall choose from ten to twenty members to serve under her. This group will form a **Thespian Branch.** There will be, therefore, about 5000 members of this association in our state and together they will form one of the most powerful forces for the uplift of our race the world has ever seen.

WHAT WILL OUR WORK BE?

Now, all the **Thespians** will have to do is to give about one concert every two months. These concerts will be furnished by the Atlanta Home Office already printed out, one copy to each member. These concerts will be easy to get up, easy to learn, easy to present, but will be the most inspiring literary programs and the highest class of entertainment ever presented to our people on so large a uniform scale.

We will charge fifteen cents at the door for all concerts; When the money has been counted, the president will pay the officers one-fourth or one-third for the use of the church as the case may be (or it might be better to call this amount a donation to the church) and the rest of the money belongs to the branch. Now let us make this point very plain. This money that has been raised does not belong to anybody a long way off. It belongs to the **Thespians** who raised it. But of course it is raised under agreement to place all net proceeds in a common treasury for the purpose of establishing the great publishing house we are talking about in this book.

PERMANENT ORGANIZATION.

Just as soon as one concert shall be given by all the branches round, a call will be issued for all the presidents to meet in a general convention in Atlanta and their railroad fare and expenses shall be paid out of the proceeds of the first concert. At this meeting we will elect our permanent officials and appoint our various executive committees. From the day of this meeting we will become a permanent and powerful reality.

We must stress the fact that these concerts will not be difficult to present. The Program Committee of the Home Office will get these concerts up. They will be sent printed out to the various presidents. After giving to each one his or her part and allowing about thirty days to learn these parts, the concert is ready. The president arranges with the officers of one of the leading churches for the use of the church. A night is appointed. Everybody works together in complete accord to make the program a success. And as we have already said **the net proceeds belong to the ones who raise it.**

Different programs will be given every two or three months, and they will be continued until each member has $25 to his or her credit and each president has one or two hundred dollars to her share according to the number of members who serve under her. The presidents in small communities will chose ten members and will be paid $100 to their share. The presidents in larger communities like Rome, Griffin, Americus will choose twenty members and will have $200 for their share out of all the proceeds. The proceeds of the concerts will be divided on a scale of four and one and eight and one. In the first group, each time the members receive one dollar around, the president is to receive four. In the second group, each time the members receive one dollar around, the president is to receive eight.

DIVIDENDS AND PROFITS

When the money we have raised has been pooled in a common treasury to be made over into the **Great Voice Publishing Company,** it is still the property of the various **Thespians,** personally, legally and in fee simple; and each and every member will hold a duly certified certificate to represent his or her amount in the big treasury; moreover, each and every member and president will draw dividends every quarter on his or her share just as if it were a house or money in the bank. In addition to this each and every member will have the right to sell his or her share according to the Thespian By-Laws and Constitution just the same as a horse or a bale of cotton. And for the protection of all concerned our organization is to be incorporated under the laws of the State of Georgia.

MAIN PURPOSE OF THE THESPIANS.

Now the main object of the Thespians is the uplift of our people from the center and bottom thru literary exercises, inspiring speakers, newspapers, pamphlets, books and magazines. Other organizations of uplift begin on the edge and top. We are going to start at the center and bottom. Thru the medium of our lyceum department we mean to send educated and thoughtful speakers into the most remote communities and the good which shall come to us thru this can scarcely be imagined. A little later it is our intention to institute the world's first Negro Chautauqua.

THE MIGHTY CHAUTAUQUA

Colored people have made various attempts to institute a chautauqua. They have failed to make any impression heretofore because of the regretable habit of our leading men to be grafters. We are going to succeed because we are going at the thing in the right way. Atlanta with her five colleges, her reputation for hospitality and her healthy altitude, is the logical and proper place for this annual chautauqua. And in a short while the Thespian Chautauqua will become a part of the history of our progress.

HOW SHALL WE START?

In order to put the big ball to rolling we are actually beginning to organize. A great number of progressive ladies have already been appointed presidents and are beginning to choose their members. We want to put the wheels to turning in our great Publishing House. Once started, it will do the biggest part of the printing for our people in this State. Simultaneously we shall begin to publish our great newspaper, the **Atlanta Voice.** We shall soon make it the most widely read race paper in the world. It is to be edited by Welborn Victor Jenkins, who is acknowledged to be one of the foremost young writers of our race.

WE WANT **YOU.**

In every community we want one lady to be our president. We want a lady who realizes that the crying need of our people is to begin to think. This will be her opportunity to come into vital touch with a mighty union. We have sent you this book because **we want you.** We are sure you are the proper person to represent us in your special community. It will be several months before we begin our actual work. All we want now is to put you on roll as a president. There are to be exactly three hundred of these high class ladies in the state. **You must be one.** You have been highly recommended to us by one of your friends. That's why we have sent you this letter made into a book so that you can read it easily.

We want you, and all you have to do now is to sign the enclosed card and mail it back to us.

NOT A SECRET ORDER.

Remember this is not a secret order. Everything we do is in broad daylight. There are no dues to pay. Our work is progress, advancement and uplift. There are no death benefits; all our benefits are in life. Our people are putting too much stress on death benefits. The Thespians believe in life benefits, in the endowments of self-dependence and a strong will to go forward. And they stress the necessity of eternal progress as the only solution of the problem which is before us.

We want you. Come with us. We want you for a president. There are no obligations. There will be some work but it will be joy and inspiration to do it. And the reward will be great indeed.

Sincerely yours,

WELBORN VICTOR JENKINS,
General Secretary Thespian Literary Association.
Home Office 523 W. Hunter St., Alanta, Ga.

CHAPTER 4

Resisting Jim Crow

Resistance to Jim Crow laws and customs, either individual forms of defiance or organized challenges, is the focus of the documents in this section.

DOCUMENT 49:
Letter and Address, Black Ministers of Washington, "Doomed to Destruction," August 13, 1910. Legislative, Judicial, and Fiscal Branch, Civil Archives Division, National Archives, Washington, D.C. Department of Justice, file 152961–3.

Courtesy National Archives.

These two letters protest the violence that erupted in the summer of 1910 in Anderson County, Texas, when African American share-croppers demanded their wages and were murdered as a result. The Committee of Colored Ministers drafted the cover letter and addressed it to President Taft to urge state and federal intervention, which never occurred.

Washington D.C.
August 13th, 1910

President William H. Taft
Dear Sir:

The undersigned have been appointed a Committee by the Colored Ministers—numbering more than 150—of the city of Washington to convey to you the enclosed address to the President and the American people relative to the murdering of 20 or more innocent and unarmed colored men near Palestine, Texas recently. It is the hope of the colored Ministers of this city, and of the many thousands whom they represent, as well as the hope of the colored people throughout America, that you may use the powers of your great Office to suppress lynching, murder and other forms of lawlessness in this country. According to the most recent and reliable statistics there are eight times more murders committed in the United States of America each year, than are committed in Great Britain, and six times more than in France, and five times more than of the German Empire. Our Nation is already the laughing stock of civilized peoples throughout the world, and unless something is done to make human life more valuable and law more universally respected, we feel that our beloved country is doomed to destruction at no distant date. We believe that you are as much interested in the suppression of lawlessness and crime in this country as we are, and we feel confident that you will do all in your power to help bring about this much to be desired end.

> We beg, sir, to remain
>> Yours very respectfully
>>>>>> (signed)
>> J. Milton Waldron, J. Anderson Taylor, W. J. Howard
>> *Committee*

To President Wm. H. Taft, and to the American People:—

We have come together tonight to make a sane protest to the reason and enlightened conscience of the great American people. We deplore the fact that such a meeting as this should be necessary. An impartial enforcement of law and unprejudiced treatment of citizens, regardless of ancestry, would leave little excuse for a meeting like this. But when so many black men are murdered without indictment, trial or conviction, as so recently happened in Texas and Florida, we feel it our duty to appeal to the American people to aid us in reenthroning law and order in every community of our country. To God, the Executive head of the Nation, and the American people we make this appeal as descendants of citizens who were, even in bondage, warm friends of the Southern white people; and who, until a half-hundred years ago made history for others, but none for themselves. Since then we have striven against race antipathy and the stigma of previous condition, and have rapidly improved in literacy, morals and economic status. In the past we put confidence in Statecraft to save us from exploitation at the behest of the strong, but the best we have ever received from it is not enough to deliver us from the troubles of which we now complain. We sought strength thru education, but the more we advance along this line, the greater the discrimination. We have bought land, built homes and established Churches, but those states as desire to do so go on disfranchising us, lynching our men on frivolous charges and unproved allegations, and widening the chasm which race differentiation has made broad enough. When progress does not promise to save a people, that people is near unto desperation. But let us appeal to the best instincts of men as long as reason has a chance or argument a hearing. While the brotherhood of man is a doctrine of our religion we must believe that this world can be made better, and ultimately set right. There is no wrong that cannot be put away by good men determined to do it. We pledge ourselves to this gigantic task, especially in agitating for the enforcement of law. It is pitiable to note that the white man who makes laws for men of other races to live under has not succeeded in ruling according to the laws he has made, nor has he the courage or fairness or courage to punish himself for the greatest crime against the State, which he has ordained—the crime of lynching. Within a month approximately a hundred citizens have suffered death or persecution in a community of the State of Texas. They have been lynched, murdered, burned and persecuted, the State apparently powerless to help them. This sad condition of racial strife, ever present like a smothering volcano ready to emit the lava of race hatred, makes it imperative for us as Colored Ministers, servants of the public and friends of justice, to make this impassioned protest—this earnest appeal:

(1) This is not intended to be an indignation meeting, but one expressive of our weakened confidence in the custodians of the law in certain sections of our country, and of an avowed sympathy for those of our people who suffer not from wrong doing, but from race hatred.

(2) We believe in democracy; which we interpret to mean government by suffrage and protection by law. The mission of the law is: justice to every man at any price. Now God's arbiter for humanity is justice; not for any one race or nation above another, but for the human race.

Humane treatment, establishing the guilt of evil doers, as a part of justice, is absolutely necessary.

(3) We urge in favor of political and judicial fairness for our people, their historic relations to the progress of our country. Traditions of beautiful sentiments and unparalleled fidelity ought to be enough to give our fathers a wreath of honor and to secure for us, their descendants, a place as men and citizens on equal terms with other men. Negro brawn and adaptability did much to make the South prosperous and beautiful and happy.

(4) We argue that the colored race deserves the appreciation of the American Nation—North and South. Besides his hundreds of years of unrequited toil, at a critical moment in the history of our country, when our brothers were torn by internecine strife from '61—'65, our people fought for liberty in the army of the Union—and worked to feed and protect the women and children of the confederacy. No slave race ever had such a record under such difficulties. No base charge of the present should rob the colored people of this glory of the past; still we are last in the hearts of our countrymen.

(5) We are alarmed that out of the wrong so generally acknowledged —the national sin of lynching and mob rule—no voice rings out sufficiently clear to check the mad career of the lawless who murder innocents whom the law has promised to protect. We ask the sympathetic consideration of the President of the U.S., the Judges of the Supreme Court, the Governors of States, the officials of law, the pulpit and press, and fair-minded people everywhere, to the end that lynching and mob rule and race riots be driven from the American commonwealth.

(6) We earnestly ask that this Government which has shown its sympathy with the weak of foreign nations by sending an army to Cuba, by joining with the powers in settling the Boxer Movement in China, by suggesting that honor had been satisfied to Russia and Japan, that is in sympathy with Russian Jews and Armenians in their suffering, that has often protected an individual abroad in the name of humanity—we insist that this Government shall protect its weak at home as well as abroad.

(7) We commend every brave man who has in the past or present, in the North or South, East or West, spoken out boldly for justice and right.

We make this appeal to the reason of all true Americans. We invoke the good office of blind-folded justice, who has no respect of persons. We appeal to the home-loving instinct of the real American—descendant of

Saxons, Teutons and Celts, whose motto is "A man's home is his castle," to espouse the cause of law for all alike. We appeal to the love that gave birth to the Golden Rule that lives in the Declaration of Independence and in the justice of the Constitution of the United States.

COMMITTEE

M. W. D. Norman,	W.D. Jarvis, President
J. M. Waldron,	E. B. Gordon,
W. J. Howard,	J. H. Randolph,
A. Sayles,	J. A. Taylor,
S. L. Corrothers,	J. I. Loving,
N. B. Marshall,	T. L. Jones,
	A. Wilbanks,
	M. W. Gibbs,
	I. N. Ross,
	A. C. Garner,
	J. I. Loving, Sec'y

DOCUMENT 50:

"Birth of a Nation" Protested Again: Opinion Club Sends Resolutions to Mayor from Faneuil Hall," *Boston Journal,* May 31, 1915.

Based upon the best-selling book *The Clansman* (1905), by Thomas Dixon Jr., *Birth of a Nation* was released in 1915 to widespread acclaim. Praised by President Woodrow Wilson, the film glorifies the Ku Klux Klan and stereotypes African Americans as bestial and uncontrollable. This article printed in the *Boston Journal*, a newspaper in print from 1903 to 1917, includes a resolution from the New Public Opinion Club that condemns the film for teaching "race prejudice, racial injustice, racial disfranchisement against colored Americans, falsifying reconstruction."

Faneuil Hall was taxed to its capacity yesterday afternoon at a public meeting held under the auspices of the New Public Opinion Club to commemorate the semi-centennial observation of Memorial Day and the fiftieth anniversary of Negro freedom.

Dr. W. E. B. Du Bois was the principal speaker, taking as his subject, "The Outlook for the Future." At the conclusion of Du Bois' address it was voted to send to Mayor James F. Curley this resolution, adopted by a rising vote:

> Colored Americans assembled under the auspices of the New Public Opinion Club, on Memorial Sunday, to be addressed by Dr. W. E. B. Du Bois, on "Fifty Years of Negro Freedom" in Faneuil Hall, sacred edifice which, as Boston's mayor rightly says, has ever stood against prejudice, contempt, injustice, enslavement of race, petitions the Boston Censor Board to stop the photoplay Birth of a Nation, which teaches race prejudice, racial injustice, racial disfranchisement against colored Americans, falsifying reconstruction.
>
> From Faneuil Hall itself, we protest the proposition that the pictured slander and disparagement of a minority race shall make licensed amusement for the rest of the people. This is but a step from that brutal tyranny when men were slaughtered to make a Roman holiday.

The meeting was presided over by President F. B. Washington, and on the platform with Dr. Du Bois were these officers of the club: Vice President Miss Crystal Bird of Boston Normal School; Secretary Nadine Wright, Radcliffe, 1917; Treasurer John Bowen; Rev. Osmond Walker, Harvard Divinity School; Miss Gertrude O'Neil of the Boston Conservatory of Music, Wesley Howard and Louria Jones.

DOCUMENT 51:
Photograph, Colored School at Anthoston, Kentucky, September 13, 1916.

Courtesy Library of Congress.

This image was taken by noted photographer Lewis Hine for the Census Bureau. It is captioned "Census 27, enrollment 12, attendance 7. Teacher expects 19 to be enrolled after work is over. 'Tobacco keeps them out and they are short of hands.' Ages of those present: 13 years = 1, 10 years = 2, 8 years = 2, 7 years = 1, 5 years = 1. Location, Henderson County, Kentucky."

Document 51

DOCUMENT 52:
Photograph, Home of Bill Reynolds and Family, October 7, 1921.

Courtesy Library of Congress.

The Reynolds family, in Minnehaha Springs, West Virginia, had to home school their two children because there was no school for African American students nearby, even though a white school was within walking distance.

Document 52

DOCUMENT 53:
Speech, Marcus Garvey, "The Confession of a Great Whiteman and Leader," Liberty Hall, New York, March 18, 1923.

In this speech, responding to a speech given by William Jennings Bryan, Marcus Garvey details the goals of the Universal Negro Improvement Association and criticizes black leaders such as W.E.B. Du Bois for their shortsightedness. Marcus Mosiah Garvey Jr. (1887–1940) was a publisher, journalist, and orator who is best known for his Back-to-Africa movement. Born in Jamaica, he founded the Universal Negro Improvement Association and African Communities League in 1914.

My subject for tonight is "The Confession of a Great White Man and Leader." Some Sunday nights ago you heard me speak of the speech made by William Jennings Bryan in Washington at a dinner where he was entertained by a large group of his own people. We commented on Mr. Bryan's speech in Liberty Hall, as well as through my front page article in the Negro World. Other Negro newspapers commented on the speech of Mr. Bryan, and these various comments led the daily "Times" of New York (I speak of the white 'Times') to request of Mr. Bryan to write an article expressing his further opinion on the matter and explain himself for what he said at the dinner in Washington. Mr. Bryan repeated everything he said this morning in his article in the daily "New York Times" and adds even more.[1] In concluding the article he said this: "My views upon the race question do not depend upon my present residence in the South;[2] they were formed long before I ever thought of living in the South; they were expressed as the occasion required, and so far as I know do not differ from the views of other white men who have had occasion to express themselves on the fundamental principles involved when these principles would apply to themselves and to their own families."

In this article of today we have Mr. Bryan repeating himself what he said in his talk in Washington a few weeks ago and adding more as expressing his attitude on the race question. He held to his idea of white supremacy and his belief that government should only be in the hands of the white man because white men are best able to interpret the needs of humanity. He concludes this article by saying that his views, he feels sure, are the views and opinion of other white people when called upon to give an opinion upon the subject. The statement of Mr. Bryan confirms the opinion and attitude of the Universal Negro Improvement Assn. of five years and confirms my stand in the matter of the Ku Klux Klan and the misrepresentation that other Negroes tried to make of my interview with that organization and the statement I made after that interview—that all white men in America feel like the Ku Klux Klan, but the only difference is that the Klan is honest enough to give expression to its opinion and carry out its attitude in defiance of any other opposition whilst others are not honest enough to give expression but feel the same way. Mr. Bryan comes out and says as a leader and statesman that his feeling and his opinion on the race question is that there should be white supremacy and that government should be in the hands of the white race because the white race can best interpret the needs of humanity; that such is the feeling of other white men when called upon to give an opinion on the same subject. This should convince us now that the majority of white people in this country feel as the Ku Klux Klan feels and Mr. Bryan feels, and that is that the power of government should rest not with the Negro race in this country, but should rest with the white men. For that they intend to fight and for that they intend to die. Now admitting that is so, and as we know it is so, what is the alternative for the Negro? The alternative is to follow in the cause of the Universal Negro Improvement Assn., that of the Negro building for himself. Hence the Universal Negro Improvement Assn. wastes no time in trying to explain itself. We do not need men like Mr. Bryan or Tillman and Vardaman to tell us that; we understand that well; we know that so long as this difference in numbers between the two opposite races that live in this country exists, the white man is going to carry out a program of white supremacy, and there will be absolutely no chance or opportunity between now and eternity for the colored man in America to take an equal place socially, politically and economically with the race that dominates. The one alternative is for the Negro not to waste his time and energy and ability in contributing to that which will make the other man great, but to use his energy and ability in contributing to build for himself. And that is where the Universal Negro Improvement Assn. differs from all the other movements in this country, in that we feel that whatsoever they do, whatsoever they say in trying to bring about a condition where colored men will co-operate side by side with the white man, at the best they are contributing to the white man's civilization, the white man's power, and are therefore wasting their energy and their ability that they should use in building for themselves.

PROGRAM OF THE U. N. I. A. CLEAN CUT

The Program of the Universal Negro Improvement Assn. is clean cut as far as our destiny in America and in other parts of the world goes, and when it comes to the carrying out of the program of the Universal Negro Improvement Assn. we need not fear the result or the consequences. This recent propaganda against us has done a great deal of good, for the simple reason that without invitation, without our request, we have brought to our support more and more a large number of men not of our race in this country who have held the view and opinion of the Universal Negro Improvement Assn. probably even before the Universal Negro Improvement Assn. came into being, and it brings to those of us who are leaders of the movement the fact that when the time comes for the Universal Negro Improvement Assn. to draw the line we will draw it with a great deal of support behind us in helping us to put the program over.

I am not going to blame Mr. Bryan for saying this, for the simple reason he is only speaking the truth as he sees it, and is only speaking the truth, as the Universal Negro Improvement Association knows it. I have a better regard and appreciation of Mr. Bryan than the men who would try to deceive us into believing that all will be well in the future when they know that the future holds nothing but darkness toward this race of ours. By our being able to understand American political psychology, by our being able to understand the intentions of the political leaders of this country, we will be placed in a better position to prepare for ourselves and to act for ourselves. We have lived under this camouflage for over fifty years, so much so that there are many of the other organizations of the race coming forth and telling us they are working towards the time when justice and equality will be meted out to the Negro in this country. Such a time will never come as far as the Negro is concerned if the Negro relies upon the mere question of humanity to solve this great problem of race. Humanity has never settled any great political program between races and nations. The appeal to humanity is a thing that has fallen flat even from the time of Jesus to the present hour. The appeal to humanity will not solve the great human problem. The only appeal that will solve the great human problem is the appeal to power, to force. The Universal Negro Improvement Association, therefore, will not waste its time advancing a purely humanitarian cause, believing that one day the dominant race will become so converted in its attitude toward the oppressed that it will hand to the oppressed and weaker peoples of the world that which we call justice and real liberty and freedom and democracy. It has never been in the ages past and will never be in the ages to come. There has been but one resort for those who are oppressed and that was the resort to power, to force, and that is where the Universal Negro Improvement Association is striking 400,000,000 Negroes of the world, endeavoring to accumulate that physical power, that mental power, that political power out of which we will be able to convince the world of our ability to protect ourselves not only in one spot but throughout the world.

Therefore I trust that you have tonight, if not before, a true conception of the program of the Universal Negro Improvement Association as far as it affects us in our American life and in our American attitude. We believe in the eternal existence of man; we believe that in the end of time only the fittest of this great human race will survive. We believe also that at the present time humanity everywhere is preparing itself for a condition through which it will live into eternity; but in this regulation of human affairs we find all peoples heretofore oppressed clamoring for a chance, clamoring for an opportunity to make their impress upon the world, to make their contribution to the world, so as to convince others of their fitness to live, of their fitness to survive, and we can do nothing less than to make some contribution to the civilization of this age. The race or the nation that is to be recognized must be the race or nation, which is capable of doing for itself. Dependent races and dependent nations will be ignored, will be pushed aside, will be weeded out, will be exterminated. It is only a question of time, and here we have it. As far as America is concerned, the great statesmen of the nation say that in the regulation of things the white man is the fittest individual to control government and to dominate government, because he is better able to interpret human needs. During the time that he has been interpreting human needs and the time that he has been regulating human society, what has he done? In that time he has brought us from freedom in our own native country to slavery, and kept us there for 250 years. That is his interpretation of the regulation of human society. Who can tell but that may be his interpretation in the next fifty years or the next hundred years? Can you, therefore, trust yourselves to his interpretation? (Cries of "No! No!") Can you, therefore, place your destiny in his hand? (Cries of "No! No!") Therefore, the only alternative for the Universal Negro Improvement Association and all sober minded Negroes is for them to draw the line and strike out for themselves, because no one can better interpret your needs than you can yourselves.

I trust, therefore, those of you who doubted that America's attitude toward the Negro is that of white supremacy—that of Government in the end is of the majority group will now be convinced by the utterances of Mr. William Jennings Bryan; and it pains me sometimes when I hear these little insignificant Negroes talking about what the white man can not do and saying that what Mr. Bryan has said is all bosh. They say what Mr. Bryan is saying is bosh and cannot be done, and all the time it is being done. It is all right for you to write in your papers saying it cannot be done, but what are you doing if they are doing it and not asking leave or license to do it? You must decide at the present time between propaganda and idle sentiment and facts. It is a fact that you have an organized strength in the country made manifest in the Ku Klux Klan and you have in conjunction with that the utterances of Mr. Bryan. Mr. Bryan when he speaks carries more weight in what he says than all the Negroes of the United States of America speaking at one time. Whatsoever Mr. Bryan says, whether he says it in Washington or Florida, carrie[s] more weight with the people of this country and the Government of the country than all our newspapers, magazines and books put together. Therefore, when a man like this talks we cannot afford to say it is idle bosh. And what has happened? I told you in regard to this Ku Klux business that these newspapers and those local politicians who talk about putting the Ku Klux Klan out of business were only playing with you and were only adopting a clever method of advertising the Klan. This morning's papers brought out that the Klan is now stronger in the Northern States than they are in the South States; that there are more Klansmen in the State of New York than there are in Texas, that there are more Klansmen in Jersey than there are in Alabama, that there are more Klansmen in Illinois than there are in Mississippi.[3] And what has happened? Last Sunday fifty Klansmen put on their robes and the leader of them occupied the pulpit of a large church in Newark,[4] and all the other Klansmen had the front seats; and in New York they were so bold and were given the right of way that one of their members died and they paraded and attended the funeral all of them in their regalia, and the New York World tries to deceive and fool us that they are going to crush the Klan.[5] What has happened? The great noise that Governor Parker in Louisiana was making that he was going to lead all the governors of the States into a great organization to crush the Klan in every State and he was going to start crushing the Klan in the State of Louisiana and when they got hold of ten of the Klansmen and accused them of killing two men in one of the towns of that State and they were making a great noise how they were going to convict them, the District Attorney of that State closed the case and said there was nothing against the Klan and has given the Klan a clean slate in the State of Louisiana.[6] It is nothing else but a skillful game of these men to advertise the Klan by showing the merit of the organization to those who never thought of it before.

So when these ignorant Negro papers talk about doing this and doing that, you will understand that when any group of white men get together in this country and talk about doing something, you had better get busy and look out for yourselves and don't think that appeal to humanity or any appeal to their Christian conduct is going to help you: it is not going to do it.

William Jennings Bryan is as big a Klansman as the Imperial Wizard himself, and not only Mr. Bryan but men bigger than William Jennings Bryan are deep down in the Ku Klux Klan and they are going to put over that program of white supremacy as sure as there is a God; and the only thing you can do is to get busy and get a country of your own and build up there so strong that not even hell and the Klan will be able to move you in the future. (Applause.)

So that my message to you tonight in Liberty Hall is to pay more and serious attention to what is going on, because within another fifty, another hundred years, especially when the world returns to its normal attitude and all these different nations are able to give more attention to their own domestic affairs, you and I will be confronted with a condition in this country, economically, that will end in nothing else but disaster for those of us who will live here at that time. I want you to understand that when the time comes for the white man to carry out his program of white supremacy for the purpose of eliminating the Negro as a political, social and industrial competitor he will not have to shoot you down, he will not have to lynch you and burn you to get rid of you. The Negro problem in America is such that economically he will grind us and push us to the wall, and in the space of two or three years he will solve the Negro problem without the Negro even realizing that the problem is already solved. The white man has laid the plan of economically forcing the Negro to the wall in another few years.

I am going back now to the bread-and-butter question. Do you know that every Negro in Liberty Hall tonight can die out by the end of this month without anybody poisoning you, without anybody putting a rope around your neck, without anybody shooting you or without anybody doing any bodily harm to you? Do you know? By starving. There is not a man in this building tonight who, if denied food for thirty days, would be able to resist death by starvation. What do I mean by that? I mean this: that we are so careless of ourselves, so careless of our future, that tonight 15,000,000 of us in America are dependent upon the white man for our daily existence, our daily sustenance and our daily bread. If the white man should say in another twenty-four hours that "I will not employ any more Negroes in my industry, on my farms or in my business," what would happen? Fifteen million Negroes would be jobless in the United States of America. And if you were kept jobless for a day or a week and rendered unable to go to the grocer to buy your provisions or to pay your rent to your landlord on the 1st or the 15th of the month and you were kept jobless for two weeks, everyone of us would have to leave our homes in Harlem and go out into the streets, unable to go to the grocer, and every one of us would be dying on the streets of New York, and I feel sure the white man would not have any objection to supplying the coffins to bury us by the hundreds, because it will be in keeping with his plan to get rid of us. Such a condition of unemployment would rid this country of 15,000,000 people just as the North American Indian was exterminated. And that was the white man's plan to get rid of the Negro problem in America up to 1913. But God Almighty sent the war and created a breach. We are still in that breach and if the 15,000,000 Negroes of America remain without action for another five or ten years and allow this country to return to normal to carry out their pre-war program, it is only a question of fifty or 100 years more when you and I will be weeded out from this Western civilization.

So the Universal Negro Improvement Association is pointing the way to destiny. There is only one relief, which is: While the world is readjusting itself now, while the world is reorganizing itself, while political boundaries are being adjusted, to pitch in and establish some political stronghold of your own. And there is no more logical place than Africa. (Applause.) The selfishness of the present-day Negro leader causes him to see only that in his lifetime he can get all that he wants and accumulate all he wants. Fellows like Du Bois will not think of the future, because they can get all they want. They have so much love for the Negro that if it comes to moving they can move to Brazil or Cuba; and as they do not like the Negro race already, it will be splendid for them to identify themselves with another race; they can be South Americans and Cubans. But you, the common people, who have nowhere to go, who have to struggle for your daily existence, you are the ones to be considered at that time, and you should see this danger that confronts us.

I trust you understand what the Universal Negro Improvement Association is driving at when we say that the time is now that we are to endeavor to create a nation of our own, and I thank God we are gradually creeping toward the realization of that dream. The strength of this movement is: being admitted by the South Africans themselves[7] and the white men who have gone to Africa; they admit that the Universal Negro Improvement Association is pressing them to the wall. The best thing you can do is to get behind the Universal Negro Improvement Association, and as they are pressing us to the wall in this Western world, let us unitedly press them to the wall in Africa. If you give to this organization for another five years the moral and financial support that we need I feel sure that we will have a new tale to give to the world and the world will have a new history to write out of the achievement of the twentieth century negro. (Applause.)

Printed in NW, 24 March 1923. Original headlines omitted.

[Notes]

1. The article, which appeared on 18 March 1923, was an amplification of Bryan's earlier address to the Southern Society of Washington on 20 February 1923 (*NYT,* 18 March 1923).

2. In 1916 Bryan and his wife, Mamie, moved to Miami. By 1923 he maintained residences in both Miami and Lincoln, Nebr. (Charles Morrow Wilson, *The Commoner: William Jennings Bryan* [New York: Doubleday, 1970], pp. 357–358; WWWA, 19227–1923).

3. No official records have been found of Klan membership and probably none ever existed. Estimates of Klan membership fluctuated widely; in 1923 membership figures ranged from 1.5 million to 4.5 million (*NYT,* 14 February 1925; Kenneth T. Jackson, *The Ku Klux Klan in the City, 1913–1930* [New York: Oxford University Press, 1967, p. 235). The Klan itself rarely boasted of over 2 million members. In the early 1920's the Klan's strength had increased markedly, especially in the Midwest and the East. By 1925 New York was estimated to have 300,420 members and Texas, 50,000; New Jersey boasted 720,000 members and Alabama 115,910; Illinois was said to have had 300,324 and Mississippi 93,040 (*NYT,* 14 February 1923; Jackson, *The Ku Klux Klan in the City,* pp. 10–12, 235–238, 289).

4. On Sunday, March 1922, forty hooded Klansmen marched into the Grace Methodist Episcopal Church in Newark, N.J. The pastor of the church, who had arranged the event, then introduced the Klan leader as "the Exalted Cyclops" and per-

mitted him to deliver a speech on the need for white Protestant supremacy. The pastor followed the address with a sermon on "Americanism" (*NYT,* 13 March 1923).

5. Probably a reference to the series of articles that appeared in the *New York World* attacking the Klan. In 1921 the *World* had run a three-week expose of the Klan which was picked up by other national newspapers and helped lead to the federal investigation of the organization. The *World* continued to publish articles on the Klan throughout the 1920s (Jackson, *The Ku Klux Klan in the City,* pp. 11–13; David M. Chalmers, *Hooded Americanism: The History of the Ku Klux Klan* [New York: Franklin Watts, 1981, pp. 42, 227, 294).

6. In September 1922 Gov. John M. Parker of Louisiana condemned the Klan for the kidnapping of five men in the small town of Mer Rouge and stated his intention to fight the Klan "to the finish" (*New York Age,* 16 September 1922). In November Parker informed federal authorities that the administration of state law had come to a virtual halt in Louisiana and that U.S. government administration of law in certain portions of the state might be necessary. The governor also instructed the attorney general to use "the full power of the State, civil and military" in an investigation of the torture and murder of two of the five kidnapped men (*New York Age,* 25 November 1922). At the annual governors' conference in December, Parker again denounced the Klan and called for federal legislation requiring the registration of secret organizations with the Department of Justice. He also requested that the governors put themselves on record against the Klan's usurpation of the judicial process (*NYT,* 15 December 1922). No federal intervention was forthcoming, however, and in March 1923 a special grand jury, many of whose members were known Klansmen, failed to return a single indictment against forty-six suspects (*NYT,* 16 March 1923). Despite this failure, Governor Parker's crusade against the Klan proved successful, and by 1924 the Louisiana Klan was in rapid decline (Jackson, *The Ku Klux Klan* in the City, p. 87).

7. A South African newspaper, *Cape Argus,* carried an article on 29 January 1923 which reported that the Garvey propaganda "among the natives of South Africa . . . is having an unsettling effect, and is beginning to cause anxiety among the white people, who have worked for the good of the natives, and among the educated natives, who foresee danger in the present situation" (*Cape Argus Cape Town,* 29 January 1923).

DOCUMENT 54:
Langton Hughes, "The Negro Artist and the Racial Mountain," *The Nation* 122 (June 23, 1926): 692–694.

Langston Hughes (1902–1967), one of the best-known writers of the Harlem Renaissance, urged African Americans to create their own voice through literature and art and not measure themselves to white standards. *The Nation* described itself as a "weekly journal of opinion, featuring progressive ideas and analysis on politics and culture, publishing since 1865." The founding prospectus held: *"The Nation* will not be the organ of any party, sect, or body. It will, on the contrary, make an earnest effort to bring to the discussion of

political and social questions a really critical spirit, and to wage war
upon the vices of violence, exaggeration, and misrepresentation by
which so much of the political writing of the day is marred" (see
Andrew L. Slap, *The Doom of Reconstruction: The Liberal Republicans
in the Civil War Era* [New York: Fordham University Press, 2006], 46).

One of the most promising of young Negro poets said to me once, "I
want to be a poet—not a Negro poet," meaning, I believe, "I want to
write like a white poet"; meaning subconsciously, "I would like to be a
white poet"; meaning behind that, "I would like to be white." And I was
sorry the young man said that, for no great poet has ever been afraid of
being himself. And I doubted then that, with his desire to run away spiritually from his race, this boy would ever be a great poet. But this is the
mountain standing in the way of any true Negro art in America—this
urge within the race toward whiteness, the desire to pour racial individuality into the mold of American standardization, and to be as little
Negro and as much American as possible.

But let us look at the immediate background of this young poet. His
family is of what I suppose one would call the Negro middle class:
people who are by no means rich yet never uncomfortable nor hungry—
smug, contented, respectable folk, members of the Baptist church. The
father goes to work every morning. He is a chief steward at a large white
club. The mother sometimes does fancy sewing or supervises parties for
the rich families of the town. The children go to a mixed school. In the
home they read white papers and magazines. And the mother often says
"Don't be like niggers" when the children are bad. A frequent phrase from
the father is, "Look how well a white man does things." And so the word
white comes to be unconsciously a symbol of all the virtues. It holds for
the children beauty, morality, and money. The whisper "I want to be
white" runs silently through their minds. This young poet's home is, I
believe, a fairly typical home of the colored middle class. One sees immediately how difficult it would be for an artist born in such a home to interest himself in interpreting the beauty of his own people. He is never
taught to see that beauty. He is taught rather not to see it, or if he does,
to be ashamed of it when it is not according to Caucasian patterns.

For racial culture that home of a self-styled "high-class" Negro has
nothing better to offer. Instead there will perhaps be more aping of things

white than in a less cultured or less wealthy home. The father is perhaps a doctor, lawyer, landowner, or politician. The mother may be a social worker, or a teacher, or she may do nothing and have a maid. Father is often dark but he has usually married the lightest woman he could find. The family attend a fashionable church where few really colored faces are to be found. And they themselves draw a color line. In the North they go to white theaters and white movies. And in the South they have at least two cars and a house "like white folks." Nordic manners, Nordic faces, Nordic hair, Nordic art (if any), and an Episcopal heaven. A very high mountain indeed for the would-be racial artist to climb in order to discover himself and his people.

But then there are the low-down folks, the so-called common element, and they are the majority—may the Lord be praised! The people who have their nip of gin on Saturday nights and are not too important to themselves or the community, or too well fed, or too learned to watch the lazy world go round. They live on Seventh Street in Washington or State Street in Chicago and they do not particularly care whether they are like white folks or anybody else. Their joy runs, bang! into ecstasy. Their religion soars to a shout. Work maybe a little today, rest a little tomorrow. Play awhile. Sing awhile. O, let's dance! These common people are not afraid of spirituals, as for a long time their more intellectual brethren were, and jazz is their child. They furnish a wealth of colorful, distinctive material for any artist because they still hold their own individuality in the face of American standardizations. And perhaps these common people will give to the world its truly great Negro artist, the one who is not afraid to be himself. Whereas the better-class Negro would tell the artist what to do, the people at least let him alone when he does appear. And they are not ashamed of him—if they know he exists at all. And they accept what beauty is their own without question.

Certainly there is, for the American Negro artist who can escape the restrictions the more advanced among his own group would put upon him, a great field of unused material ready for his art. Without going outside his race, and even among the better classes with their "white" culture and conscious American manners, but still Negro enough to be different, there is sufficient matter to furnish a black artist with a lifetime of creative work. And when he chooses to touch on the relations between Negroes and whites in this country with their innumerable overtones and undertones, surely, and especially for literature and the drama, there is an inexhaustible supply of themes at hand. To these the Negro artist can give his racial individuality, his heritage of rhythm and warmth, and his incongruous humor that so often, as in the Blues, becomes ironic laughter mixed with tears. But let us look again at the mountain.

A prominent Negro clubwoman in Philadelphia paid eleven dollars to hear Raquel Meller sing Andalusian popular songs. But she told me a few weeks before she would not think of going to hear "that woman," Clara Smith, a great black artist, sing Negro folksongs. And many an upper-class Negro church, even now, would not dream of employing a spiritual in its services. The drab melodies in white folks' hymnbooks are much to be preferred. "We want to worship the Lord correctly and quietly. We don't believe in 'shouting.' Let's be dull like the Nordics," they say, in effect.

The road for the serious black artist, then, who would produce a racial art is most certainly rocky and the mountain is high. Until recently he received almost no encouragement for his work from either white or colored people. The fine novels of Chestnut go out of print with neither race noticing their passing. The quaint charm and humor of Dunbar's dialect verse brought to him, in his day, largely the same kind of encouragement one would give a side-show freak (A colored man writing poetry! How odd!) A clown (How amusing!).

The present vogue in things Negro, although it may do as much harm as good for the budding colored artist, has at least done this: it has brought him forcibly to the attention of his own people among whom for so long, unless the other race had noticed him beforehand, he was a prophet with little honor. I understand that Charles Gilpin acted for years in Negro theaters without any special acclaim from his own, but when Broadway gave him eight curtain calls, Negroes, too, began to beat a tin pan in his honor. I know a young colored writer, a manual worker by day, who had been writing well for the colored magazines for some years, but it was not until he recently broke into the white publications and his first book was accepted by a prominent New York publisher that the "best" Negroes in his city took the trouble to discover that he lived there. Then almost immediately they decided to give a grand dinner for him. But the society ladies were careful to whisper to his mother that perhaps she'd better not come. They were not sure she would have an evening gown.

The Negro artist works against an undertow of sharp criticism and misunderstanding from his own group and unintentional bribes from the whites. "O, be respectable, write about nice people, show how good we are," say the Negroes. "Be stereotyped, don't go too far, don't shatter our illusions about you, don't amuse us too seriously. We will pay you," say the whites. Both would have told Jean Toomer not to write *Cane*. The colored people did not praise it. The white people did not buy it. Most of the colored people who did read *Cane* hate it. They are afraid of it. Although the critics gave it good reviews, the public remained indifferent. Yet (excepting the work of Du Bois) *Cane* contains the finest prose written by a Negro in America. And like the singing of Robeson, it is truly racial.

But in spite of the Nordicized Negro intelligentsia and the desires of some white editors we have an honest American Negro literature already with us. Now I await the rise of the Negro theater. Our folk music, having achieved world-wide fame, offers itself to the genius of the great individual American Negro composer who is to come. And within the next decade I expect to see the work of a growing school of colored artists who paint and model the beauty of dark faces and create with new technique the expressions of their own soul-world. And the Negro dancers who will dance like flame and the singers who will continue to carry our songs to all who listen—they will be with us in even greater numbers tomorrow.

Most of my own poems are racial in theme and treatment, derived from the life I know. In many of them I try to grasp and hold some of the meanings and rhythms of jazz. I am sincere as I know how to be in these poems and yet after every reading I answer questions like these from my own people: Do you think Negroes should always write about Negroes? I wish you wouldn't read some of your poems to white folks. How do you find anything interesting in a place like a cabaret? Why do you write about black people? You aren't black. What makes you do so many jazz poems?

But jazz to me is one of the inherent expressions of Negro life in America: the eternal tom-tom beating in the Negro soul—the tom-tom of revolt against weariness in a white world, a world of subway trains, and work, work, work; the tom-tom of joy and laughter, and pain swallowed in a smile. Yet the Philadelphia clubwoman is ashamed to say that her race created it and she does not like me to write about it. The old subconscious "white is best" runs through her mind. Years of study under white teachers, a lifetime of white books, pictures, and papers, and white manners, morals, and Puritan standards made her dislike the spirituals. And now she turns up her nose at jazz and all its manifestations—likewise almost everything else distinctly racial. She doesn't care for the Winold Reiss portraits of Negroes because they are "too Negro." She does not want a true picture of herself from anybody. She wants the artist to flatter her, to make the white world believe that all Negroes are as smug and as near white in soul as she wants to be. But, to my mind, it is the duty of the younger Negro artist, if he accepts any duties at all from outsiders, to change through the force of his art that old whispering "I want to be white," hidden in the aspirations of his people, to "Why should I want to be white? I am a Negro—and beautiful!"

So I am ashamed for the black poet who says, "I want to be a poet, not a Negro poet," as though his own racial world were not as interesting as any other world. I am ashamed, too, for the colored artist who runs from the painting of Negro faces to the painting of sunsets after the manner of the academicians because he fears the strange un-whiteness of his own features. An artist must be free to choose what he does, certainly, but he must also never be afraid to do what he might choose.

Let the blare of Negro jazz bands and the bellowing voice of Bessie Smith singing Blues penetrate the closed ears of the colored near-intellectuals until they listen and perhaps understand. Let Paul Robeson singing "Water Boy," and Rudolph Fisher writing about the streets of Harlem, and Jean Toomer holding the heart of Georgia in his hands, and Aaron Douglas drawing strange black fantasies cause the smug Negro middle class to turn from their white, respectable, ordinary books and papers to catch a glimmer of their own beauty. We younger Negro artists who create now intend to express our individual dark-skinned selves without fear or shame. If white people are pleased we are glad. If they are not, it doesn't matter. We know we are beautiful. And ugly too. The tom-tom cries and the tom-tom laughs. If colored people are pleased we are glad. If they are not, their displeasure doesn't matter either. We build our temples for tomorrow, strong as we know how, and we stand on top of the mountain, free within ourselves.

DOCUMENT 55:
"The Yokinen Trial," *Baltimore Afro-American,* March 7,
1931, 7.

Courtesy of the Afro-American.

This article documents a rare trial held by the Communist Party to
charge August Yokinen of white chauvinism. Held in the Harlem
Casino on February 28, 1931, the trial attracted two thousand spec-
tators and resulted in the expulsion of Yokinen. It is a rare glimpse
of a bi-racial effort to address racial prejudice.

August Yokinen, white, a member and janitor of the Finnish Workers'
Club, 15 W. 126th Street, facing a workers jury at the Harlem Casino,
116th Street and Lenox Avenue, on charges of showing race prejudice
against Negroes, was indefinitely expelled from the party.

A mixed crowd of about 2,000 crowded the hall until police turned
them away because of lack of space. It was the first public Communist
trial held in the United States, but according to a member of the party's
secretariat, more will take place if its members fail to carry out the program laid down.

Thousands of leaflets were distributed, especially in Harlem, and
letters were sent to many working class organizations to send delegates.
One hundred thirteen organizations responded with 211 delegates.

Alfred Wagenknecht, white, presided as judge, while C. A. Hathaway,
also white, a leading member of the Communist party and editor of the
Daily Worker, was prosecutor.

The offense with which Yokinen was charged, occurred about two
months ago when Harold Williams, and other workers attended a dance
at the Finnish Hall and were pushed into a corner, shunned and even
threatened with being ejected.

Hathaway branded Yokinen's actions as being detrimental to the
working class struggle achieved by working class solidarity and greatly
in discord with the party program. Yokinen, according to the prosecutor, showed a chauvinistic tendency by not coming to the rescue of these
workers and by saying: "If Negroes come into the dance hall and pool-

room they will want to use our baths ("for which they are justly proud," said Hathaway) and I for one do not want to bathe with a Negro."

Hathaway recalled the case of discrimination against Lewis, a Negro worker at Stalingrad, by a white engineer from the U.S., who was tried for the act, and deported from the Soviet Union; he also recalled the Gastonia strike where the white workers saved Otto Hall from a lynching mob by rushing him to another town.

Richard B. Moore, national Negro director of the International Labor Defense, who was the Communist candidate for state attorney-general, was counsel for the defense. He asked the jury not to be severe with Yokinen after admitting that his client was guilty of a grievous crime, but to place the blame where it rightfully belongs. "The vicious bourgeois system, the damnable capitalist system, which preaches corruption and discrimination, is the real criminal," he said.

Moore pointed out that Yokinen was not as schooled as were some of our comrades, who practiced these same tendencies and were never brought to trial and that he spoke and understood very little English and was therefore not able to read the documents and instructions from the party organs that the prosecutor offered as exhibits.

"Let us not yell for the blood of Yokinen, but examine ourselves to see how far we have contributed to this thing with which the defendant is charged.

"I would rather have my head severed from my body by the lynchers than be expelled from the Communist International," shouted Moore. At this the crowd broke into tremendous applause and cheering.

The jury, composed of seven Negro workers, including a woman, and seven white workers, selected by the workers present, retired after the attorneys had summarized, and remained out for about thirty minutes, and after quite a bit of deliberation returned with a verdict of guilty. Eleven voted for expulsion.

The verdict proclaimed that he be expelled with one condition: that he might be re-admitted to the party after he had demonstrated in deeds his solidarity with the Negro workers and proved his worthiness by performing among other tasks (1) the selling of an adequate number of *The Liberator,* organ of the League of Struggle for Negro Rights, and (2) also to join this organization; (3) to lead demonstrations against certain restaurants that discriminate against Negroes in Harlem; (4) to immediately go to the Finnish Club, call a mass meeting and give them the report of the trial, couched in such terms as to destroy white chauvinistic tendencies in the club, and (5) to carry on in the club a persistent struggle for the admittance of Negro workers and the granting of all privileges, including use of the poolroom, bathroom and restaurant.

All during the procedure Yokinen sat with bowed head.

Never before in the history of his membership in the party had Moore met defeat from another speaker, regardless of the nature of the discussion or debate, and it is the general opinion of the masses that he more than credited himself against Hathaway.

DOCUMENT 56:

Photograph, Trainman Signaling from a Jim Crow Coach, St. Augustine, Florida, January 1943.

Courtesy Library of Congress.

Gordon Parks took this image for the Office of War Information. Segregated transportation was common throughout the American South and was one of the core components of Jim Crow.

Document 56

DOCUMENT 57:

Letter from Boston Scottsboro Defense Committee, April 20, 1933. Henry Wadsworth Longfellow Dana Collection (MSS1033), Box 1, Folder 4.

Courtesy Special Collections, Robert W. Woodruff Library, Emory University.

> This letter, signed by members of the Boston Scottsboro Defense Committee, asks for contributions to fund a fifth trial for the Scottsboro boys, estimated to cost fifteen thousand dollars. The nine Scottsboro boys—black teenagers who were accused of raping two white girls on a freight train traveling from Chattanooga to Memphis on March 25, 1931—were repeatedly found guilty by all-white juries in the South. The case and the imprisonment of the men lasted more than twenty years and became an international cause for justice.

April 20th, 1933

Dear Friend:

On Sunday, April 9th, an all-white jury filed into the Decatur court-room. With grins on their faces, they delivered a verdict of legal lynch-ing for Heywood Patterson, first of the nine innocent Negro boys tried on framed rape charges. Today, Heywood Patterson stands condemned to die June 16th.

This verdict was asked by Wade Wright, Morgan County solicitor, and Attorney General Thomas E. Knight, Jr. of Alabama, who disregarded all the testimony presented and demanded a verdict based solely on sec-tional, racial and religious prejudice and hatred.

The other eight boys were taken suddenly to Birmingham for safe-keeping as mobs of farmers jammed the town, lynch-gangs came in from Scottsboro, Huntsville and other sections. Fiery crosses were burned, hardware stores reported they were sold out of ammunition, sold exclusively to whites.

Returning from Alabama recently, Samuel S. Leibowitz, chief trial coun-sel, said, "I want to say that had it not been for the International Labor Defense, those nine boys would be in their coffins now, buried back of the county jail."

"This verdict would not hold in any Supreme Court in the United States," said General George W. Chamlee, Scottsboro defense counsel and noted Southern attorney.

A lynch verdict, after two years of intense struggle . . . a struggle <u>for</u> nine lives—<u>against</u> denial of elementary human rights to thirteen million Negroes.

Friends of the Scottsboro Boys say, "Now this fight is only beginning." Certainly it needs renewed strength. The appeal from the lynch verdict, (for which the record alone will cost above $5,000), the preparation of defense of the other boys, must go forward today.

We call on you to sent whatever money you can . . . and send it quickly. When you have done that, ask your friends to do the same.

Help save nine innocent Negro Scottsboro Boys!

> Sincerely,
> [signed]
> William L. Patterson
> National Secretary
> INTERNATIONAL LABOR DEFENSE

DOCUMENT 58:
A. Philip Randolph, "Why Should We March?" *Survey Graphic* 31 (November 1942): 488–489.

A. Philip Randolph (1889–1979) was a leader in civil rights and the founder of the Brotherhood of Sleeping Car Porters, the first African American union. Along with Bayard Rustin and A. J. Muste, he planned a 1941 march on Washington in protest of segregation in the armed forces. When the Fair Employment Act was issued, with pressure from Randolph, the march was cancelled. Randolph and the March-on-Washington Movement, however, did not disband. In this 1942 article, he details his demands to end Jim Crow in "housing, education, transportation and every other social, economic, and political privilege." In print from 1921 to 1952, *Survey Graphic* was a companion to the journal *Survey,* which focused on social work. The publication focused on political and sociological research of national and international issues, such as unionization, anti-Semitism, and fascism. According to the editor, Paul Kellogg, in a December 1937 issue, the magazine relied on "social team play," bringing together writers from different fields and with varied perspectives to debate issues that were not commonly discussed in mainstream publications.

Though I have found no Negroes who want to see the United Nations lose this war, I have found many who, before the war ends, want to see the stuffing knocked out of white supremacy and of empire over subject peoples. American Negroes, involved as we are in the general issues of the conflict, are confronted not with a choice but with the challenge both to win democracy for ourselves at home and to help win the war for democracy the world over.

There is no escape from the horns of this dilemma. There ought not to be escape. For if the war for democracy is not won abroad, the fight for democracy cannot be won at home. If this war cannot be won for the white peoples, it will not be won for the darker races.

Conversely, if freedom and equality are not vouchsafed the peoples of color, the war for democracy will not be won. Unless this double-barreled thesis is accepted and applied, the darker races will never wholeheartedly fight for the victory of the United Nations. That is why those familiar with the thinking of the American Negro have sensed his lack of enthusiasm, whether among the educated or uneducated, rich or poor, professional or non-professional, religious or secular, rural or urban, north, south, east or west.

That is why questions are being raised by Negroes in church, labor union and fraternal society; in poolroom, barbershop, schoolroom, hospital, hair-dressing parlor; on college campus, railroad, and bus. One can hear such questions asked as these: What have Negroes to fight for? What's the difference between Hitler and that "cracker" Talmadge of Georgia? Why has a man got to be Jim-Crowed to die for democracy? If you haven't got democracy yourself, how can you carry it to somebody else?

What are the reasons for this state of mind? The answer is: discrimination, segregation, Jim Crow. Witness the navy, the army, the air corps; and also government services at Washington. In many parts of the South, Negroes in Uncle Sam's uniform are being put upon, mobbed, sometimes even shot down by civilian and military police, and on occasion lynched. Vested political interests in race prejudice are so deeply entrenched that to them winning the war against Hitler is secondary to preventing Negroes from winning democracy for themselves. This is worth many

divisions to Hitler and Hirohito. While labor, business, and farm are subjected to ceilings and floors and not allowed to carry on as usual, these
interests trade in the dangerous business of race hate as usual.

When the defense program began and billions of the taxpayers'
money were appropriated for guns, ships, tanks and bombs, Negroes
presented themselves for work only to be given the cold shoulder. North
as well as South, and despite their qualifications, Negroes were denied
skilled employment. Not until their wrath and indignation took the
form of a proposed protest march on Washington, scheduled for July 1,
1941, did things begin to move in the form of defense jobs for Negroes.
The march was postponed by the timely issuance (June 25, 1941) of the
famous Executive Order No. 8802 by President Roosevelt. But this order
and the President's Committee on Fair Employment Practice, established thereunder, have as yet only scratched the surface by way of eliminating discriminations on account of race or color in war industry. Both
management and labor unions in too many places and in too many ways
are still drawing the color line.

It is to meet this situation squarely with direct action that the March
on Washington Movement launched its present program of protest
mass meetings. Twenty thousand were in attendance at Madison Square
Garden, June 16; sixteen thousand in the Coliseum in Chicago, June 26;
nine thousand in the City Auditorium of St. Louis, August 14. Meetings
of such magnitude were unprecedented among Negroes.* The vast
throngs were drawn from all walks and levels of Negro life—business-
men, teachers, laundry workers, Pullman porters, waiters, and red caps;
preachers, crapshooters, and social workers; jitterbugs and Ph.D.'s. They
came and sat in silence, thinking, applauding only when they considered the truth was told, when they felt strongly that something was
going to be done about it.

The March on Washington Movement is essentially a movement of
the people. It is all Negro and pro-Negro, but not for that reason anti-
white or anti-Semitic, or anti-Catholic, or anti-foreign, or anti-labor. Its
major weapon is the non-violent demonstration of Negro mass power.
Negro leadership has united back of its drive for jobs and justice.

---

*In view of charges made that they were subsidized by Nazi funds, it may not be
amiss to point out that of the $8,000 expenses of the Madison Square meeting every
dime was contributed by Negroes themselves, except for tickets bought by some liberal white organizations.

"Whether Negroes should march on Washington, and if so, when?" will be the focus of a forthcoming national conference. For the plan of a protest march has not been abandoned. Its purpose would be to demonstrate that American Negroes are in deadly earnest, and all out for their full rights. No power on earth can cause them today to abandon their fight to wipe out every vestige of second class citizenship and the dual standards that plague them.

A community is democratic only when the humblest and weakest person can enjoy the highest civil, economic, and social rights that the biggest and most powerful possess. To trample on these rights of both Negroes and poor whites is such a commonplace in the South that it takes readily to anti-social, anti-labor, anti-Semitic and anti-Catholic propaganda. It was because of laxness in enforcing the Weimar constitution in republican Germany that Nazism made headway. Oppression of the Negroes in the United States, like suppression of the Jews in Germany, may open the way for a fascist dictatorship.

By fighting for their rights now, American Negroes are helping to make America a moral and spiritual arsenal of democracy. Their fight against the poll tax, against lynch law, segregation, and Jim Crow, their fight for economic, political, and social equality, thus becomes part of the global war for freedom.

PROGRAM OF THE MARCH ON WASHINGTON MOVEMENT

1. We demand, in the interest of national unity, the abrogation of every law which makes a distinction in treatment between citizens based on religion, creed, color, or national origin. This means an end to Jim Crow in education, in housing, in transportation and in every other social, economic, and political privilege; and especially, we demand, in the capital of the nation, an end to all segregation in public places and in public institutions.

2. We demand legislation to enforce the Fifth and Fourteenth Amendments guaranteeing that no person shall be deprived of life, liberty or property without due process of law, so that the full weight of the national government may be used for the protection of life and thereby may end the disgrace of lynching.

3. We demand the enforcement of the Fourteenth and Fifteenth

Amendments and the enactment of the Pepper Poll Tax bill so that all barriers in the exercise of the suffrage are eliminated.

4. We demand the abolition of segregation and discrimination in the army, navy, marine corps, air corps, and all other branches of national defense.

5. We demand an end to discrimination in jobs and job training. Further, we demand that the F.E.P.C. be made a permanent administrative agency of the U.S. Government and that it be given power to enforce its decisions based on its findings.

6. We demand that federal funds be withheld from any agency which practices discrimination in the use of such funds.

7. We demand colored and minority group representation on all administrative agencies so that these groups may have recognition of their democratic right to participate in formulating policies.

8. We demand representation for the colored and minority racial groups on all missions, political and technical, which will be sent to the peace conference so that the interests of all people everywhere may be fully recognized and justly provided for in the post-war settlement.

DOCUMENT 59:
E. W. Eckard, "How Many Negroes 'Pass'?" *American Journal of Sociology* 52 (May 1947): 498–500.

Courtesy American Journal of Sociology.

This article was written in response to a theory proposed in *Collier's* magazine on August 3, 1946, that estimated that nearly thirty thousand Negroes pass annually as whites to escape the strictures of Jim Crow. The article concludes that a more accurate number between 1930 and 1940 was twenty-six hundred.

How Many Negroes "Pass"?

The article in *Collier's* of August 3, 1946, entitled "Who Is a Negro?" reawakened my interest in the subject of Negro "passing." The upshot of this article may be stated briefly: A large number of light-skinned Negroes pass over into the white race each year; the author, Herbert Asbury, surmises 30,000 annually.

The original interest in this subject came from contact with persons who were accepted as whites but who reputedly possessed Negro blood. In some cases the physical features of these individuals were similar to those of the Negro, while in most cases there was very little easily detected similarity. Further intermarriage with whites seemed to reduce the Negroid appearance; the writer knows of no instance in which a child displays more Negroid features than its part-Negro parent. Generally, such persons had one-sixteenth or less of Negro blood.

What is meant by "passing"? The chance occasional "passing" of the light Negro to get a Pullman berth, a meal, a hotel room, or just for the hell of it cannot be included. It is agreed that this type of passing occurs, but there is no way to measure the amount. We are really concerned with the type of passing in which the light-skinned Negro becomes permanently accepted as white. This type of passing leads to intermarriage with whites, and the descendants are legally and socially a part of the white race.

If it is true that each year 30,000 Negroes pass over and become accepted as whites, the gradual assimilation of the Negro race is on its way, provided that the Negro population ceases increasing. But there is always the important question: Is this figure correct? This writer decided to investigate for himself.

Study reveals that the above conclusion is based upon questionable data and statistical methods. The statistical methods employed in arriving at the estimate that 30,000 Negroes "pass" the color line each year include the use of crude birth rates and death rates and various devices for forming conclusions from use of statistical samples. These methods will give credible results only if used properly.

The total population of the United States in 1930 and 1940 was 122,775,046 and 131,669,275, respectively. The respective Negro population for the same years in the United States was 11,891,143 and 12,865,518, with the Negro population being 9.7 per cent of the total in 1930 and 9.8 per cent in 1940.[1] If 30,000 Negroes "pass" the color line each year, they amount to only .023 of 1 per cent of the total population and .25 of 1 per

1. Preceding figures are taken from the census of the United States for 1930 and 1940. The editors of the *Journal* and the writer wish to acknowledge suggestions from Henry S. Shryock, Jr., chief, Population Statistics Section, Population Division Bureau of the Census, while this paper was in preparation.

cent of the Negro population in 1940. The attempt to arrive at a number that is such a small part of the total population by approximate methods cannot bring forth an acceptable answer. For example, an error of 1 per cent of the Negro population will amount to 110,000 which is much larger than the alleged number of Negroes "passing" each year.

An attempt was made to follow each age group of whites and Negroes through several decades to find out if there were a decrease in the number of Negroes that could not be accounted for because of deaths or emigration and if there were a corresponding increase of whites. But this plan was abandoned because of the small size of the units involved and because not all states submitted official death-registration data prior to 1930.

By 1930 all states except Texas registered deaths and submitted the data to the Bureau of the Census. Texas commenced this practice in 1933. Hence, vital statistics for the decade 1930–40 are far more complete than for any previous decade.

In order to use the largest group available and to remove as many chances of error as possible, the following procedure was adopted:

1. The 1930 population of each race was taken from official census figures which are obtained by actual count.

2. Immigration data were taken from the *Statistical Abstract of the United States* and were based on Department of Justice figures.

3. The deaths among the 1930 population of each race were taken from census figures; the deaths occurring of children born subsequent to 1930 were excluded. The deaths for the state of Texas were estimated for the period prior to 1933. Since Mexicans are included as "white" and their deaths listed as among "other races" prior to 1935, an estimate of 25,000 deaths is added to "white" deaths.

4. The 1930 population, plus immigration, minus deaths among the 1930 population, will equal the 1940 population, age ten and above, provided all counts are exact to the last man. This statement will apply to each race if there is no "passing."

5. The figure for the 1940 population of each race, age ten or above, was taken from the census and compared with the result obtained by Number 4.

This method retains the advantage of keeping a large mass of population and removes the necessity for using birth registrations which are incomplete.

According to the official census of 1930 there were 110,286,740 whites in the United States at that time. The excess of immigration to the United States over emigration from the United States was 209,804. The number of deaths among the 1930 white population was 10,841,000. The last figure was obtained by subtracting the deaths among the children born subsequent to 1930 from the total number of deaths listed for the death-registration area of the United States during the decade 1930–40. Since Texas was not included in the death-registration area before 1933, the number of deaths for Texas was estimated and added. Also the number of Mexican deaths from 1930 to 1934 was estimated and included. Thus, 110,286,740 + 209,656—10,866,000 = 99,630,544, which is the calculated number of whites age ten or above in 1940. According to the census of 1940 there were 99,656,414 whites in the United States age ten or above in 1940. If these figures were exact to the individual, they would indicate that the white race had received 25,870 (99,656,414—99,630,544) members from an outside source.

The census states that the Negro population of the United States for 1930 was 11,891,143. The net effect of immigration and emigration was small, an excess of 1,648 emigrants from the United States. The deaths among the 1930 Negroes, obtained as the similar figure for the whites, from 1930 to 1940 was 1,541,558. Thus, 11,891,143—1,648—1,541,558 = 10, 347,937. The census figure for the 1940 Negro population age ten or above is 10,321,892. If all counts concerning Negroes were exact, 26,045 (10,347,937—10,321,892) of them became accepted as whites in that decade.

From the above it appears that the Negroes lost 26,045 the decade from 1930 to 1940 and that the whites gained 25,870.

The estimation of Texas deaths prior to 1933 and Mexican deaths prior to 1935 introduces the possibility of an error, probably less than 4,000 for the whites and less than 300 for the Negroes. Failure to register deaths in every instance and failure to count population accurately will introduce the possibility of additional errors. The author does not claim the degree of accuracy suggested by the approximate equality of Negro losses and white gains shown by the figures above.

From the above data we may conclude that Negroes "passed" into the white race at the rate of 2,600 per year during the decade from 1930 to 1940. Owing to errors, the author believes that the number was actually much less.

CONCLUSIONS

It is possible that in a decade such as the one from 1920 to 1930 there may have been more economic inducement for Negroes to become accepted as whites than from 1930 to 1940. But before 1930 the registration of deaths was too incomplete to achieve a very great degree of accuracy with research on the subject.

There are, in the main, two conclusions to be drawn from the information included in Table 1:

1. The number of Negroes "passing" over to the white race from 1930 to 1940 was very small, probably less than 2,000 per year.[2]

2. The second conclusion depends upon the validity of the first. At the rate of 2,000 per year it will take 6,000 years to assimilate the 12,000,000 Negroes in the United States, and this only if the Negroes maintain a stationary population, which they do not.

2. This conclusion is supported by John H. Burma, "The Measurement of Negro 'Passing,'" *American Journal of Sociology*, LII, Part I (July, 1946), 18–22. Mr. Burma uses different statistics.

TABLE 1

COMPARISON OF WHITE AND NEGRO POPULATION GROUPS
UNITED STATES, 1930–40*

	White	Negro
1930 population	110,286,740	11,891,143
Immigration 1930–40	209,804	1,648 (Emigration 1930–1940)
Deaths among 1930 population	10,866,000	1,541,558
Calculated 1940 population age ten or above	99,630,544	10,347,937
1940 population age ten or above	99,656,414	10,321,892
Calculated change	25,870 (Apparent loss)	26,045 (Apparent gain)

*Data taken from Bureau of the Census publications, 103 0–40. Data on immigration are from *Statistical Abstract of the United States* (Department of Justice figures).

Actually, they have been increasing at the rate of approximately 100,000 per year for the last thirty years.

Thus, the notion of white assimilation of the black is unrealistic and without factual ground.

UNIVERSITY OF ARKANSAS

DOCUMENT 60:
"A. Clayton Powell Supports Randolph," *Washington Afro-American*, April 6, 1948.

This newspaper account documents Adam Clayton Powell's support of A. Philip Randolph's testimony before the Armed Services Committee of the U.S. Senate to encourage African Americans to resist the draft. Powell was an influential African American member of the U.S. House of Representatives from 1945 to 1971 and was an outspoken critic of Jim Crow laws and policies.

WASHINGTON.—Representative Adam C. Powell, Jr. (Democrat, New York), testifying last Friday before the Senate's Armed Services Committee, fully supported A. Philip Randolph's civil disobedience threat to keep colored youth out of a Jim Crow army, and called on 60,000 fellow ministers to preach that doctrine. He declared:

"I want to assure you that the testimony given you by Mr. A. Philip Randolph on March 3 did most emphatically state the mood of the vast majority of the 15,000,000 colored Americans. He did not overestimate it."

Tired of Hypocrisy

"They are sick and tired of the hypocritical pretense at democracy now being evidenced by our Congress. . . ."

Can't Be Frightened

"We are not going to be frightened by the cry of 'Treason.' We, the colored people, for over 400 years have been the most loyal element of this democracy.

"If the finger of treason can be pointed at anyone, it must be pointed at those of you who are traitors to our Constitution and to our Bill of Rights."

Not Enough Jails

"There aren't enough jails in America to hold the colored people who will refuse to bear arms in a Jim Crow army.

"If you threaten our leaders, then the 60,000 pulpits of the colored church will thunder through their ministers, against the immoral hypocrisy of you, the leaders.

"I dare you to arrest 60,000 ministers of God in order to whitewash your un-Americanism."

Congress Scored

"Step by step, this Congress is pushing the colored people's backs against the wall. Last March you refused to accept my amendment and you set up a permanent Nurse Corps for the Armed Services which rigidly excluded colored women. You are now planning to present a bill authorizing a permanent Women's Auxiliary to the Armed Services.

"The bill again rigidly excludes colored people, despite the fact that I appeared before the House Armed Services Committee and presented my amendments, but they were overwhelmingly defeated."

Will Seek Amendment

"And now you think you can ram Universal Military Training down the throats of the colored people.

"Well you can't. We won't take it. We refuse to bear arms in un-American Jim-Crow armed services. That choice is forced upon us by our God, our conscience, our Constitution, and the Bill of Rights.

"When UMT comes before the House, I promise you I will fight vigorously and militantly to amend it so that there will be complete non-segregation in every phase of our armed services."

DOCUMENT 61:

National Council of Negro Women, Inc., "Wednesdays in Mississippi," 1965, African American Miscellany (#1032), Box 1, Folder 13.

Courtesy Special Collections, Robert W. Woodruff Library, Emory University.

This excerpt of a typescript provides general background on the state of Mississippi from the 1960 Federal Census, including statistics on education, economics, and voting. The document is intended to educate African American women from outside the state who will be working to help promote the civil rights movement.

WEDNESDAYS IN MISSISSIPPI
SPONSORED BY
NATIONAL COUNCIL OF NEGRO WOMEN, INC.

GENERAL BACKGROUND MATERIAL

Some general information about the state of Mississippi might prove to be interesting and important background material for WIMS teams going to Mississippi this summer. Much of the statistical information has been taken from the 1960 Federal Census Reports; other reports are from articles in the Southern press.

A look at the characteristics of the population is enlightening in many respects. Only 17 of the 82 counties in Mississippi have cities with over 10,000 population. 33 counties have cities with populations of 2,500–10,000, and 32 counties (more than one third) have no urban places listed in the Federal census. This population structure may well be one of the reasons why communication within the state is so difficult.

42.3% of the population in Mississippi is Negro, 57.7% is white. The median age of Negroes is considerably lower than that for whites in the state, 18.6 years, compared to 28.5 years. This is obviously important economically, and the explanation for these figures lies in the higher Negro birth rate, and the emigration from the state of Negroes in the 18–64 age groups.

EDUCATION

The picture of education in Mississippi, compared to the national picture, is rather appalling. The illiteracy rate in 1960 was 4.9%, compared to the national average of 2.4% (more than <u>twice</u> as high). In 1961, this was reflected in the fact that 50.1% of the Mississippi draftees failed the mental test, compared with 18.8% on the national level.

It must be pointed out that 66.7% of the total male population of Mississippi 25 years or older, from 13 counties with over 55% Negro population, have not completed eight years of schooling, while nationally this is true of 55% of the Negro males and only 20% of white males. In one county, one half of the adults did not complete more than 4th grade. In all 13 of the Delta counties, almost 30% of the males have not completed more than 4 years of school.

The white population, 25 years and older, completed 11 years of schooling, compared to six years for the Negro in Mississippi. This represents the median figure. . . .

The low level of education for Negroes is reflected partially in the fact that there are only 50 Negro doctors in the state—one for every 18,000 Negroes.

Despite the difference in educational standards, only 19 out of 150 school districts in Mississippi have met the March 4 deadline for compliance with the school integration provisions of the Civil Rights Act. The state stands to lose $23 million a year in federal funds if more districts do not decide to comply soon.

PROJECT HEAD START

"In our time, literacy is the most important vocational skill of all. Today's society—and, even more, tomorrow's—needs masses of educated men . . . To be uneducated is not only to be unproductive but to be virtually unemployable."*

As further evidence of the problem, in 1950, only 8% of the nation's cotton crop was harvested mechanically. In 1962, 70% was harvested mechanically. "As one Mississippi planter pointed out recently, the skills needed to operate some of the farm machines nowadays is almost as great as the skill needed to pilot an airplane. This poses a real challenge to cotton states' educators. (<u>Memphis Commercial Appeal,</u> November 17, 1963.)

"As the U. S. Commission on Civil Rights concluded in 1961, a principal reason for continued Negro poverty is the lack of motivation on the part of many Negroes to improve their educational and occupational status.'"*

To reverse the effects of a starved environment, the public schools nationally should begin admitting children in poor neighborhoods at age 3 or 4, instead of at 5 or 6. (Mississippi has no compulsory education or kindergartens.) "The nursery school probably holds the key to the Negro's future—but a very different kind of nursery school from the ones with which most Americans are familiar."* (Italics added)

Project HEAD START is not a nursery school experience, but it attempts to help overcome the poverty of experience that Negro children, who are both poor and forced into ghettos, endure.

ECONOMICS

The economic picture in Mississippi is also most disturbing, although there are encouraging signs of improvement on the horizon, thanks chiefly to the federal government.

The median white family income in the state in 1960 was $4209. The comparable figure for non-whites was $1444. In the three counties with over 75% Negro population, annual family income was under $2000. Among 25 additional counties with over 50% Negro population, 16 have median family incomes under $2000, eight have incomes of $2000-$2999, and only one has a median income of $3000-$3999. In the latter, Washington County, the Negro family income was $1597, compared to the white family income of $5560.

The poorest county in the United States is the Delta county of Tunica, where half of the families have an annual income of less than $1260. ($3000 is the national poverty level.) This county is 79.2% Negro. There are only 97 factory jobs in the county and 82% of the farms are operated by tenants. Half of the adults completed no more than 4th grade. Because of the high birth rate, only 36% are in the 21–65 year-old income-producing age bracket.

"By finding industrial jobs for Negroes in Tunica County, improving educational standards there, encouraging Negro home ownership,

---

*Charles Silberman, writing in Columbia College Today, Fall, 1964.

reducing the unusually high Negro birth rate and encouraging development of additional farm enterprises, we could establish patterns adaptable to other portions of Mississippi's large Negro population." (Tupelo Daily Journal, December 2, 1964.)

There are some encouraging signs, however, thanks to the economic force of federal funds, and the Civil Rights Act's provisions. The Mississippi Economic Council has publicly urged an end to racial oppression, and its statement has been endorsed by 50 local Chambers of Commerce. There is a fear of economic boycotts and of further loss of industry to the state. Investment in new plants in the state dropped 28% in 1963.

Governor Johnson has been working very hard to try to change the state's image. His aim is to get Mississippi off the bottom of the nation's economic ladder. One third of the operating budget of the state comes from federal sources. He can hardly afford to give up this money, so he is being forced to comply with Title VI. Johnson has recently urged county officials to take advantage of poverty funds available to the state. They will be participating to the extent of $35,000,000.

In March, Hodding Carter, Editor of a liberal newspaper, the Delta Democrat-Times, said that there is more inclination to go along with the law—even federal law—than possibly ever before in the state's history.

VOTING

In order to avoid having federal registrars swarm in to take over the duties of county officials, Mississippi Attorney General Patterson has asked for a special session of the Mississippi Legislature to repeal the Mississippi laws used to keep Negroes from voting. He has also asked for repeal of the constitutional provision requiring "good moral character," and the required interpretation of the State Constitution. Hodding Carter reported this information in the Delta Democrat-Times, April 12, 1965. . . .

THE ROLE OF THE OUTSIDER IN MISSISSIPPI

The following quote, taken from the Christian Century, March 17, 1965, expresses the role of the outsider in Mississippi from the point of view of Mississippi's Negro citizens.

"The role of the outsider is indispensable to the Mississippi Negro in his struggle for human rights. Had the freedom movement never come to McComb the situation would probably be unchanged today. Most Negroes now active in the struggle see this clearly. One has been quoted as saying: 'We are just captives and can't move at all. Discrimination goes on around here by law. The people who come in open up the situation, give us moral support, and then the whole world hears about it.' . . . No major social change will be effected by the dominant group, which has constructed its society on the basis of suppressing and exploiting another group . . . The McComb story illustrates this point, for the statement of the white citizens *followed* the cessation of violence, it did not *cause* it." (Italics added)

Although not all white Mississippians share this view, many, including several with whom we will be working, recognize the need for support from the outside at this time of crisis and tension in their state.

CHAPTER 5

Dismantling Jim Crow

This final section examines the multiple ways in which Jim Crow was challenged and eventually dismantled, illustrating the transition from nearly a century-long period of segregation to integration, brought forth by the *Brown v. Board of Education* decision (1954), the Civil Rights Act (1964), and the Voting Right Act (1965).

DOCUMENT 62:
"Marian Anderson Sings," *New York City Amsterdam News*, April 15, 1939, 17.

The famous contralto Marion Anderson, who had performed all over the world, was denied use of Constitution Hall by the Daughters of the American Revolution (DAR), and also the use of a public high school auditorium by the Board of Education of the District of Columbia, called by the editors the place "where discrimination is probably more acute than in other city in the United States." Eleanor Roosevelt resigned her membership in the DAR and, with the help of Harold Ickes, Secretary of the Interior, and others, obtained for Anderson's use the Lincoln Memorial. Between seventy-five thousand and one hundred thousand persons were present for the concert. Reaction against the DAR was severe in some quarters, but most Southern newspapers condemned the First Lady's actions.

Never in the history of the nation's capital has such an enormous crowd gathered to pay tribute to any person as gathered in Potomac Park here Sunday to pay tribute to Marian Anderson, who was presented in a free concert at Lincoln Memorial by Howard University and Associated Sponsors.

Although Captain P. J. Carroll, in change of the Potomac Park police, estimated the crowd at a little more than 75,000, other observers set the figure at nearer 100,000 and said that the crowd was even greater than that which greeted Col. Charles Lindbergh when he was honored here after his famous non-stop flight to Europe.

Beginning Saturday morning, excursion trains, buses and private cars began converging on Washington from New York, the New England states, New Jersey, Pennsylvania, Delaware, Maryland, Virginia, North and South Carolina, and by nightfall every available room in hotels, the Y.M.C.A. and Y.W.C.A. was filled. Many, who had no friends in the city, slept in their cars all night.

Frost was in the air in the early morning, after a slight snowfall, and, for a time, it was believed that the weather would cause the concert to be postponed until Easter Monday; but before noon the sun was shining in a cloudless sky, and a little after noon, even before workmen carried the piano up the twelve marble steps to the memorial, a city-wide movement began toward Potomac Park.

People making up the audience were fifty percent Negro and represented every walk of American life. Here in the nation's capital, where discrimination is probably more acute than in any other city in the United States, black and white waited side by side in almost reverent silence and in complete harmony for as long as two hours, to hear the world's greatest singer.

Mothers carrying babies arrived early in order to find choice spots but by 4 o'clock—a full hour before the concert was scheduled to begin—the steps and wide landing before the Memorial were crowded and park police were having difficulty keeping the throng behind the roped-off sections reserved for the sponsors, the press and special guests.

Also before 4 o'clock the parking place on Constitution Avenue which the Police Department had reserved for 5,000 cars was completely taken and vehicles were parked as many as twelve blocks away, many passengers taking taxis from their parked cars to Potomac Park.

The crowd itself, thickest at the foot of Lincoln Memorial, stretched almost to the Washington Monument along both sides of the pool. As an evidence that the program was clearly audible to everyone, after each number persons as far as six blocks away from the singer could be seen applauding.

Although the crowd was unusually orderly, park police had great difficulty in keeping it from rushing Miss Anderson off her feet at the end of the concert. The signal to close in on the singer was seemingly set off by a small colored boy dressed in a lumberjacket who darted from the crowd after Miss Anderson's speech and shyly shook her hand.

DOCUMENT 63:

"Negro Veterans Return," Social Sciences Institute, Fisk University, "The Postwar World Begins," *A Monthly Summary of Events and Trends in Relations* 3, no. 1-2, 3, 4, and 6 (August–December 1945–January 1946).

Courtesy Fisk University.

Fisk University's Social Science Institute summarized events of 1945–46 in its *A Monthly Summary of Events and Trends in Race Relations*. This excerpted portion, *"Negro Veterans Return,"* is a pessimistic account of opportunities awaiting returning American soldiers in the fields of education, business, agriculture, and other areas of employment, which proved to be all too true.

THE POSTWAR WORLD BEGINS

I

NEGRO VETERANS RETURN

One of the most important race relations jobs of the next ten years will be the full integration of minority group veterans into a post-war world. There are 900,000 Negroes serving today in the armed forces. By the end of the war well over a million will have been in uniform. Large scale demobilization is now taking place. Ultimately then, a million Negro GI's, each with three or four dependents or close family connections, will be discharged. This means that a third of the entire Negro group will be directly affected by the post-war opportunities available to Negro veterans and the use they can make of their rights and benefits.

What are the opportunities open to the Negro veteran and what are his plans? Using the reports on the "Post-War Plans of the Soldier" compiled by the Armed Service Forces and data as to the number of Negroes serving in the Army released by the Adjutant General's Office, it is possible to get a good picture of what Negro GI's are planning and to estimate the number of men falling into the various types of plans. First of all, there will be a substantial amount of post-war migration, the pattern of which will correspond roughly to movements already made by the Negro worker during the war. The net effect of these movements will be a heavy out-migration from the agricultural regions of the South with a considerable increase in the Negro populations of the Northeast and Pacific Coast states. While it is difficult to estimate the numerical volume of such migration, it should total about 300,000 men. Most of the migration planned is from one region to another, involving long distances, and hence will tend to be permanent.

Education

Almost every Negro veteran will be entitled to at least one year's education at any type of school he chooses, on any academic level, and may take this schooling wherever he wishes throughout the United States. He may also attend approved schools in foreign countries. Among Negro enlisted men 43.5 percent, an aggregate of 522,000 men, have made some plans for returning to school after the war. This total includes men with a very wide range of plans for full-time schooling, 32,000 of whom will be returning to the South. These are the men who will wish to resume high school or college studies broken off by the war. While the majority of these men are young—eighty-eight percent are under twenty-five years of age, and eighty-five percent are single—nearly a third, 17,000 men, have had less than four years of high school education.

Although some Negro veterans will take advantage of specific vocational training rights, most men will receive their benefits under the general education clauses in the GI Bill of Rights. The Bill has two qualifications particularly important for Negroes. First, the veteran must be acceptable to the school and meet its academic standards. Second, the school he chooses must be on the approved list submitted by the state to the Veterans Administration. Let us see what these two qualifications mean for the Negro veteran.

Because of the formal segregation in education in the South, the

Negro veteran will be subject to the differential in the quality and quantity of education available for Negroes and whites. The facts of this differential treatment have been told and retold for years. The 112 Negro colleges, having a present over-crowded enrollment of 50,000 students, will be expected to absorb, at the minimum, about 22,000 Negro veterans. The southern Negro veteran will probably not be told by his sources of information that he may go to any college outside the South. Neither will the counselors at Negro colleges be likely to urge him to go elsewhere, as these colleges have a vested financial interest in his attendance.

The 10,000 men who plan to return to full-time school below the college level in the South, must find their education in the very few, inadequate, and already crowded high schools provided for Negroes.

Outside the South the Negro veteran will be confronted by a high informal barrier; although there is no formal segregation, the majority of schools either will not take Negro students or do it grudgingly and often on a quota basis.

Since many states are lax about their standards of approval, all veterans will be exposed to the danger of being exploited by opportunists who start new schools or use their control of existing institutions merely to make money from government tuition payments. The Negro veteran, because he is mainly excluded from attending old and well established institutions, is highly susceptible to the inducements offered by these "sheepskinners." This will be especially true in the South where approval standards are very low, particularly where Negro education is concerned.

Business

About twelve percent, 144,000 men, have some fairly well formulated plans for owning a business after the war. Contained in this group are 84,000 men with definite plans, 49,000 of whom will be returning to the South. The type of establishment that Negro GI's are predominantly planning is the small one-man retail or service business having a low capitalization met partly out of savings and partly by borrowing.

There are very stringent requirements that must be met before a veteran can get a government guaranteed loan. The veteran must satisfy the lending agency, governmental or private, that his ability and experience, and the conditions under which he proposes to pursue his business, are such that there is a reasonable likelihood of success. Of the Negro GI's definitely planning business, only an eighth, 13 percent, were self-employed before the war. However, half of the men with definite plans have had previous experience as employees in the type of business they wish to own. It is doubtful whether this previous experience is adequate, in many cases, to enable the men to obtain a loan, or to operate a business of their own effectively. In general, it may well be that the widespread myth of the Negro's inability to operate a successful business will bar him from obtaining loans.

While 84,000 Negro GI's are definitely planning to own a business, mainly in the retail and service fields, the number of establishments in these fields owned by Negroes before the war was only 29,827. Moreover, it is exactly in these types of establishments, regardless of the color of the owner's skin, where the rate of failure is high.

There is a paradox facing the prospective Negro businessman whose success is largely dependent upon Negro patronage. Outside the South credit is relatively easier to obtain but he must compete fiercely with white-owned business for customers; in the South, credit will be difficult to get, but his clientele will be far more assured.

Agriculture

Almost all the ten percent of Negro GI's, 120,000 men, who have either definite or tentative plans for full-time farming will be returning to the South. Of the men with definite plans, a group of about 84,000, a very high proportion were full-time farmers before they went into the armed forces. Most of these men received their previous experience working on the family farm. Over half of the Negro GI's who plan to operate a farm intend to invest not more than $1,000; less than ten percent intend to invest as much as $4,000. This small investment indicates that most of the men will be operating farms at the subsistence level.

In obtaining guaranteed loans for farms, Negro veterans are faced with much the same restrictions as confront them in getting business loans. The processing of farm loans is handled by the Department of Agriculture, and the Negro veteran interested in agriculture must go to the local office of the Department's county extension agent. The county agents in the plantation South often have an attitude on economic, social, and racial questions similar to that held by the large landowners.

The question is, will the county agent and the local community in the South be more interested in a square deal for the returning Negro veteran than they have been in the past for Negro civilians?

A ray of hope for the Negro veteran desiring a loan is that the GI Bill of Rights also makes each veteran eligible for a loan under the Bankhead-Jones Farm Tenant Act to the same extent as if he were a tenant. This act is administered by the Farm Security Administration which has been the main federal agency helping Negro farmers in the South.

Southern agriculture has long been greatly overcrowded and during the war more crops than were grown in the pre-war years have been produced by fewer men, using larger farms, more machinery, and increased capitalization. With the close of the war, the trend toward increased mechanization of farming in the South will be accentuated. Only by mechanization and large scale farming can the South hope to compete with the price of cotton determined in the world market. These new large farms will be owned by wealthy white landowners. In cold fact this means that the Negro in agriculture is at the very bottom of the economic heap.

Other Employment

A surprisingly large group, twenty-one percent, constituting 252,000 Negro GI's, have plans for public employment after the war. Of this group, 108,000 men have definite plans.

Because of the sweeping advantages granted veterans under the Veterans' Preference Act of 1944, the Civil Service for many years to come will be made up largely of veterans. Government jobs hold particular attraction for Negro veterans owing to the relative lack of racial discrimination. Due to the impetus given to public employment of Negroes by the policies of the Roosevelt administration, it is not surprising to find that eight percent of the Negro veterans want federal jobs rather than state or municipal. A large majority of the men planning federal employment have worked for the government before the war and a third of these men desire a job in a different occupational group than the one they were in before joining the armed forces.

While the Negro veteran's chances for a job are better in the Civil Service than at almost any point in the employment structure of our society, the number of jobs available in the post-war period will meet only a fraction of the demand. The total number of Negroes in public employment in April, 1944, was about 200,000 in contrast to fewer than 60,000 in the same month of 1940. It is obvious that with the contraction of public employment after the war, Negro veterans will experience considerable difficulty in carrying out their plans.

Of the 700,000 Negro veterans who plan to join the general labor force as workers after the war, 400,000 will be returning to the South. Almost all of these men were employees before they joined the armed forces. However, their re-employment rights will be of little benefit to them as only a fifth of the men have definite plans for returning to their old job and employer. Further, only a third are even planning to return to the same kind of work they did before the war. Negroes have been trained in many skilled fields—as pilots, mechanics, radio technicians and operators—and will not be content in the menially unskilled employment of traditional Negro jobs.

The single basic issue confronting Negro veterans who plan to enter the labor market as workers is whether or not there will be a reasonably high level of employment in the reconversion and post-war periods. Between April, 1940, and April, 1944, the employment of Negroes in civilian jobs increased by almost a million, the occupational shift being mainly from the farm to the factory. But, looking to the post-war period, it must be noted that the Negro worker has made his greatest employment gains in occupations such as semi-skilled factory jobs, which will suffer the highest rate of lay-off once the war is ended. Further, the Negro's occupational gains have been in those industries—iron and steel, munitions, aircraft and ship building—which will experience the greatest decline and most radical reconversion adjustments.

For the 400,000 Negro veterans returning to the South as workers there may be no jobs of any kind. The South remains industrially underdeveloped despite the emergency aid of defense industry, and even during the war there was a surplus labor force. This surplus will be swelled now that the war has ended by the closing of defense plants and the coming home of millions of veterans looking for jobs.

The theory behind much of the administration, evolved to give the veteran adequate aid in re-establishing himself, is based on the belief that the local community can best handle the problems of its own veterans. The right to decide whether a veteran may enroll in a school rests with the local school he wishes to attend. Whether the veteran may make a loan for a business or farm rests with the local bank or other agency which will decide whether he meets the requirements for a loan. The veteran's re-employment in his old job is handled by the re-employment committeeman of his local draft board. A new job will depend upon the policies of local industry and the local United States Employment Office.

For the white veteran the theory of allowing each local community to take care of its own has a certain validity. It is true that with federal and state aid providing the channels through which local decisions are implemented, the community can give individualized special service to its own veterans. And the Negro veteran will receive individualized and special treatment in an ironical sense; it is at the level of the local community where he had always suffered the most discrimination.

At three points the Negro veteran will have difficulty not encountered by the white veteran. First, he will have less access to places in which he may obtain information about his benefits and where he should apply for them. In the South he will have to utilize "jim-crow" veterans' information centers, or no information centers at all. Second, once he has obtained information, he will be subject to careless treatment and possible discrimination in the offices where his rights are administered. Lastly, he has the very special problem, particularly in the South, that, even if he were to obtain sufficient information, if he were to meet absolutely no differential treatment in the offices of administering agencies, he would still not have the wide choice of schools, loan institutions, or jobs open to the white veteran.

Therefore, at many points of contact with society where veterans must act to change their plans into reality, the white GI will be considered first a veteran, secondly and incidentally a white man; the Negro GI will often be considered first a Negro, secondly and incidentally a veteran.

DOCUMENT 64:
Augusta Strong, "Lily White Traditions Tumbling," *Daily Worker,* April 25, May 2, and May 13, 1954.

This series of vignettes, described by African American Augusta Strong, recounts gains in voting and voter registration and the nomination and, in some cases, election of black Americans in places as diverse as Jefferson County, Alabama; East St. Louis, Missouri; and Newark, New Jersey. As optimistic as these accomplishments were, many years of struggle remained ahead. The *Daily Worker* was the newspaper of the American Communist Party.

A

A Negro attorney has entered the Democratic primary here . . . as a candidate for a seat in the state legislature. Arthur D. Shores, a former vice-president of the National Association for the Advancement of Colored People, is running for one of seven seats in the House of Representatives from Jefferson County. He is one of 27 candidates in the primary which will be held May 4, followed by a run-off election the first of June.

Though the proportion of Negro voters to whites is still small in this area, Negroes comprise about one third of the population and over the last two decades, especially, have organized a strong movement to win the right to vote.

Shores has participated actively in this movement. In 1944 when the white primaries were being challenged before the Supreme Court, he attempted to file as a candidate in the Jefferson County primaries.

His application was thrown out, however, when Democratic party officials found out that he was a Negro. Though the Supreme Court has since outlawed the white primary, the Alabama Democratic machine today uses as its symbol a white rooster with the slogan "White Supremacy."

The symbol still has meaning in the state. Alabama is one of six Southern states which retains the poll tax. The Alabama Board of Registrars still has absolute power to determine "educational" and "character" qualifications for voters. In the Birmingham area, white voters are estimated to outnumber the Negroes 15 to 1, though Negroes comprise more than one third of the population.

Election gains were made by Negro voters in two other areas of the South during April, again indicating results won from the wide right-to-vote movement of recent years.

The first Negro city councilman took his seat in the Joplin, Missouri Council April 13, after an election won with the support of large numbers of white voters. M. W. Dial, principal of the Lincoln School, was elected as one of five councilmen-at-large, running fifth in a field of 26 candidates, in which he was the only Negro.

In Opelousas, Louisiana, local leaders proudly reported that for the first time in a city election, 2,000 registered Negro voters turned out for the mayoralty election.

The weight of their votes—there are 5,000 registered voters in the city—carried the election of candidate Percy Ledoux.

Negro leaders were elated over their success in defeating Mayor T. W. Huntington, who had held office for 13 years. They attributed the victory to the fact that white workers, for the first time had united their voting strength with Negroes, for the good of both groups. They hailed the end of the atmosphere of terror that had kept Negroes from the polls previously. Mayor-elect Ledoux, in a postelection speech promised the appointment of Negro police and juvenile officers.

Daily Worker, April 25, 1954.

B

Recent and forthcoming electoral contests throughout the nation include a growing number of Negro candidates running for local offices, sometimes with the endorsement of major parties, often as independents. Many of the contests, even for minor offices, are of more than ordinary significance since they occur, in many instances, in areas where Negroes have only recently overcome voting barriers or have only recently won the fight for public office.

EAST ST. LOUIS, Ill.—Dr. Arthur M. Jackson was elected last week to the hitherto lily-white School Board in a popular election. In this city, which maintained segregated schools until four years ago, he ran second in a field of 12 candidates, with 8,856 votes.

CROWLEY, La.—The election of two Negro candidates to City Council in this city of 15,000 is being hailed here as an accepted fact, upon the withdrawal of two white candidates for the post.

Both were unopposed in the Democratic primary. David L. May, high school principal and Joseph A. Pette, barber shop operator, will break the jimcrow barriers here for the first time when they are installed in the Council in July. Both men were supported by the winning mayoralty candidate, chief of police, and many white voters.

The victory for May, a World War II vet, came after many defeats, since he first sought public office 10 years ago. Pette, also a veteran, had been a leader in the fight to win admission of Negroes to state supported universities equally with white students.

TUSKEGEE, Ala.—Mrs. Jessie Guzman, editor of the Negro Yearbook, an educator for 33 years, is opposing a white attorney for the position of the Macon County School Board—for the first time in this Black Belt county.

An all-white school board presides over the 25,771 Negroes and 4,777 whites in Macon County. Mrs. Guzman is campaigning on a platform of "democratic distribution of public school funds" and seeking the "welfare of all children regardless of race."

OTHER ALABAMA contests in which candidates are pioneering for the May 4 primaries are in Birmingham and Mobile. In Jefferson County, Dr. Arthur D. Shores has qualified to run in the Democratic primary for state legislature; he is president of the Alabama Progressive Democratic Association. . . .

In Mobile County which has more than 5,000 registered Negro voters, three are running for posts on the County Democratic Committee. Two thousand Negro voters have registered since Dec. 15 when poll tax laws were modified. E. D. Nixon of Montgomery, a leader of the National Association for the Advancement of Colored People, has filed for a similar post at Montgomery.

ST PETERSBURG, Fla.—The Rev. W. R. Johnson is a candidate for the School Board of Pinellas County. Active in clerical circles and in civic groups, he says of his bid for election: "My reason for entering the race . . . is that I feel it is high time for the Negroes of Pinellas County to have a share of the responsibility of operating the schools of our county."

NEWARK, N.J.—Three Negroes are running for seats in the City Council in May 11 elections. Despite a Negro population of 76,000, there are and have been no representatives in the Council. Irving Turner is supported by the Voters Independent Council; Harry Hazelwood has CIO endorsement; Roger Yancey has the support of many Negro civic leaders.

Daily Worker, May 2, 1954

C

A freedom rally in this all-Negro town last week drew 5,000 participants, who adopted a resolution to raise a defense fund of $100,000 for civil rights and cheered speakers calling for "first-class citizenship in Mississippi."

The gathering marked the third annual meeting of the Regional Council of Negro Leadership, headed by Dr. T. R. M. Howard, a Mississippi physician, who founded the statewide organization.

Dr. Howard told the crowd assembled in a huge tent, "We are on a great crusade in Mississippi and it will not end until the humblest share-cropper has received full citizenship rights.

"Most of the things you hear about Mississippi are true, but we are not going to ask God to fight our battles. Instead, we are going to use dollars and fight until we are free."

Thurgood Marshall, NAACP counsel, was the main speaker. Marshall had been invited, with leading Negro lawyers and leaders from Georgia, Alabama, Louisiana, Texas, Arkansas and Tennessee, to discuss a new approach to problems if the Supreme Court outlaws segregated schools in the South.

Marshall emphasized the NAACP campaign for full freedom by 1963:

"Come hell or high water. We'll be free by 1963," he declared. "The question of civil rights and the question of the treatment of Negroes in the U.S. is no longer a question on the local or national level.

"It has become an international question, one that is watched closely by all other nations, especially Russia."

Placards bearing the slogan "Liberty and Justice for all" were carried in the parade preceding the meeting. Mayor B. R. Green of Mound Bayou delivered the welcome address.

The meeting was widely featured in the Negro press, with the Atlanta Daily World urging all Georgia leaders to follow the example of Mississippi and set up similar organizations for funds to be used "in the struggle for first class citizenship and the holding of gains that might come to us."

The Mound Bayou fund is specifically being raised to file suits against sheriffs and circuit clerks in county offices who deny Negroes the right to register as voters.

Daily Worker, May 13, 1954

DOCUMENT 65:
Brown v. Board of Education of Topeka, 347 U.S. 483, 1954.

Overturning earlier Supreme Court decisions, such as *Plessy v. Ferguson, Brown v. Board of Education of Topeka* declared that "separate educational facilities are inherently unequal" in a unanimous decision—an obvious blow to Jim Crow. Implementation of the decision was far more complicated. The decision was argued on December 9, 1952, reargued on December 8, 1953, and decided on May 17, 1954. The syllabus is included here; for the full text of the decision visit http://www.nationalcenter.org/brown.html.

Syllabus

Segregation of white and Negro children in the public schools of a State solely on the basis of race, pursuant to state laws permitting or requiring such segregation, denies to Negro children the equal protection of the laws guaranteed by the Fourteenth Amendment—even though the physical facilities and other "tangible" factors of white and Negro schools may be equal.

(a) The history of the Fourteenth Amendment is inconclusive as to its intended effect on public education.

(b) The question presented in these cases must be determined not on the basis of conditions existing when the Fourteenth Amendment was adopted, but in the light of the full development of public education and its present place in American life throughout the Nation.

(c) Where a State has undertaken to provide an opportunity for an education in its public schools, such an opportunity is a right which must be made available to all on equal terms.

(d) Segregation of children in public schools solely on the basis of race deprives children of the minority group of equal educational opportunities, even though the physical facilities and other "tangible" factors may be equal.

(e) The "separate but equal" doctrine adopted in **Plessy v. Ferguson, 163 U.S. 537**, has no place in the field of public education.

(f) The cases are restored to the docket for further argument on specified questions relating to the forms of the decrees.

Opinion
WARREN

MR. CHIEF JUSTICE WARREN delivered the opinion of the Court.

These cases come to us from the States of Kansas, South Carolina, Virginia, and Delaware. They are premised on different facts and different local conditions, but a common legal question justifies their consideration together in this consolidated opinion.

In each of the cases, minors of the Negro race, through their legal representatives, seek the aid of the courts in obtaining admission to the public schools of their community on a nonsegregated basis. In each instance, they had been denied admission to schools attended by white children under laws requiring or permitting segregation according to race. This segregation was alleged to deprive the plaintiffs of the equal protection of the laws under the Fourteenth Amendment. In each of the cases other than the Delaware case, a three-judge federal district court denied relief to the plaintiffs on the so-called "separate but equal" doctrine announced by this **Court in Plessy v. Fergson, 163 U.S. 537.** Under that doctrine, equality of treatment is accorded when the races are provided substantially equal facilities, even though these facilities be separate. In the Delaware case, the Supreme Court of Delaware adhered to that doctrine, but ordered that the plaintiffs be admitted to the white schools because of their superiority to the Negro schools.

The plaintiffs contend that segregated public schools are not "equal" and cannot be made "equal," and that hence they are deprived of the equal protection of the laws. Because of the obvious importance of the question presented, the Court took jurisdiction. Argument was heard in the 1952 Term, and reargument was heard this Term on certain questions propounded by the Court.

Reargument was largely devoted to the circumstances surrounding the adoption of the Fourteenth Amendment in 1868. It covered exhaustively consideration of the Amendment in Congress, ratification by the states, then-existing practices in racial segregation, and the views of proponents and opponents of the Amendment. This discussion and our own investigation convince us that, although these sources cast some light, it is not enough to resolve the problem with which we are faced.

At best, they are inconclusive. The most avid proponents of the post-War Amendments undoubtedly intended them to remove all legal distinctions among "all persons born or naturalized in the United States." Their opponents, just as certainly, were antagonistic to both the letter and the spirit of the Amendments and wished them to have the most limited effect. What others in Congress and the state legislatures had in mind cannot be determined with any degree of certainty.

An additional reason for the inconclusive nature of the Amendment's history with respect to segregated schools is the status of public education at that time. In the South, the movement toward free common schools, supported by general taxation, had not yet taken hold. Education of white children was largely in the hands of private groups. Education of Negroes was almost nonexistent, and practically all of the race were illiterate. In fact, any education of Negroes was forbidden by law in some states. Today, in contrast, many Negroes have achieved outstanding success in the arts and sciences, as well as in the business and professional world. It is true that public school education at the time of the Amendment had advanced further in the North, but the effect of the Amendment on Northern States was generally ignored in the congressional debates. Even in the North, the conditions of public education did not approximate those existing today. The curriculum was usually rudimentary; ungraded schools were common in rural areas; the school term was but three months a year in many states, and compulsory school attendance was virtually unknown. As a consequence, it is not surprising that there should be so little in the history of the Fourteenth Amendment relating to its intended effect on public education.

In the first cases in this Court construing the Fourteenth Amendment, decided shortly after its adoption, the Court interpreted it as proscribing all state-imposed discriminations against the Negro race. The doctrine of "separate but equal" did not make its appearance in this Court until 1896 in the case of **Plessy v. Ferguson**, supra, involving not education but transportation. American courts have since labored with the doctrine for over half a century. In this Court, there have been six cases involving the "separate but equal" doctrine in the field of public education. In **Cumming v. County Board of Education, 175 U.S. 528**, and **Gong Lum v. Rice, 275 U.S. 78**, the validity of the doctrine itself was not challenged. In more recent cases, all on the graduate school level, inequality was found in that specific benefits enjoyed by white students were denied to Negro students of the same educational qualifications. **Missouri ex rel. Gaines v. Canada, 305 U.S. 337; Sipuel v. Oklahoma, 332 U.S. 631; Sweatt v. Painter, 339 U.S. 629; McLaurin v. Oklahoma State Regents, 339 U.S. 637.** In none of these cases was it necessary to reexamine the doctrine to grant relief to the Negro plaintiff. And in **Sweatt v. Painter**, supra, the Court expressly reserved decision on the question whether **Plessy v. Ferguson** should be held inapplicable to public education.

In the instant cases, that question is directly presented. Here, unlike **Sweatt v. Painter**, there are findings below that the Negro and white schools involved have been equalized, or are being equalized, with respect to buildings, curricula, qualifications and salaries of teachers, and other "tangible" factors. Our decision, therefore, cannot turn on merely a comparison of these tangible factors in the Negro and white schools involved in each of the cases. We must look instead to the effect of segregation itself on public education.

In approaching this problem, we cannot turn the clock back to 1868, when the Amendment was adopted, or even to 1896, when **Plessy v. Ferguson** was written. We must consider public education in the light of its full development and its present place in American life throughout the Nation. Only in this way can it be determined if segregation in public schools deprives these plaintiffs of the equal protection of the laws.

Today, education is perhaps the most important function of state and local governments. Compulsory school attendance laws and the great expenditures for education both demonstrate our recognition of the importance of education to our democratic society. It is required in the performance of our most basic public responsibilities, even service in the armed forces. It is the very foundation of good citizenship. Today it is a principal instrument in awakening the child to cultural values, in preparing him for later professional training, and in helping him to adjust normally to his environment. In these days, it is doubtful that any child may reasonably be expected to succeed in life if he is denied the opportunity of an education. Such an opportunity, where the state has undertaken to provide it, is a right which must be made available to all on equal terms.

We come then to the question presented: Does segregation of children in public schools solely on the basis of race, even though the physical facilities and other "tangible" factors may be equal, deprive the children of the minority group of equal educational opportunities? We believe that it does.

In **Sweatt v. Painter**, supra, in finding that a segregated law school for Negroes could not provide them equal educational opportunities, this Court relied in large part on "those qualities which are incapable of objective measurement but which make for greatness in a law school." In **McLaurin v. Oklahoma State Regents**, supra, the Court, in requiring that a Negro admitted to a white graduate school be treated like all other students, again resorted to intangible considerations: ". . . his ability to study, to engage in discussions and exchange views with other students, and, in general, to learn his profession." Such considerations apply with added force to children in grade and high schools. To separate them from others of similar age and qualifications solely because of their race generates a feeling of inferiority as to their status in the community that may affect their hearts and minds in a way unlikely ever to be undone. The effect of this separation on their educational opportunities was well stated by a finding in the Kansas case by a court which nevertheless felt compelled to rule against the Negro plaintiffs:

Segregation of white and colored children in public schools has a detrimental effect upon the colored children. The impact is greater when it has the sanction of the law, for the policy of separating the races is usually interpreted as denoting the inferiority of the negro group. A sense of inferiority affects the motivation of a child to learn. Segregation with the sanction of law, therefore, has a tendency to [retard] the educational and mental development of negro children and to deprive them of some of the benefits they would receive in a racial[ly] integrated school system.

Whatever may have been the extent of psychological knowledge at the time of **Plessy v. Ferguson**, this finding is amply supported by modern authority. Any language in **Plessy v. Ferguson** contrary to this finding is rejected.

We conclude that, in the field of public education, the doctrine of "separate but equal" has no place. Separate educational facilities are inherently unequal. Therefore, we hold that the plaintiffs and others similarly situated for whom the actions have been brought are, by reason of the segregation complained of, deprived of the equal protection of the laws guaranteed by the Fourteenth Amendment. This disposition makes unnecessary any discussion whether such segregation also violates the Due Process Clause of the Fourteenth Amendment.

Because these are class actions, because of the wide applicability of this decision, and because of the great variety of local conditions, the formulation of decrees in these cases presents problems of considerable complexity. On reargument, the consideration of appropriate relief was necessarily subordinated to the primary question—the constitutionality of segregation in public education. We have now announced that such segregation is a denial of the equal protection of the laws. In order that we may have the full assistance of the parties in formulating decrees, the cases will be restored to the docket, and the parties are requested to present further argument on Questions 4 and 5 previously propounded by the Court for the reargument this Term. The Attorney General of the United States is again invited to participate. The Attorneys General of the states requiring or permitting segregation in public education will also be permitted to appear as amici curiae upon request to do so by September 15, 1954, and submission of briefs by October 1, 1954.

It is so ordered.

* Together with **No. 2, Briggs et al. v. Elliott et al.,** on appeal from the United States District Court for the Eastern District of South Carolina, argued December 9–10, 1952, reargued December 7–8, 1953; **No. 4, Davis et al. v. County School Board of Prince Edward County, Virginia, et al.,** on appeal from the United States District Court for the Eastern District of Virginia, argued December 10, 1952, reargued December 7–8, 1953, and **No. 10, Gebhart et al. v. Belton et al.,** on certiorari to the Supreme Court of Delaware, argued December 11, 1952, reargued December 9, 1953.

DOCUMENT 66:
Conrad Lynn, "The Southern Negro Stirs," *American Socialist* 3 (February 1956): 7–9.

This article is by Syracuse Law School graduate and civil rights lawyer Conrad J. Lynn, who both defended civil rights leaders and participated in many antiracist demonstrations. Author of *There Is a Fountain: An Autobiography of a Civil Rights Lawyer,* he was

recipient of the Roy Wilkins Civil Rights Award. In this article, he
describes the increasing incidents of black resistance to the injustices of Jim Crow and predicts a rapidly mounting increase in even
more action.

The most inspiring area in the United States is the old South. The rest
of the country exclaims in horror at the Till mutilation-murder and the
sickening whitewash of its perpetrators. The cowardly Belzoni shoot-
ings, the bullwhip and shotgun reigns of a Sheriff McCall in Florida, or
a Byrd, Strider of Mississippi, expose the hideous visage of race dictatorship for all the world to see. Who can blame other Americans for
decrying the hanging out of such dirty linen? But they view the scene
from only one angle of vision. While the masses of Negroes accepted
an economically depressed, socially inferior status, it was seldom necessary for the ruling class openly to employ such brutal tactics. Lynching
was the prerogative of the poor white and the petty shopkeeper. It
served the function of keeping the Negro in his place while the upper
class remained carefully off stage. Now, such aloofness can no longer be
pretended. A social structure is being shaken and the Southern aristocrat may soon have his back against the wall.

The Southern "way of life" was constructed around the turn of the
century after the Negro had enjoyed a shortlived emancipation. The
Southern pattern was less of a crazy quilt than the more hypocritical
Northern accommodation. A tiny Negro business and professional class
was permitted to exist but in a strictly segregated locale. It was reasoned,
with some justification, that pressure from below could thus be siphoned
off and the educated Negro could be given a stake as a minor partner of
Jim Crow.

But two world wars have loosened the grip of the traditional ruling
classes everywhere and at last the semi-feudal rulers of the South are
confronted with the handwriting on the wall. The cotton-picking
machine has chased the poor white from the fields as tenant farmer or
overseer, and he has found employment in the Texas oilfields or in the
many new industries that find his labor cheaper than in the unionized
North. He is even painfully learning in the sugar refinery strikes in
Louisiana and in the longshore struggles of the Gulf ports that he has

a fundamental identity of interest with the despised blacks. The lesson is being learned slowly but inescapably.

Is it any wonder, then, that the ruling class in the South has openly assumed the helm in the savage struggle to smash the Negro back? The amalgamation of the White Citizens Councils into the Federation for Constitutional Government finds a score of ex-Governors and ex-Senators lined up with such active politicians as Talmadge, Eastland, Fielding Wright, Griffin and Strom Thurmond. Appropriately, a major industrialist, John U. Barr, is its chairman. One of its first acts was to put out feelers for alliance with Rumely and Mervin K. Hart. Thus, a special brand of American fascism appears on the scene.

Numberless anonymous little Negroes who trudged to the polls to vote, who dared to challenge Jim Crow on buses, who petitioned for non-segregated schools, are compelling a polarization of forces. In most instances these actions have been without the sanction of their major spokesman, the National Association for the Advancement of Colored People. Winfred Lynn was denied support when he refused to submit to induction in a segregated Army. Irene Morgan did not have official approval for sitting in the "white" section of a bus in 1946. The national office of the NAACP hesitates to endorse the fight of Andrew Wade and his white friends, the Bradens, for a home in an unsegregated neighborhood of Louisville.

What is true of the national body, however, is not true of the branches of this organization. When the writer was jailed in Petersburg, Va., in 1947, for refusing to move to the "colored" section of a bus, the local branch of the NAACP was quick to come to his aid. Local Negro leaders of the battle for equality in the South almost uniformly come from indigenous chapters in the various states. McCoy and Howard of Mississippi, the youthful Carl Gray of Montgomery, Ala., Simkins of Columbia, S.C., Calhoun of Georgia, to mention only a few, are all active NAACP members.

Until the recent past the NAACP has been dominated by its Northern constituents. The Northern middle-class Negro has accepted a second-class status which is for the most part not as galling as that suffered by his Southern brother. At the same time, influential in his councils, are liberal whites like Mrs. Eleanor Roosevelt and H. B. Lewis, whose hearts bleed for the Negro but who are anxious that the Negro not be too ready to bleed for himself. Inevitably the influence of this faction must wane as the struggle in the South intensifies.

Why is it that among the most prosperous Negroes in the South we find many of the most militant fighters for social emancipation? A glance at Morocco, the Gold Coast, or Indochina, affords a clue to the answer. In many respects the situation of the Negro in the South is analogous to that of oppressed colonials. Regardless of his economic station, he is barred in many crucial areas from participation in the national life. From this circumstance, however, we need not adopt the Communist deduction of "self-determination for the Black Belt." As much as any non-accepted group, the Negro in America seeks integration into the general body politic.

While the leadership of the current struggle has come from the educated middle-class Negro, as the fight deepens, the Moses Wrights among the downtrodden masses come to the fore. This is a sure sign that this campaign differs fundamentally from all that have preceded it. Every previous upsurge of the Negro has resulted in a compromise with his inferior status consolidated at a slightly higher level than that which existed before. Now his fight coincides with the stirring of that vast world of color in Asia and Africa, awakening from a millenium of apathy. The lowliest Negro veteran remembers his experiences in Asia and Europe. The impact of a changing economic organization arouses obscure impulses for more participation in society's benefits. "The Negro in America is the great proletarian. The white worker can dream of rising to middle-class status but the Negro is a worker in uniform, so to speak, a uniform he cannot take off: his skin. When such a group, deliberately kept for generations at the bottom of the social structure, begins to stir and raise its head, the whole edifice feels the shock." (D. MacDonald, *Politics,* February 1944.)

In the South, the Negro knows that his battle admits of no further compromise. The basis of the decision of the United States Supreme Court that segregation, *per se,* is discrimination, makes this implicit. That decision was itself only a recognition of the world struggle for men's allegiances. Any doubt that the final contest for integration has been joined can be resolved by a visit to a Southern Negro church, such as the one in Lake City, South Carolina, which was burned to the ground by the blind and desperate mob. In this cultural center of the Negro one is likely to hear on any occasion the singing of "O Freedom":

And before I'll be a slave
I'll be buried in my grave
And go home to my Lord
And be free.

The conflict assumes innumerable forms. In Augusta, Ga., the Negroes win the right to vote and throw out of office a reactionary Board of Education wedded to segregation. In Montgomery, Ala., a young Negro woman refuses to heed an order of a bus driver to give up her seat to a white woman. Three policemen drag her in chains to jail. Three days later Carl Gray leads a boycott of 40,000 Negroes who walk as much as five miles to work rather than submit any longer to Jim Crow on buses. The Negro taxi-drivers cut their fare for their brothers to ten cents and even some white employers, in grudging admiration, call for their Negro servants in their own cars.

In Orangeburg, S. C, the White Citizens Council decrees the firing from jobs of Negroes who sign a petition for an unsegregated school system. The Negroes, who are in the majority there, place a selective boycott on the leaders of the Council. Economic ruin stares these worthies in the face. The Godchaux refinery in Louisiana hires armed thugs to break up the strike of Negro and white workers. The union quietly provides all its members with the weapons of self-defense.

In Louisville, Ky., a white man, [Carl] Braden, sells a home to a Negro friend, Andrew Wade, in an unsegregated neighborhood. Hoodlums stirred up by the real estate interests fire shots into the house. Friends of Wade, Negro and white, volunteer to move into his house with guns to protect home and family. In the dead of night a bomb is thrown under the home, partially destroying it. Wade sends his wife and baby away and grimly stays on with his rifle.

In Milford, Del., young white toughs set out to beat up Negroes in the black ghetto. They are thrown back and punished so severely by the erstwhile lowly blacks that the police have to rescue them. In Mississippi a bloody showdown impends as the whites and blacks sweep the hardware stores bare of guns and ammunition and the white banking authorities announce that they will no longer extend credit on the crops of the Negroes this spring.

Nor does the Negro stand alone in the area of the fight. Small groups of dedicated whites all over the South risk everything to stand by his side, foreshadowing the ultimate reawakening of the disadvantaged whites. The history of Populism and of native socialism in this region is ample testimony to the revolutionary potential of the Southern masses. Don West in Dalton, Ga., the Bradens in Louisville, Charlie Jones in Chapel Hill, Minter, Cox and Editor Hazel Smith of Mississippi, have but taken up the cause of their forebears.

Finally, the remainder of the country is profoundly affected by the course of this crucial struggle. For the first time, any obscure region in the South knows that the acts of the hooded mob in the dead of night may be exposed by a Murray Kempton, or a Desmond, or even an anonymous field hand in Mississippi who writes to a Chicago paper of the terror in his neighborhood. Unquestionably the Negro will experience attacks of mounting intensity as native fascism plays its last cards. But who can doubt the eventual outcome?

DOCUMENT 67:

"Southern Manifesto: Declaration of Constitutional Principles," *Congressional Record,* 84th Congress, 2nd Session, March 12, 1956, 4460–4461, 4515–4516.

This document, created in 1956, was signed by nineteen senators and seventy-seven congressmen from Alabama, Arkansas, Florida, Georgia, Louisiana, Mississippi, North Carolina, South Carolina, Tennessee, Texas, and Virginia. All the signers were Democrats, with the exception of Republicans Joel Broyhill and Richard Poff of Virginia. There were several notable southern politicians, such as senators Lyndon B. Johnson of Texas and Albert Gore Sr. and Estes Kefauver of Tennessee, who did not sign the document.

The unwarranted decision of the Supreme Court in the public school cases is now bearing the fruit always produced when men substitute naked power for established law.

The Founding Fathers gave us a Constitution of checks and balances because they realized the inescapable lesson of history that no man or group of men can be safely entrusted with unlimited power. They framed this Constitution with its provisions for change by amendment in order to secure the fundamentals of the government against the dangers of temporary popular passion or the personal predilections of public officeholders.

We regard the decision of the Supreme Court in the school cases as a clear abuse of judicial power. It climaxes a trend in the Federal Judiciary undertaking to legislate, in derogation of the authority of Congress, and to encroach upon the reserved rights of the States and the people.

The original Constitution does not mention education. Neither does the 14th Amendment nor any other amendment. The debates preceding the submission of the 14th amendment clearly show that there was no intent that it should affect the system of education maintained by the States. . . .

In the case of *Plessy* v. *Ferguson* in 1896 the Supreme Court expressly declared that under the 14th amendment no person was denied any of his rights if the States provided separate but equal public facilities. This decision has been followed in many other cases. It is notable that the Supreme Court, speaking through Chief Justice Taft, a former President of the United States, unanimously declared in 1927 in *Lum* v. *Rice* that the "separate but equal" principle is "within the discretion of the State in regulating its public schools and does not conflict with the 14th amendment."

This interpretation, restated time and again, became a part of the life of the people of many of the states and confirmed their habits, customs, traditions, and way of life. It is founded on elemental humanity and commonsense, for parents should not be deprived by Government of the right to direct the lives and education of their own children. . . .

This unwarranted exercise of power by the Court, contrary to the Constitution, is creating chaos and confusion in the States principally affected. It is destroying the amicable relations between the white and Negro races that have been created through 90 years of patient effort by the good people of both races. It has planted hatred and suspicion where there has been heretofore friendship and understanding.

Without regard to the consent of the governed, outside agitators are threatening immediate and revolutionary changes in our public schools systems. If done, this is certain to destroy the system of public education in some of the states.

With the gravest concern for the explosive and dangerous condition created by this decision and inflamed by outside meddlers:

We reaffirm our reliance on the Constitution as the fundamental law of the land.

We decry the Supreme Court's encroachments on rights reserved to the States and to the people, contrary to established law, and to the Constitution.

We commend the motives of those States which have declared the intention to resist forced integration by any lawful means.

We appeal to the States and people who are not directly affected by these decisions to consider the constitutional principles involved against the time when they too, on issues vital to them may be the victims of judicial encroachment.

Even though we constitute a minority in the present Congress, we have full faith that a majority of the American people believe in the dual system of government which has enabled us to achieve our greatness and will in time demand that the reserved rights of the States and of the people be made secure against judicial usurpation.

We pledge ourselves to use all lawful means to bring about a reversal of this decision which is contrary to the Constitution and to prevent the use of force in its implementation.

In this trying period, as we all seek to right this wrong, we appeal to our people not to be provoked by the agitators and troublemakers invading our States and to scrupulously refrain from disorder and lawless acts. . . .

DOCUMENT 68:

Cartoon, "The Negro, The Ape," c. 1957. National Citizens Protective Association, St. Louis, Missouri, J. D. Rowlett Collection, 1954–1972 and n.d., ac 1971–0299M, Folder 3, White Sentinel.

Courtesy Georgia Archives.

This overtly white supremacist cartoon draws upon fairly typical stereotypes of African Americans by comparing them to apes and was published in protest to the *Brown v. Board of Education* decision and the crisis over the desegregation of Central High School in Little Rock, Arkansas.

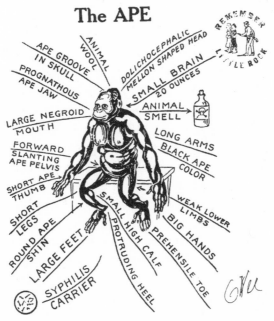

DOCUMENT 69:
Nick Aaron Ford, "Consider the Negro Teacher," *New Republic,* April 15, 1957, 14–15.

Courtesy New Republic.

Morgan State College professor Nick Aaron Ford writes of the claims of many that the likely sufferers of the 1954 Supreme Court desegregation order will be white and black students and parents, but then focuses on the problems black teachers have faced pre-integration and now face post-integration, suggesting they are likely the greatest losers. He is correct in some respects, as many black administrators and teachers were forced out of their field when schools were consolidated and integrated.

Since the Supreme Court's decision three years ago outlawing racial segregation in the public schools, much sympathy has been expanded on the "victims" of the Court order. Some have said that the worst sufferers from this "monstrous" deed are white parents who from birth have known only "white superiority," who have never doubted the reality of the stereotype of Negro crap-shooters, razor-wielders, sex fiends or superstitious clowns. We are asked to picture these parents dying a thousand deaths each morning as their children trudge off to school where a few black students may be cowering on the grounds and in the buildings.

Others may suggest that it is the white children who are most to be pitied. For are not these youngsters being forced to listen to the incorrect (or worse) language of Negro pupils, and are they not at the impressionable age when they will imitate the bad habits of Negro schoolmates —and at the same time voluntarily form close friendships with them?

There are those, too, who are sure that the Court's decision has been hardest on Negro parents—parents who have learned through bitter experiences of unemployment, economic reprisals and brutality to accept their status as "inferiors," parents who feel more at ease living in black ghettos and moving among people who have at least an understanding of their unrealized dreams, parents who live with fear as their children leave home each morning to sit in classrooms and play during recess with the sons and daughters of white supremacists.

I have also heard it said that the Negro children themselves are the real martyrs in this de-segregation struggle. Suddenly lifted from a school situation of mutual respect and cordiality where they were encouraged to join wholeheartedly in every kind of extracurricular activity, they now are thrust into an electric atmosphere; their talents are rejected everywhere outside the classroom; and, at the same time, they are expected to perform at the level of the best of their classmates. When some of them fail miserably, all of them are condemned as poor educational risks. When some of them fight back when jeered by mobs, all of them are classed as juvenile delinquents. When some of them make high grades, they are considered unrepresentative of their race. When they form little groups of their own for study or for play, they are accused of preferring segregations to integration. When they actively seek comradeship among their white fellow-students, they are charged with forcing "social equality."

And what of the white teacher? If education is problem-solving, here indeed—in the new relationships that must follow in the wake of the Court decree—is a problem to be solved. But might it not be difficult for an intelligent white teacher of social studies to read the Declaration of Independence with a straight face when he knows some children who are looking up at him would be beaten severely should they insist on the Declaration's full and prompt implementation? It would be equally painful for such a teacher to read and interpret the Constitution of the United States to a mixed class when he knows that the parents of some of his students have been assaulted, even killed, for attempting to exercise the right to vote. Furthermore, if there is such a vast difference between the rate of learning and the quality of academic achievement of white and Negro children because of race (as a small minority of psychologists contend), must there not be an *Educational Psychology for Negroes* and a manual on *Methods of Teaching Arithmetic to Negro Children,* and how can the harassed teacher master all the new pedagogical texts necessary to make him understand how to teach the two Negro children in his class of 35 and carry on his regular class schedule at the same time?

But the individual whose dilemma concerns me most, because I know him best, is the Negro teacher. In many sections of the South, he faces the choice of swearing *opposition* to the Constitution of the United States and thereby retaining his job, or swearing *allegiance* to the

Constitution and losing his job. Last summer, 17 teachers in one Southern state showed me contracts they were given which required that they sign affidavits swearing their opposition to integration in public schools and affirming their disinterest in teaching in an integrated situation. In another state, I was shown contracts for Negro teachers which were subject to cancellation or renewal at the end of each 30-day period, depending upon the conduct of the signer. Since some of the teachers had satisfactorily held their positions for as long as 20 years, it seemed obvious that "conduct" referred specifically to attitudes toward integration.

The dilemma of the Negro teacher is not due wholly to integration. Under the "separate but equal" doctrine which antedated the Supreme Court decision of May 17, 1954, other contradictions had to be endured. A former Negro colleague of mine, who had been principal of a rural high school for 11 years, was awarded the degree of Masters of Arts after many summers of study at a Western university. Upon his return from the graduating exercises, the county superintendent of education called him in to inform him that his contract would not be renewed for the next year. He was assured that his work had been eminently satisfactory, but unfortunately his M.A. degree plus his 11 years of teaching entitled him under state law to a salary higher than that of the white high school principal who had no graduate degree. And since the county authorities had no intention of paying a Negro more than a white man occupying a similar position, the only alternative was to secure another Negro principal with less training and no tenure.

But although the threat to the Negro teacher's professional security is serious, the undermining of his morale is catastrophic. Some Negroes in all occupations have resigned themselves to martyrdom. They defy all demands to compromise their principles or suppress their opinions, even though such defiance may mean hardship for themselves and their families. But the vast majority of peace-loving and law-abiding Negroes avoid the hero's lonely stand. Like their white counterparts, they will fight for their rights if they must, but they are prepared to pay for peace and comfort with outward conformity. Many will sign contracts with affidavits opposing integration; while in the silence of their souls they will shout, "Down with segregation!"

Not only is the Negro teacher's livelihood jeopardized, but his intellectual competence is questioned as well. He may attend the same graduate schools as his white colleagues and receive the same degrees based on the same requirements, but in the push toward integration he is usually referred to as an inferior teacher. Part of the very evidence which helped to destroy the "separate but equal" doctrine rests on the assumption that a school with an all-Negro faculty, even though the buildings and equipment may be superior, does not provide an education equal to that provided by an all-white faculty. Any school with an all-Negro faculty and an all-Negro student body is classified as inferior; white schools with all-white faculties are never thus classified, except on the basis of such criteria as buildings and equipment.

The fact is that in several large cities in the South, the average Negro teacher has more academic training and more tenure than his white colleague, which is not surprising since white college graduates have a far larger assortment of occupations open to them at higher salaries than do Negroes. And since the teaching profession represents for the Negro one of the highest paid white collar occupations available, once a Negro qualifies for a teaching position he generally remains until retirement— improving his status and salary by periodic attendance at summer school.

Finally, although the Negro teacher knows there is no fate more bleak than a loss of faith in the only political doctrine that guarantees freedom and equality for all, the application of this doctrine is so half-hearted in many sections that his hope drains away. He knows democracy means equal opportunities for employment based on merit alone, but he sees teaching positions go begging in the South and the North while thousands of his race with first-class teaching certificates are forced to take menial jobs in domestic service because boards of education will not even examine their applications and educational credentials. In cities which have already accepted the principal of integration, brilliant and experienced Negro teachers are passed over when promotions open up.

I dwell on the problems of the Negro teacher because it seems to me so evident that the survival of America as a free and responsible nation depends so largely on the devotion and moral integrity of our teachers. Any deprivation which encourages despair, which robs educators of their dignity, self-respect and chance for advancement robs the whole nation. Unless we are resolved to apply the teachings of our democratic tradition to teachers, what hope is there that the next generation of Americans will understand and deeply care about the decencies that make America worth saving?

DOCUMENT 70:
"Thoughts of a White Citizen Council Member" and
"Reply," *Clinical Sociology Review* (1958): 27–32.

Tuskegee Institute professor Charles G. Gomillion was dean of the
school of education and later dean of students as well as of the college of arts and sciences. Active in civic affairs, he led successful boycotts against racist businesses in Tuskegee. The exchange between
the two correspondents is clearly no contest, with Gomillion's well-
reasoned and temperate response to the racist's screed clearly
demonstrating the differences in the quality of the minds of the two
writers.

Thoughts of a White Citizen Council Member

To Charles Gomillion:

Who I am is unimportant. The important thing is that I'm a southerner from Lake Charles, Louisiana, and I have a few things to say to
you. I have just finished reading an article in a Coronet magazine labeled
The Integration Fight is Killing Tuskegee.

You and your ideals make me sick. You and the rest of the colored
race had it made before you started all this integration crap. I belong to
a branch of the White Citizens Council here in Lake Charles, La. I just
want you and the rest of your friends to know that we will never inte-
grate! We will stop integration if it takes bloodshed!

A few years ago I knew several negro boys my age. We were fairly
good friends. Now, I would not speak to them because of what their
race is trying to pull. Now I hate all niggers.

Its people like you who are leading the rest of the negro's down the
wrong trail.

I do not think of myself as better than a negro. But I believe that if
I want segregation and the majority of the people in the south want segregation we should be able to have it. In fact, we are going to have it!

I believe in the negro having everything that I have, just as long as
he stays on his side of the fence.

I don't want to see intermarriage between a colored man and white
women. It may happen up in yankee land but it won't happen here.

In short, Gomillion, you and your associates are fighting a losing battle. And I assure you there (are) many like I who are ready to fight anywhere, any sort of way for segregation. And as far as the Supreme Court is concerned they can go to hell! If they want another civil war they will sure as hell get it.

If you don't like it in the south why not move to the north. Those damn Yankees love niggers. Don't they?

The letter above was not dated, was not signed, and did not carry a street address. The envelope was postmarked "Lake Charles, La., Feb. 26. 1959 6:30 P.M. It was addressed to "Charles G. Gomillion, Tuskegee Institute, Tuskegee, Alabama."

Reply

March 7, 1959

The Southerner
Member of a Branch of a White Citizens Council
Lake Charles, Louisiana
Author of the letter to Charles G. Gomillion,
    Tuskegee Institute, Tuskegee, Alabama;
    Postmarked February 26, 1959

Dear Sir:

Thank you for the very informative letter which you sent me. It happens that I was not at home when it was delivered. Please pardon my delay in responding. Some of the delay is due to my uncertainty as to whom or where to send the reply. I regret that in your effort to enlighten me you neglected to identify yourself by name or address. This failure makes it impossible for me to send you a personal and private reply, which I should like to do. Since this is not possible, I think that it is courteous that I endeavor to have it published, in the hope that you will discover that your effort was not in vain.

I regret that you underestimate your importance. Who you are *is* important. Your behavior affects many persons, even me. Because you are important, and because my well-being, directly or indirectly, is affected by your conception of yourself and of your relation to others, I hope that you will consider how important you are.

You are more than "a southerner from Lake Charles, Louisiana"; you are *an American,* I presume, and one who has probably read the

Declaration of Independence, and the Constitution of the United States of America. It is quite likely, also, that you have pledged allegiance to the Flag of the United States, our Homeland. I am inclined to believe that at some time in the past you have professed to believe in the concept of democracy, the principle of equality of opportunity. I am inclined to believe, further, that basically you are a "good American," because you have chosen (1) to inform me of your affiliation, and of your intention, (2) to warn me of impending danger, and (3) to advise me as to what I should do. For this I am grateful.

Congratulations on your reading *CORONET,* which magazine frequently contains important articles. Unfortunately, however, the title of the article which you read, "The Integration Fight is Killing Tuskegee," is misleading. If Tuskegee is being killed, it is not being killed by the "integration fight." If it is being killed, might it not be by short-sighted, narrowminded, and undemocratic public officials and citizens who deprive some American citizens of civil rights and opportunities by refusing to register them, and by gerrymandering a city? Those in favor of integration did not reduce the size of the city, nor did they propose to abolish a county. They do not seek to destroy the integrity and the prestige of an historic municipality; they try to build its resources, enhance its prestige, and make it a model for democratic living and progress.

By this time, I hope that you have recovered from your illness. I regret that you were made "sick" by me and my ideals. Whenever I am responsible for the illness of anyone, I am unhappy.

I am sorry that you have decided not to speak to the Negroes whom you have known "because of what their race is trying to pull." Is it fair to them? Have *they* mistreated you? Have you asked them whether or not they are in favor of what you think "their race is trying to pull"? I regret even more your development of the capacity to "hate." Hatred is both expensive and dangerous. It takes time and effort to hate. And when one is hating, he cannot be loving. When he is acting on hatred, he cannot be engaged in noble efforts. Persons who hate are unhappy persons. Many of them are afraid, and fear is dangerous. Many persons who are afraid find it difficult to resist the temptation to engage in vice or crime. Love is much more satisfying, and honorable, than hatred. Please examine your present emotional content, and see if you might not want to talk with your one-time "fairly good" Negro friends. If you listen to them, and objectively examine their civic status and opportunities, you might discover in them something which you admire. If you discover in them nothing which elicits your respect, you would rise to the challenge if you would decide to meet and work with them in an effort to help them become worthy of your respect, and possibly of your love. If you do not think of yourself "as better than a negro," then you can afford to do this.

I am glad that you believe "in the negro having everything I have." If by "everything" you mean the civic status and opportunities to which you have access, that is exactly what Negroes are working for. When you are willing for "the negro" to have everything you have "just as long as he stays on his side of the fence," you write as if you and he are not in the same field. You and he are living in the United States of America one nation, indivisible. Where is the fence that divides? How can the Negro stay on "his side of the fence" if he does not see any fence, and if the Federal Government does not recognize the existence of any fence?

There are many implications which can be drawn from your statement that you "don't want to see intermarriage between a colored man and white women." Polygyny is not legal in the United States. Do you mean to imply that there is the possibility that two or more white women might become the wives of a colored man? Or do you mean to imply that intermarriage between a white man and a colored woman would meet with your approval? Or that you are not interested in what the white woman might think about the extramarital relations of the white man and the colored woman? Since no man is able to marry a woman if she says "No," do you imply that there are some white women who could not, or would not say "no"? Does your statement suggest that there are some white women whose judgment you do not trust? In the United States, is not legal marriage between healthy persons considered more honorable, and more in keeping with the moral code of our culture, than illegal extra-marital relations?

You err when you say that my associates and I are "fighting." We are not "fighting." We are simply working hard to be good, productive Americans. We are trying diligently to get the same kind of education you and your associates want so that we may be able to make contributions to the culture which are comparable to those which you and your associates make. We do not want to fight; we want to learn and earn. We do not want to shed blood; we want to maintain the peace. We regret that you threaten to shed blood.

It happens that I cannot answer your question as to whether or not "damn Yankees love niggers." I have never asked anyone I know whether or not he loved me. Those whom I know seem to love justice, fair play, the Golden Rule, and recognize and respect the rights of their fellow Americans. I do know that they have allowed me many more opportunities to develop my mind and my cultural interests and competencies than have Southern white Confederates.

As for leaving the South, I am not interested. I was born in the South, and attended the public elementary school in my native state, South Carolina. Although the educational opportunities in the county in which I lived were grossly inferior to those provided for white youth, as reported by white citizens, I did have the opportunity to read the Declaration of Independence, and the Constitution of the United States, and I believed what I read. I believed that I was a full citizen of this Nation, and that this was a land of opportunity, where the law-abiding and the industrious could prosper. I believed, also, that it was the duty of every American citizen to contribute constructively to the development of his Fatherland. I have spent my past years studying the arts of peace, not the science of war. Professionally, I have sought to enlighten and heal the minds of youth and men, not to poison them. My mission is to shed light, not blood, and I hope that I may be permitted to shed it in the South before the more martial-minded shed blood. Because I believe firmly that those who live by the sword shall perish by the sword. I am not now prepared "to fight anywhere, any sort of way." I am a worker, not a fighter.

As sincere as I think you are, I hope that the United States Supreme Court will not take your suggestion to "go to hell." To "go to hell" would be cowardly. There is too much work yet to be done in America. The Supreme Court in some of its recent decisions has been merely trying to implement the American value of equality of opportunity, and to rectify the unfortunate decision of the 1896 Court. The present Court now knows that if Western Civilization is to survive, it will need contributions from citizens who have developed themselves to the optimum, and this can be done only when opportunities are unrestricted. We can either work cooperatively and honorably, and try to compete successfully with undemocratic opponents, or we can waste our resources, efforts, and time, and wait for subjugation. What is your choice?

I hope that if you have read this letter you will accept it in the spirit in which it is written. It is not my desire to offend. I do not threaten you. I am sorry that you hate me. I do not hate you. This might not be of any value to you, but it makes me feel good. I can sleep at night, and I can study and work during the day. I do not have to plan courses of action designed to shed blood. I am a student, eager to learn, and would appreciate an opportunity to meet and confer with you. Those who really know me say that I am gentle, kind, and generous. I invite you and your associates to meet with my associates and me in friendly fellowship. You might discover that we are good Americans. If you observe that we are un-American, you could have us arrested and imprisoned. *Don't kill us! Don't shed our blood!* Let the constituted legal authorities do that.

> Very truly yours,
> Charles G. Gomillion
> Box 31
> Tuskegee Institute, Alabama

DOCUMENT 71:
"Youth March for Integrated Education," *Congressional Record,* May 20, 1959, vol. 105, 8694–8698.

This portion of a series of articles, by student writers and U.S. Representative Charles C. Diggs Jr. (D-Michigan), reflects the actions of twenty-six thousand students who converged on Washington, D.C., on April 18, 1959, and demanded an end to school segregation. A. Phillip Randolph, labor and civil rights leader and founder of the Brotherhood of Sleeping Car Porters, initiated the march. The last in the series, a student list of proposals, was presented to Deputy Assistant to the President Gerald D. Morgan. Presidential aide E. Frederic Morrow, the only African American in Eisenhower's administration, was present at the meeting but had no authority. Morgan afforded them fifteen minutes and explained that the president was on one of his frequent golfing vacations. Eisenhower, unsympathetic to their cause, never met with civil rights leaders.

YOUTH MARCH FOR INTEGRATED EDUCATION

A

REPRESENTATIVE DIGGS'S STATEMENT

Mr. DIGGS. Mr. Speaker, in the CONGRESSIONAL RECORD of April 20, 1959, beginning on page 6352 under the heading "Washington Window," there appear comments and several newspaper articles referring to the April 18, 1959, youth march on Washington for integrated schools. Inserted in the RECORD by the gentleman from Georgia [Mr. FORRESTER], these materials are used in an attempt by implication to link the youth march with Communist Party movement. I should like to set the RECORD straight on this piece of slander.

The 1959 youth march was very fully and objectively covered by Washington and other daily newspapers around the country. It involved nearly 26,000 white and Negro students from all parts of the Nation and outstanding, substantial, national personalities, both white and Negro, from the fields of Government, labor, religion, entertainment, and other interests. It was definitely a large action and, in that respect, indication of the growing demand on behalf of school integration and the enforcement of all constitutionally guaranteed civil rights. A delegation of these youth from the march was received at the White House by Deputy Assistant to the President Gerald D. Morgan, and Presidential Aide E. Frederick Morrow.

By including, among the newspaper clippings in this April 20 discourse, an article published in the Communist Party's Sunday Worker on the subject of the youth march, an attempt is made to infer a connection between the two. Of course, the Communist press would comment upon this march. It, too, is the press and reports on events of national interest. Of course, the Communist Party, through its press, would imply sympathy toward a cause that is humanitarian or just, however feigned its sympathy as a means to its own end. This is the Communist Party tactic—the avowing of itself as the savior for mankind's every just cause. Why else, as a Nation, are we concerned about its attempts to identify with India's, Africa's, China's, the world's needs, its unrelenting efforts to win alignments through expressions of sympathy and profferings of economic, technological, and even military assistance to nations in need? Who denies that there is hunger and disease and slavery and economic oppression and deprivation of human rights in the world and that these are the causes of which communism, on the one hand, is saying, "I am the way to overcome them," and democracy, on the other hand, is saying, "No, I am the way"?

It is ironic that with those who have some vested interest in the continuation of segregation between the races and oppression of the rights of Negro citizens, anything having to do with the democratic ideals of justice, equality, liberty, and opportunity between and for all men must somehow be linked up with communism. It is more ironic that this inference and charge should come from such groups when the truth is it is this group's very position on race relations and civil rights which is the boon to communism. During my 5 years in Congress, I have observed all kinds of positions on questions of race relations and civil rights. There are those of my colleagues, who while not in favor of integration, at least command respect for their human reasonableness in the level and character of their opposing fight. On the other hand, there is that small band of vitriolic and demagogic diehards whose approach to these issues is so completely divorced of reason and at such an animalistic level that while they defeat their own efforts to sell their blind hatred and bigotry to thinking people, they nevertheless make fodder for the Communist cause. The use of inference as a tactic for hurling vitriolic unreasoned charges is not subtle and does not escape attention and the evaluation it deserves.

Congressional Record, May 20, 1959, vol. 105, p. 8694.

B
WHY WE MARCH: THE CALL

On April 18, thousands of American young people will march in the Nation's Capital in the largest demonstration of youth in our history. The will come from all parts of the country, by bus, plane, train, and car, and will represent all faiths. In Washington, they will be joined together in great union of protest and action—the youth march for integrated schools.

We March for Real Democracy—Now

For over a century, the American Negro has been brutally and undemocratically denied the rights guaranteed to all citizens by our Constitution. The traditional rights of free speech, of suffrage, of due process, of equal protection under the law have been withheld from millions of Americans. And today, a minority of southern racist leaders is endangering our free educational system. This minority is threatening to close public schools, leaving thousands of our young people stranded, barred from the benefits of sound education.

Is this the way of real democracy?

We march to protest the century-long mistreatment of Negro citizens. They have waited long enough. We march to demand real democracy—now.

We March in Defense of the Supreme Court

Because of its recent decisions in behalf of equal educational opportunities for the Negro, the Supreme Court has been subjected to a battery of vicious attacks. Dangerous attempts have been launched to curb the power of the judicial branch of Government, which has moved courageously to defend the rights of Negroes. We protest against these attacks and call upon the executive and legislative branches to back up the Supreme Court in its reflection of the will of the majority.

We March for Civil Rights Legislation

Once again, Congress is being presented with an alternative: either to strengthen American democracy or to retreat before the campaign of the Dixiecrats. The procivil rights majority in Congress, greatly reinforced by the November elections, will have the opportunity to pass the Douglas-Celler-Javits-Powell bill, which goes a long way in helping the Negro and other minorities to achieve equality in all areas of life.

But time and time again, Congress has compromised the will of the people. We march to protest minority rule in Congress, and to demand the passage of the Douglas bill. We march to demand an immediate end to the spectacle of Congressional double-dealing that encourages resistance to the law and deforms the democratic process.

Civil rights legislation is long overdue. We march for just laws—now.

We March for Executive Action

We march to confront the President directly with the conviction of young people that he must use all of his powers to bring about the speedy integration of the schools. Specifically, we call upon him to speak out morally for the Supreme Court decision of May 17, 1954, and to use his influence to destroy the disease of segregation.

We March as Part of Our Democratic Duty

When the wheels of government are slow in expanding our democracy (less than 500 students have been integrated in the deep South), when they get bogged down in compromises and maneuvers, we have the moral obligation in a democratic society to register our protest—through action. The essence of democratic government is the participation of the people themselves. Our failure to move against undemocratic practices leaves the field open to forces hostile to democracy.

Throughout our history, dramatic action by deeply concerned people has served to awaken the whole nation to its sense of duty. The power of the democratic idea symbolized by a vast march of sincere, earnest, disciplined, and dedicated people will influence those who have not yet taken a clear stand. Such a demonstration presses forward the cause of democracy and social progress in the courts, legislature, and all areas of American life.

Thus, American young people march not only to demonstrate solidarity with their embattled fellow students of the South, but for the deepening and reinforcing of our democracy. *We demand for every American every single right guaranteed by the Constitution, political, civil, and social and until we get these rights, we will never cease to protest and assail the ears of America.* We will continue to march, to petition, to demonstrate, and to persuade. It is our responsibility to do so.

We march on April 18 for the total victory of equal rights for all. We can no longer endure compromises and delays. We want a program for speedy integration—and we won't take no for an answer.

Come to Washington on April 18.

YOUTH MARCH FOR INTEGRATED SCHOOLS

Congressional Record, as cited, p. 8695. The sentence italicized by the editor is taken—without acknowledgment—from the Niagara Address of 1906, written by Dr. Du Bois—see my *Documentary History*, vol. 1, p. 907. . . .

E
PRESIDENTIAL DELEGATION STATEMENT

Four African-American young people—three female, ranging from seventeen to twenty-six years of age—were seen by a president's assistant for fifteen minutes. He told them President Eisenhower was vacationing in Georgia and shared their concerns. They left at his office this statement:

In the light of the considerations which we discuss below, we respectfully urge that you give consideration to the following proposals, which we feel would enable the Federal Government to place its weight behind the movement for the integration of the schools:

1. The Chief Executive should make an explicit moral as well as legal commitment of the full resources of the Federal Government to the objective of achieving orderly, effective, and speedy integration of the schools.

2. The Chief Executive should place his weight behind the passage of a truly effective civil rights bill in the present session of Congress. As far as school integration is concerned, we believe that the Douglas-Javits-Celler bill is by far the most comprehensive and effective piece of legislation before Congress. It deserves, we feel, the full support of the administration.

The Douglas-Javits-Celler bill is an historic and statesmanlike proposal. It empowers the Federal Government to move into the center of the school picture and to undertake, on a nationwide basis, careful and constructive planning of the Nation's march toward integration. It provides the expert counseling, the financial aid, and the legal authority necessary to achieve this end.

The several admirable features of the bills introduced on behalf of the administration likewise merit vigorous support, especially those adding to the protection of the right to vote.

3. The Chief Executive should call a White House conference of youth and student leaders, chosen from national and regional organizations, both North and South, to discuss ways in which youth may participate in the implementation of the Supreme Court decision.

4. The Chief Executive should intervene in the case of Asbury Howard, Jr., the 18-year-old Negro youth from Bessemer, Ala., who has been sentenced to the chain gang for 1 year for coming to the defense of his father when the latter was attacked by a mob. Cases such as this must be brought to the attention of the Nation and of the State authorities if a wrong is to be redressed and justice done.

We make these recommendations in the light of the following urgent considerations:

1. Nearly 5 years have elapsed since the Supreme Court ruled that in the field of education "separate but equal" has no place. But today only some 800 of 2,890 biracial school districts in Southern and border States have begun desegregation even on a token basis. In five States, there has been no desegregation in public education. In the past 3 years, the number of districts instituting new desegregation plans has shrunk to a mere handful.

2. This situation is not acceptable to the youth and the students of the United States. For us, the youth, the question of school integration is the central moral issue of our time. Not only are the rights of minorities at stake; American democracy itself, and the supremacy of our Government, the very survival of the Constitution, are at issue.

We must point out that American youth have made strong and repeated affirmation of their support for the Supreme Court decision and the integration of the schools. Among the most recent demonstrations of this are the following:

(a) In August 1957, when the delegates of over 300 student governments, representing over 1 million students, expressed their belief at the U.S. National Student Association's 10th National Student Congress, that—

Segregation in education by race is incompatible with human equality. It is now also unconstitutional. In the face of ethical concepts, legal requirements, and global ramifications, there can be no justification for delay in the implementation of the Supreme Court decision.

(b) At the National Student Conference of the YMCA and YWCA held last December at the University of Illinois;

(c) At the 1958 convention of the National Federation of Catholic College Students held in San Francisco;

(d) At the 11th National Student Congress last August when delegates from 50 southern campuses expressed their desire for the abolition of segregation;

(e) At the 1958 youth march in Washington, when 10,000 students expressed their moral support for integration.

The petition campaign and youth march for integrated schools, with its 20,000-member march, its quarter of a million signatures, and its nationwide support, has won more support among the young people than any other national campaign or issue in the past 15 years.

3. Concern over the integration of the U.S. schools is not limited to this country. The delegates from the 75 national unions of students outside the Communist bloc, meeting in Lima, Peru, at the International Student Conference this spring, condemned the continued practice of racial segregation in our country. Similar grave concern was expressed at the World Assembly of Youth held in New Delhi last summer.

4. As young Americans, we appreciate the difficulties confronting those who work to implement integration of the schools. We commend the efforts of the courts, the Civil Rights Commission, and members of the administration such as Attorney General Rogers and Secretary Flemming on behalf of integration. Yet, if massive resistance has been defeated in Virginia, it is very much alive in South Carolina, Georgia, Alabama, Mississippi, Louisiana. The leaders of the Deep South do not seek time to accommodate to integration, but to block it altogether. They do not wish to discuss compliance with the law but ways to evade it.

5. The crisis that centers around the integration of the schools is a national question. It affects school systems and national minorities in all parts of our land. It must, we feel, have the fullest attention of the Federal Government if a solution is to be reached, if the Nation is to have the leadership for progress, for the creation of a truer, fuller democracy that it so deeply needs.

Congressional Record, as cited, pp. 8697–98.

DOCUMENT 72:
Photograph, March on Washington for Jobs and Freedom, August 28, 1963.

Courtesy Library of Congress.

More than 250,000 people attended the event in Washington, D.C., making it the largest demonstration in the nation's capital and one of the first to be covered by television. At the march, Martin Luther King Jr. delivered his now famous "I Have a Dream" speech. Originally opposed by John F. Kennedy, the march ultimately generated support for the Civil Rights Act (signed into law by President Lyndon B. Johnson on July 2, 1964). This landmark act officially ended segregation in public facilities and in employment, effectively nullifying Jim Crow laws throughout the nation. For the full text of that document, visit http://www.eeoc.gov/policy/vii.html.

DOCUMENT 73:
Photograph, Civil Rights March from Selma to Montgomery, March 1965.

Courtesy Library of Congress.

The Selma to Montgomery march for voting rights was one of the most significant events of the civil rights movement. The photograph, taken by Peter Pettus, documented a peaceful phase of the march. On "Bloody Sunday" (March 7, 1965), the event turned violent as six hundred of the participants were heading east out of Selma on U.S. Route 80. On Edmund Pettus Bridge, the police attacked the marchers with clubs and tear gas, driving them back to Selma. Two days later, Martin Luther King Jr. led a second, more symbolic march to the bridge. To gain protection from local law enforcement, the leaders of the march asked for federal protection, and Federal District Court judge Frank M. Johnson Jr. ruled in their favor. He said: "The law is clear that the right to petition one's government for the redress of grievances may be exercised in large groups . . . these rights may be exercised by marching, even

Document 72

Document 73

along public highways." Beginning on Sunday, March 21, the twenty-five thousand marchers covered twelve miles a day and reached the state capital four days later. This march helped garner support for the Voting Rights Act of 1965.

DOCUMENT 74:
Voting Rights Act, 1965, 1970, 1975, and 1982 Amendments.

This important civil rights legislation outlawed literacy tests as a requirement for suffrage and allowed for Department of Justice oversight over voter registration and changes to districting. The act essentially enforced the provisions of the Fifteenth Amendment ninety-five years after its passage. President Lyndon B. Johnson signed the act on August 6, 1965, at a time when barely one-third of eligible African American voters in the United States

were registered. The act, excerpted here, is significant for another
reason as well, because it is the most dramatic shift in the relationship between the federal and state governments since Reconstruction. For the entire document, visit http://www.usdoj.gov/
crt/voting/intro/intro_c.php. The following is the "Introduction
to the Federal Voting Rights Laws," written by the U.S. Department of Justice.

The Voting Rights Act of 1965
The 1965 Enactment

By 1965 concerted efforts to break the grip of state disfranchisement
had been under way for some time but had achieved only modest success overall and in some areas had proved almost entirely ineffectual.
The murder of voting-rights activists in Philadelphia, Mississippi, gained
national attention, along with numerous other acts of violence and ter-
rorism. Finally, the unprovoked attack on March 7, 1965, by state troop-
ers on peaceful marchers crossing the Edmund Pettus Bridge in Selma,
Alabama, en route to the state capitol in Montgomery, persuaded the
President and Congress to overcome Southern legislators' resistance to
effective voting rights legislation. President Johnson issued a call for a
strong voting rights law and hearings began soon thereafter on the bill
that would become the Voting Rights Act.

Congress determined that the existing federal anti-discrimination
laws were not sufficient to overcome the resistance by state officials to
enforcement of the 15th Amendment. The legislative hearings showed
that the Department of Justice's efforts to eliminate discriminatory election practices by litigation on a case-by-case basis had been unsuccess-
ful in opening up the registration process; as soon as one discriminatory
practice or procedure was proven to be unconstitutional and enjoined,
a new one would be substituted in its place and litigation would have to
commence anew.

President Johnson signed the resulting legislation into law on
August 6, 1965. Section 2 of the Act, which closely followed the language
of the 15th Amendment, applied a nationwide prohibition against the
denial or abridgment of the right to vote on the literacy tests on a
nationwide basis. Among its other provisions, the Act contained special

enforcement provisions targeted at those areas of the country where Congress believed the potential for discrimination to be the greatest. Under Section 5, jurisdictions covered by these special provisions could not implement any change affecting voting until the Attorney General or the United States District Court for the District of Columbia determined that the change did not have a discriminatory purpose and would not have a discriminatory effect. In addition, the Attorney General could designate a county covered by these special provisions for the appointment of a federal examiner to review the qualifications of persons who wanted to register to vote. Further, in those counties where a federal examiner was serving, the Attorney General could request that federal observers monitor activities within the county's polling place.

The Voting Rights Act had not included a provision prohibiting poll taxes, but had directed the Attorney General to challenge its use. In Harper v. Virginia State Board of Elections, 383 U.S. 663 (1966), the Supreme Court held Virginia's poll tax to be unconstitutional under the 14th Amendment. Between 1965 and 1969 the Supreme Court also issued several key decisions upholding the constitutionality of Section 5 and affirming the broad range of voting practices that required Section 5 review. As the Supreme Court put it in its 1966 decision upholding the constitutionality of the Act: "Congress had found that case-by-case litigation was inadequate to combat wide-spread and persistent discrimination in voting, because of the inordinate amount of time and energy required to overcome the obstructionist tactics invariably encountered in these lawsuits. After enduring nearly a century of systematic resistance to the Fifteenth Amendment, Congress might well decide to shift the advantage of time and inertia from the perpetrators of the evil to its victims" *(South Carolina v. Katzenbach, 383 U.S. 301, 327–328 [1966]).*

The 1970 and 1975 Amendments

Congress extended Section 5 for five years in 1970 and for seven years in 1975. With these extensions Congress validated the Supreme Court's broad interpretation of the scope of Section 5. During the hearings on these extensions Congress heard extensive testimony concerning the ways in which voting electorates were manipulated through gerrymandering, annexations, adoption of at-large elections, and other structural changes to prevent newly registered black voters from effectively using the ballot. Congress also heard extensive testimony about voting discrimination that had been suffered by Hispanic, Asian, and Native American citizens, and the 1975 amendments added protections from voting discrimination for language-minority citizens.

In 1973, the Supreme Court held certain legislative multi-member districts unconstitutional under the 14th Amendment on the ground that they systematically diluted the voting strength of minority citizens in Bexar County, Texas. This decision in *White v. Regester,* 412 U.S. 755 (1973), strongly shaped litigation through the 1970s against at-large systems and gerrymandered redistricting plans. In *Mobile v. Bolden,* 446 U.S. 55 (1980), however, the Supreme Court required that any constitutional claim of minority vote dilution must include proof of a racially discriminatory purpose, a requirement that was widely seen as making such claims far more difficult to prove.

The 1982 Amendments

Congress renewed in 1982 the special provisions of the Act, triggered by coverage under Section 4 for twenty-five years. Congress also adopted a new standard, which went into effect in 1985, providing how jurisdictions could terminate (or "bail out" from) coverage under the provisions of Section 4. Furthermore, after extensive hearings, Congress amended Section 2 to provide that a plaintiff could establish a violation of the Section without having to prove discriminatory purpose.

Timeline

1828—Thomas Dartmouth "Daddy" Rice, an actor who became famous for performing a stereotypical black character, Jim Crow, in blackface is born.

1863—President Abraham Lincoln signs the Emancipation Proclamation on January 1.

The Freedman's Bureau (officially named the Bureau of Refugees, Freedmen, and Abandoned Lands) is established on March 3 by an act of Congress to aid newly freed slaves in the former Confederate states.

Lincoln is shot on April 14. He died the next day. On May 29, President Andrew Johnson announces his policy for Reconstruction.

On November 24, Mississippi becomes the first state to enact a black code, most Southern states follow suit.

The Thirteenth Amendment to the Constitution, outlawing slavery in the United States, is ratified on December 18.

1866—A Republican Congress overcomes a presidential veto and passes the Civil Rights Act on April 9, 1866, which bestows citizenship upon native-born Americans, with the exception of Native Americans. It is passed in response to black codes (laws passed in the South in 1865 that promoted segregation) and forms the basis of the Fourteenth Amendment.

The Ku Klux Klan is established on December 24 by six Confederate veterans in Pulaski, Tennessee, to oppose Reconstruction and maintain white supremacy through violence.

1867—Congress enacts the first Reconstruction Act on March 2, dividing the former Confederacy into military districts.

The second Reconstruction Act is passed on March 23; the third, on July 19.

On April 1, the Ku Klux Klan holds its first national convention in Nashville, Tennessee.

1868—The fourth Reconstruction Act is passed by Congress on March 11, 1968.

The Fourteenth Amendment to the Constitution, ratified on July 28, grants African Americans equal protection under the law.

1870—Hiram R. Revels of Mississippi is elected to the U.S. Senate, making him the first black member.

The Fifteenth Amendment to the Constitution gives African American men the right to vote. Though ratified on March 30, its provisions would not be fully realized for almost a century. Many southern states pass poll-tax laws to restrict the black vote in response.

On May 31, Congress passes the First Enforcement Act to address violence and civil rights violations.

1871—The Second Enforcement Act is passed on February 28.

On March 4, black representatives to the U.S. Congress begin their terms: Joseph H. Rainey, Robert DeLarge, Robert Brown Elliott, Benjamin S. Turner, and Josiah T. Walls.

On April 20, the Third Enforcement Act (called the Ku Klux Klan Act) is passed.

1872—The Freedman's Bureau Act expires on June 10, and the bureau dissolves.

P.B.S. Pinchback of Louisiana becomes the first black governor, though only for thirty-five days.

1873—In the Slaughterhouse Cases, the Supreme Court rules that the Fourteenth Amendment protects only rights derived from federal, not state, citizenship.

1875—The Civil Rights Act, passed on March 1, grants equal access to public accommodations, including inns, theaters, public conveyances on land or water, and "other places of public amusement." That act is nullified in an 1883 Supreme Court decision.

Also in March, Congress fails to pass the Fourth Enforcement Act.

1876—The Compromise of 1877 gives Republican Rutherford B. Hayes the presidency in exchange for a return of home rule to the South, essentially ending the promise of Reconstruction. By April 24, Hayes has withdrawn federal troops from the South.

1883—On October 15, the Supreme Court declares the Civil Rights Act of 1875 unconstitutional, paving the way for the passage of Jim Crow laws.

1884—On February 8, Congress repeals the Second Enforcement Act, giving states full control over elections.

1896—On May 18, in *Plessy v. Ferguson,* the Supreme Court upholds "separate but equal," essentially making Jim Crow the law of the land.

1900—Charles Carroll publishes his book *The Negro: A Beast,* charging that blacks are the tempters of Eve, rapists, and more akin to apes.

There are 117 blacks lynched in 1900.

1905—The Niagara Movement, the precursor to the NAACP, is established to fight for integration and voting rights.

Thomas Dixon's novel *The Clansman* is published. The book serves as the basis for the movie *Birth of a Nation.*

1906—Race riots in Greensburg, Indiana, erupt as African Americans move north to escape Jim Crow.

1908—Jack Johnson defeats Tommy Burns on December 26 to become the first black heavyweight boxing champion.

1909—On February 12, the National Association for the Advancement of Colored People (NAACP) is established in New York City. It is first called the National Negro Committee.

1913—Woodrow Wilson begins to segregate the federal government.

1915—The Ku Klux Klan is re-established on Stone Mountain, Georgia.

D. W. Griffith's film *Birth of a Nation,* which celebrates the Ku Klux Klan, is released.

1917—On April 17, the United States enters World War I. Nearly 300,000 black men serve in segregated units, and three regiments receive the Croix de Guerre for valor.

1919—Whites attack blacks in race riots in Chicago, Houston, Little Rock, Harlem, New York, Baltimore, New Orleans, Washington, D.C., and many other cities during Red Summer.

1931—On April 6, nine black teenagers, known as the Scottsboro Boys, go on trial for raping two white women. The defendants are convicted, but all are free by parole, appeal, or escape by 1950.

1936—On August 9, Jessie Owens becomes the first American to win four gold medals during the Olympics, challenging Adolph Hitler's theory of racial superiority.

1942—The Congress of Racial Equality (CORE) is established in Chicago to fight for civil rights using direct-action protests.

1944—On April 3, in *Smith v. Allwright,* the Supreme Court rules that the "white primary" is unconstitutional.

Swedish economist Gunnar Myrdal publishes *An American Dilemma,* which describes Jim Crow as a national and international embarrassment. It will eventually be cited as evidence in *Brown v. Board of Education.*

1947—On April 10, Jackie Robinson joins the Brooklyn Dodgers, becoming the first black player in major league baseball.

1948—On May 3, the Supreme Court rules in *Shelley v. Kraemer* that lower courts cannot enforce restrictive housing covenants.

President Harry S. Truman desegregates the U.S. military with an Executive Order 9981 on July 26.

1950—Gwendolyn Brooks becomes the first African American to win a Pulitzer Prize for *Annie Allen,* her volume of poetry.

1954—The Supreme Court overturns the principle of "separate but equal" in *Brown v. Board of Education* on May 17. Thurgood Marshall, who later will become the first African American Supreme Court justice, serves as the lead attorney for the NAACP.

1955—On August 28, fourteen-year-old Emmett Till is lynched near Money, Mississippi. In September, Roy Bryant and J. W. Milam are found not guilty of his murder.

On December 1, Rosa Parks is arrested for refusing to give up her seat to a white passenger on the city bus, beginning the Montgomery Bus Boycott. A year later the buses are desegregated.

1957—The Southern Christian Leadership Conference (SCLC) is established by Martin Luther King Jr., Ralph David Abernathy, Fred Shuttlesworth, and Bayard Rustin to coordinate the battle for civil rights in the South.

On September 25, President Dwight D. Eisenhower sends the 101st Airborne to Little Rock, Arkansas, to resolve a crisis over the desegregation of Central High School.

1958—On June 30 the U.S. Supreme Court rules, in *NAACP v. Alabama,* that the constitution guarantees the NAACP freedom of assembly and is permitted to keep membership rolls a secret.

1960—In February, four students at the North Carolina Agricultural and Technical College sit at a segregated Woolworth lunch counter in Greensboro, North Carolina, beginning a sit-in movement across the South. In April, Shaw University students establish the Student Nonviolent Coordinating Committee (SNCC) to coordinate the effort.

President Dwight D. Eisenhower signs the Civil Rights Act on May 6, allowing federal inspection of local voter registration polls. It also provides for penalties for anyone who obstructs someone's attempt to register to vote or actually vote.

1961—Through Executive Order 10925, President John F. Kennedy creates the Committee on Equal Employment Opportunity to ensure that projects funded by federal monies are free of racial bias, thus beginning affirmative action.

CORE sends student volunteers South in May on "freedom rides" to test laws prohibiting segregation in interstate travel. During Freedom Summer, 1,000 volunteers participate.

1962—James Meredith becomes the first African American student enrolled at the University of Mississippi.

1963—On June 12, Medgar Evers, a NAACP field secretary in Mississippi, is murdered outside his home. Byron De La Beckwith is tried but is not convicted until 1994.

On August 28, half a million people gather at the Lincoln Memorial to participate in the March on Washington and hear Martin Luther King Jr. deliver his "I Have a Dream" speech.

On September 15, a bomb kills four girls at Sixteenth Street Baptist Church in Birmingham, Alabama.

1964—The Twenty-fourth Amendment eliminates poll taxes for national elections.

On June 21, civil rights workers James E. Cheney, Andrew Goodman, and Michael Schwerner are murdered. Their bodies are discovered on August 4 near Philadelphia, Mississippi.

The Civil Rights Act, signed on July 2 by President Lyndon B. Johnson, makes discrimination in public accommodations by employers illegal.

On December 10, Martin Luther King Jr. receives the Nobel Peace Prize.

1965—On February 21, Malcolm X is shot on stage at the Manhattan Audubon Ballroom in Harlem.

A fifty-mile march from Selma to Montgomery, Alabama, in March helps galvanize support for the Voting Rights Act.

On August 6, the Voting Rights Act is signed by President Lyndon B. Johnson, making local laws, including literacy tests, illegal. It is renewed again in 1970.

Discussion Questions

1. How were the laws and customs of Jim Crow passed from generation to generation?

2. What does the song "Jump Jim Crow" (document 1) reveal about assumptions about race in America before the Civil War? In what way might that song and the long tradition of minstrelsy influence African American musical performers (see document 59)?

3. What does the Voting Rights Act of 1965 (document 74) share in common with the Fifteenth Amendment (document 13)?

4. How does the lithograph "The Shackle Broken by the Genius of Freedom," 1874 (document 15), reflect Robert B. Elliott's January 6, 1874, speech (available at http://www1.law.nyu.edu/davisp/neglectedvoices/ElliotJan061874.html)?

5. How does Edmund Kirke's "How Shall the Negro Be Educated?" (document 21) anticipate arguments made by Booker T. Washington in the "Atlanta Compromise" speech (document 22)?

6. What does document 35 reveal about Jim Crow outside the Deep South?

7. How could art and literature during the Harlem Renaissance be considered a form of resistance against Jim Crow?

8. Why was passing during Jim Crow so controversial in both the black and white community?

9. Compare the images "The Negro and the Ape" (document 68) and "Jim Crow Jubilee" (document 2).

10. Analyze the two responses to *Plessy v. Ferguson:*

Justice Henry Brown wrote the majority opinion, excerpted here:

> We consider the underlying fallacy of the plaintiff's argument to consist in the assumption that the enforced separation of the two races stamps the colored race with a badge of inferiority. If this be so, it is not by reason of anything found in the act, but solely because the colored race chooses to put that construction upon it. . . . The argument also assumes that social prejudice may be overcome by legislation, and that equal rights cannot be secured except by an enforced commingling of the two races. . . . If the civil and political rights of both races be equal, one cannot be inferior to the other civilly or politically. If one race be inferior to the other socially, the Constitution of the United States cannot put them upon the same plane.

Justice John Marshall Harlan wrote the dissenting opinion, excerpted here:

> I am of the opinion that the statute of Louisiana is inconsistent with the personal liberties of citizens, white and black, in that State, and hostile to both the spirit and the letter of the Constitution of the United States. If laws of like character should be enacted in the several States of the Union, the effect would be in the highest degree mischievous. Slavery as an institution tolerated by law would, it is true, have disappeared from our country, but there would remain a power in the States, by sinister legislation, to interfere with the blessings of freedom; to regulate civil rights common to all citizens, upon the basis of race; and to place in a condition of legal inferiority a large body of American citizens, now constituting a part of the political community, called the people of the United States, for whom and by whom, through representatives, our government is administrated. Such a system is inconsistent with the guarantee given by the Constitution to each State of a republican form of government, and may be stricken down by congressional action, or by the courts in the discharge of their solemn duty to maintain the supreme law of the land, anything in the Constitution or laws of any State to the contrary notwithstanding.

Sample Assignments

There are multiple online resources that provide useful pedagogical approaches to understanding the Jim Crow era. One of the best is a Web site (http://www.jimcrowhistory.org), originally created in support of the PBS series *The Rise and Fall of Jim Crow,* produced by WNET in New York in 2002. The following assignments are intended for high school and university students but can be modified to accommodate a variety of audiences.

Assignment 1: Oral History Project

For this assignment, students will complete an hour-long oral history with an informant who had firsthand experience with Jim Crow.

> Step 1: Review "The Intergenerational Discussion Guide" at http://www-tc.pbs.org/wnet/jimcrow/jimcrowguide.pdf?mii=1.

> Step 2: Review the following oral history resources that detail the various steps involved in conducting an oral history.

Southern Oral History Program (SOHP), University of North Carolina, Chapel Hill, Southern Historical Collection; http://www.sohp.org/howto/index.html.

"How To: Resources for Planning and Conducting Oral History Interviews" includes *The SOHP Guidebook,* SOHP interview forms, and a bibliography of more than fifty oral history resources. The interview forms include a cover sheet, interview agreement, interview agreement with restrictions, life history form, and proper word form. *The SOHP Guidebook* includes guidelines on designing an oral history project; advice on conducting, cataloguing, and transcribing interviews; notes on budgets and equipment needs; and ten interviewing tips.

Step-by-Step Guide to Oral History, Judith Moyer; http://www.dohistory.org/on_your_own/toolkit/oralHistory.html.

Developed by historian and educator Judith Moyer, this thorough guide to oral history offers suggestions and strategies for collecting and preserving oral history. Topics range from an explanation of how and why to collect oral history to guidelines for planning and conducting an interview, including initial research, locating individuals, choosing equipment, and asking productive questions. Moyer also addresses a number of important conceptual and ethical issues related to conducting and using oral histories, including questions of accuracy, the limits of oral history, strategies for overcoming specific interview problems, and twenty questions to help interviewers learn from their experience

Making Sense of Oral History, Linda Shopes.

This very useful Web site (http://historymatters.gmu.edu/mse/oral) provides an excellent overview of just what oral history is, how to conduct oral histories, and how to use and interpret oral histories in a larger historical context.

Library of Congress, Learning Page; http://international.loc.gov/learn/lessons/oralhist/ohstart.html.

This oral history lesson, intended for middle and high school students, presents social history content and topics through the voices of ordinary people. It draws on primary sources from the American Memory Collection, American Life Histories, 1936–1940. Using excerpts from the collection, students study social history topics through interviews that recount the lives of ordinary Americans. Based on these excerpts and further research in the collections, students develop their own research questions. They then plan and conduct oral history interviews with members of their communities.

Oral History Association, http://alpha.dickinson.edu/oha/pub_eg.html.

Since its founding in 1967 the Oral History Association (OHA) has grappled constantly with developing and promoting professional standards for oral historians.

Step 3: In conjunction with a faculty member, review the legal and ethical issues related to oral history, especially as they apply to the Institutional Review Board (IRB) and oral history release forms. For sample forms, visit http://www.talkinghistory.org/listeningroom/ interview_release_form_1.pdf.

Step 4: Select an informant, prepare questions, and conduct the interview.

Step 5: Transcribe the interview and answer the following questions, drawn from http://historymatters.gmu.edu/mse/oral/ summary.html.

1. Who is the narrator?

   What is the narrator's relationship to the events under discussion?

   What stake might the narrator have in presenting a particular version of events?

   What effect might the narrator's social identity and position have on the interview?

   How does the narrator present himself or herself in the interview?

   What sort of character does the narrator become in the interview?

   What influences (personal, cultural, social) might shape the way the narrator expresses himself or herself?

   Consider especially how the events under discussion are generally regarded and how popular culture might shape the narrator's account.

2. Who is the interviewer?

   What background and interests does the interviewer bring to the topic of the interview?

   How might this affect the interview?

   How do the interviewer's questions shape the story told?

Has the interviewer prepared for the interview?

How adept is the interviewer in getting the narrator to tell his or her story in his or her own way?

What effect might the interviewer's social identity and position have on the interviewee and, hence, the interview?

How might the dynamic between narrator and interviewer affect what is said in the interview?

Does the interviewer have a prior relationship with the interviewee?

How might this affect the interview?

3. What has been said in the interview?

How has the narrator structured the interview?

What is the plot of the story?

What does this tell us about the way the narrator thinks about his or her experience?

What motifs, images, and anecdotes does the narrator use to encapsulate experience?

What can this tell us about how the narrator thinks about his or her experience?

What does the narrator avoid or sidestep?

What topics does the narrator especially warm to or speak about with interest, enthusiasm, or conviction?

What might this tell us?

Are there times when the narrator doesn't seem to answer the question posed?

What might be the reason for this?

Are there significant factual errors in the narrative?

Is it internally consistent?

How might you account for errors and inconsistencies?

Is the narrator's account consistent with other sources, other interviews?

How can you explain any discrepancies?

4. For what purpose has this interview been conducted?

   How might the purpose have shaped the content, perspective, and tone of the interview?

5. What are the circumstances of the interview?

   What effect might the location of the interview have on what was said in the interview?

   If anyone other than the interviewer and interviewee were present, what effect might the presence of this other person have on the interview?

   Do you know the mental and physical health of the narrator and interviewer?

   What effect might these factors have on the interview?

Assignment 2: Racial Etiquette in the Era of Jim Crow

Jim Crow was a series of federal and state laws that formalized segregation in economic, political, and legal life from Reconstruction to the civil rights movement, but it was also a system by which black and white America negotiated social relationships. For this assignment, students will focus on the specific unwritten codes of conduct that were transmitted to both races from generation to generation to understand how such a system perpetuated itself.

Step 1: Review the first-person narratives at http://www.jim crowhistory.org/resources/narratives/Theme_Etiquette.htm.

Step 2: Read chapter 1, "The Etiquette of Race Relations," from Jennifer Ritterhouse's book *Growing Up Jim Crow: How Black and White Southern Children Learned Race* (Chapel Hill: University of North Carolina Press, 2006).

Step 3: Consider the following questions:

What kind of social relations between races are made obvious in these interviews?

How did racial etiquette change as children grew older?

What happened when racial etiquette was breached?

How did one's political point of view shape one's response to racial codes and mores?

Additional Resources

Doyle, Bertram Wilbur. *The Etiquette of Race Relations in the South: A Study in Social Control*. Chicago: University of Chicago Press, 1937.

Hale, Grace Elizabeth. *Making Whiteness: The Culture of Segregation in the South, 1890–1940*. New York: Pantheon, 1998.

Assignment 3: Passing in Jim Crow America

There were multiple ways of resisting Jim Crow, but one of the most dangerous and complex involved African Americans who passed as white. Individuals who chose to pass as white often had to sever family and community ties and live in constant fear of being discovered.

Step 1: Read the following online essays:

"Passing for White in Jim Crow America," by Wendy Ann Gaudin; http://www.jimcrowhistory.org/resources/lessonplans/hs_es_passing_for_white.htm.

"Resisting Jim Crow," by Ronald F. Davis; http://www.jimcrow history.org/history/resisting2.htm.

Step 2: Read the novel *Passing,* published in 1929 by Nella Larsen, and consider the following questions:

If Nella Larsen's intended audience for *Passing* was primarily white, as with many Harlem Renaissance novels, what does that reveal about the novel's overall theme?

How does Larsen's novel debunk the notion that race is biologically rooted? In what way does it expose race as a construct that is defined by history and culture?

How might the novel be read as a critique of the black middle class?

What do the ending and Clare's death reveal about the viability and danger of passing in Jim Crow America?

Additional Resources

Calloway, Licia M. *Black Family (Dys)Function in Novels by Jessie Fauset, Nella Larsen, and Fannie Hurst.* New York: Peter Lang, 2003.

Christian, Barbara. *Black Women Novelists: The Development of a Tradition, 1892–1976.* Westport, CT: Greenwood Press, 1980.

Davis, Thadious M. *Nella Larsen: Novelist of the Harlem Renaissance, a Woman's Life Unveiled.* Baton Rouge: Louisiana State University Press, 1994.

Hutchinson, George. *In Search of Nella Larsen: A Biography of the Color Line.* Cambridge: Harvard University Press, 2006.

Larsen, Nella. *An Intimation of Things Distant: The Collected Fiction of Nella Larsen.* Ed. Charles R. Larson. New York: Anchor Books, 1992.

ANNOTATED BIBLIOGRAPHY

Books

Ashmore, Harry S. *Civil Rights and Wrongs: A Memoir of Race and Politics, 1944–1994.*
New York: Pantheon Books, 1994.

> As executive editor the *Arkansas Gazette* and author of a series of Pulitzer
> Prize–winning editorials during 1957, Ashmore was both an active participant in
> and concerned observer of the politics of race after World War II. His memoir
> begins during the war, when Jim Crow was still very much alive, and shows how
> the desegregation effort shaped the second half of the twentieth century.

Ayres, Edward L. *The Promise of the New South: Life after Reconstruction.* New York:
Oxford University Press, 1992.

> Along with James M. McPherson's *Battle Cry of Freedom* (1988) and Eric Foner's
> *Reconstruction* (1988), Ayres's book represents a flowering of scholarship on this
> period in American history, with particular focus on political, cultural, and social
> change. Ayres aims "to understand what it meant to live in the American South
> in the years after Reconstruction." Ayres's focus on the role the railroads played
> in giving rise to commercial and industrial growth while simultaneously encour-
> aging segregation is particularly useful in understanding this period.

Chafe, William Henry, Raymond Gavins, and Robert Korstad, eds., *Remembering Jim
Crow: African Americans Tell About Life in the Segregated South.* New York: New
Press, 2003.

> Using Duke University's Center for Documentary Studies' Behind the Veil pro-
> ject, this book and audio collection draws upon interviews of a diverse range of
> individuals from twenty-five communities in ten states. It seeks to examine how
> "African Americans developed their own life, hidden and estranged from the lives
> of white people." Two one-hour CDs of the radio documentary produced by
> American Radio Works, a transcript of that program, fifty rare photographs from
> the Jim Crow era, biographical information, and a bibliography are included.
> The volume is a sequel to *Remembering Slavery: African Americans Talk about Their
> Personal Experiences of Slavery and Emancipation,* edited by Ira Berlin, Marc
> Fabreau, Steven F. Miller, and Robin D. G. Kelley (New York: New Press, 2000).

Dailey, Jane. *Before Jim Crow: The Politics of Race in Postemancipation Virginia.* Chapel
Hill: University of North Carolina, Press, 2000.

> Dailey, an associate professor of history at The Johns Hopkins University and
> coeditor of *Jumpin' Jim Crow: Southern Politics from Civil War to Civil Rights,* exam-
> ines the history of Virginia's Readjuster Party, an interracial coalition in the post-
> Emancipation South that sought cooperative between races.

Franklin, John Hope. *Reconstruction after the Civil War.* Chicago: University of Chicago Press, 1994.

First published in 1961, Franklin's landmark study helped shape the field for the next four decades. Franklin's work, which describes the reasons for the failure of Reconstruction, focuses on several important topics organized as chapters: "The Aftermath of the War"; "Presidential Peacemaking"; "Reconstruction: Confederate Style"; "Confederate Reconstruction under Fire"; "Challenge by Congress"; "The South's New Leaders"; "Constitution-Making in the Radical South"; "Reconstruction—Black and White"; "The Era Begins to End"; and "The Aftermath of 'Redemption.'" At 226 pages, it is a concise introduction to the topic.

Gilmore, Glenda Elizabeth. *Gender and Jim Crow: The Political Culture of Reconstruction.* Chapel Hill: University of North Carolina Press, 1996.

Gilmore's study focuses on segregation in North Carolina at the turn of the century as it developed in response to the growing independence of white women. As black men were demonized as sexual predators, black women worked in the white community to generate some measure of interracial cooperation.

Hale, Elizabeth Grace. *Making Whiteness: The Culture of Segregation in the South, 1890–1940.* New York: Pantheon Books, 1998.

This cultural history examines how whiteness was constructed in the post–Civil War era. Hale argues that whites in the North and South embraced a collective identity of superiority, and this volume fits nicely with Ian Haney-Lopez's *White by Law: The Legal Construction of Race* (1995) and David Theo Goldberg's *Racist Culture: Philosophy and the Politics of Meaning* (1993) and *Racial Subjects: Writing on Race in America* (1997).

Hanchett, Thomas W. *Sorting Out the New South City: Race, Class, and Urban Development in Charlotte, 1875–1975.* Chapel Hill: University of North Carolina Press, 1998.

Hanchett takes Charlotte, one of the South's largest and fastest growing cities, and examines how it was transformed from a rural village to an economic hub of the nation's textile industry. Of specific interest here is Hanchett's argument that racial and economic segregation was the result of social and political upheaval in the 1880s that created race-specific neighborhoods. That trend has continued through urban renewal efforts.

Klarman, Michael J. *From Jim Crow to Civil Rights: The Supreme Court and the Struggle for Racial Equality.* London and New York, Oxford University Press, 2004.

Klarman, a professor of constitutional law, presents a thoughtful analysis of the Supreme Court's focus on race, with careful attention to national and international forces that shaped late-nineteenth- and twentieth-century decisions such as *Plessy v. Ferguson* and *Brown v. Board of Education.* His conclusion that the *Brown* decision galvanized opposition to desegregation warrants serious consideration. The book was nicely timed to coincide with the fiftieth anniversary of *Brown.*

Robert W. Gordon, Kent Professor of Law and Legal History at Yale argues, *"From Jim Crow to Civil Rights* is a bold, carefully crafted, deeply researched, forcefully argued, lucidly written history of law and legal-change strategies in the civil rights movement from the 1880s to the 1960s, and a brilliant case study in the power and limits of law as a motor of social change. Among the hundreds of recent books on the history of civil rights and race relations, Klarman's is one of the most original, provocative, and illuminating, with fresh evidence and fresh insights on practically every page."

Lhamon, W. T., Jr. *Jump Jim Crow: Lost Plays, Lyrics, and Street Prose of the First Atlantic Popular Culture*. Cambridge: Harvard University Press, 2003.

A follow-up to his book *Raising Cain: Blackface Performance from Jim Crow to Hip Hop* (2000), Lhamon's book focuses on the character of Jim Crow as portrayed by Thomas D. Rice. He offers a detailed introduction and primary sources and criticism, valuable to students of vernacular music's relationship to race in America.

Litwick, Leon. *Trouble in Mind: Black Southerners in the Age of Jim Crow*. New York: Alfred A. Knopf, 1998.

C. Van Woodward said that Litwack's book is "the most complete and moving account we have had of what the victims of the Jim Crow South suffered and somehow endured."

Myrdal, Gunnar. *An American Dilemma: The Negro Problem and Modern Democracy*. New York: Harper and Row, 1944.

The Carnegie Corporation commissioned Swedish economist Gunnar Myrdal (1898–1987) to direct a study of the condition of African Americans in the United States in 1938. Myrdal hired forty-eight writers, including Ralph Bunche and Kenneth B. Clark, to aid in the research, which was published in two volumes in 1944. Myrdal makes an argument that race relations in America are a moral, not a sociological problem. Myrdal's work was cited in the *Brown v. Board of Education* decision as an authoritative source on the impact that the concept of "separate but equal" had on the African American psyche. In 1964, the *Saturday Review* asked twenty-seven scholars, "What books published during the past four decades most significantly altered the direction of society?" Myrdal's book was second only to John Maynard Keynes's *The General Theory of Employment, Interest, and Money* (1936). Myrdal shared the Nobel Prize with Friedrich von Hayek in 1974.

Newby, I. A. *The Development of Segregationist Thought*. Homewood, IL: The Dorsey Press, 1968.

This volume offers a series of essays from the late nineteenth to middle of the twentieth century focused on various aspects of segregationist thought in America. The essays address political, scientific, legislative, and moral reasons for supporting segregation and are particularly useful in understanding supporters of Jim Crow.

Ritterhouse, Jennifer. *Growing Up Jim Crow: How Black and White Southern Children Learned Race*. Chapel Hill: University of North Carolina Press, 2006.

Ritterhouse focuses on how black and white children in the South learned the unspoken racial etiquette of Jim Crow and concludes that parental instruction was an important factor. It is a fascinating study of how people ate, drank, walked, sat, stood, and communicated; and her first chapter, "The Etiquette of Race Relations," is particularly instructive.

Smith, Graham. *When Jim Crow Met John Bull: Black American Soldiers in World War II*. Britain, NY: St. Martin's Press, 1987.

Smith's book focuses on the 130,000 black soldiers who were stationed in Great Britain between 1942 and 1945: whether African Americans should have been stationed there, how Britain responded to a segregated army, and what this experience reveals about race relations in a comparative context.

Stalcup, Brenda, ed. *Reconstruction: Opposing Viewpoints*. San Diego: Greenhaven Press, 1995.

An interestingly conceived book, it is divided into four major topics regarding Reconstruction and, in each, presents divergent viewpoints written by contemporaries on various contentious subtopics; one is entitled "Blacks Should Have / Should Not Have the Right to Vote." The book is useful to stimulate vigorous intellectual discussion.

Wilson, Theodore Branther. *The Black Codes of the South*. Tuscaloosa: University of Alabama Press, 1965.

This well-researched summary of the black codes that came into being immediately after the end of the Civil War, during what some have called "Confederate Reconstruction," describes in summaries and also state by state those legislative acts that were intended to both control and re-indenture the recently freed slaves. Largely repealed when Congress wrested control of Reconstruction away from President Andrew Johnson, many black codes later became the basis for some of the Jim Crow legislation that occurred after Reconstruction, which often proved harsher than the black codes. University of Alabama professor Brantner wrote his book during the height of civil rights discord in Alabama and is, for the most part, dispassionate and fair-minded. Some of the conclusions reached at the end of the book would cause pause today, but perhaps the remarkable thing is, given the times and circumstances, how even-handed the book is.

Woodward, C. Vann. *The Origins of the New South: 1877–1913* (Baton Rouge: Louisiana State University Press, 1951).

Written over half a century ago, Woodward's book is still one of the most important books about Reconstruction through World War I in the South. Most historians who followed in his footsteps were informed by Woodward's conclusions. He focuses on how the Redeemers, largely pro-business whites, dominated political life and extended economic incentives to industry, railroads, and insurance companies often at the expense of spending in education and social programs. The book details various challenges to this system, notably Populism and Progressivism.

Woodward, C. Vann. *The Strange Career of Jim Crow.* New York: Oxford University Press, 2001.

Published a year after the Supreme Court's landmark *Brown v. Board of Education* (1954) case, *The Strange Career of Jim Crow* was once called "the historical Bible of the civil rights movement" by Martin Luther King Jr. The book examines the early history of Jim Crow laws and argues that segregation was not widespread until the 1890s. Named one of the one hundred nonfiction works of the twentieth century, *The Strange Career of Jim Crow* has sold almost a million copies and remains, in the words of David Herbert Donald, "a landmark in the history of American race relations."

Wormser, Richard. *The Rise and Fall of Jim Crow.* New York: St. Martin's Press, 2003.

Wormser's book, a guide to the PBS series of the same name, offers a concise history of the Jim Crow era. Covering the period from 1865 to 1954, the book is primarily focused on the southern experience and draws heavily upon personal narratives of ordinary people as well as Booker T. Washington, Ida B. Wells, and Strom Thurmond. Wormser concludes, "Though Jim Crow is no longer codified in the laws, and the racial climate has decidedly improved, white supremacy is still a vital part of the American psyche." As an additional bonus, the book includes more than one hundred photographs.

Films

There are numerous films and documentaries that offer a useful perspective on the Jim Crow era, including: *Birth of a Nation* (1915), *Within Our Gates* (1919), *Gone with the Wind* (1939), *To Kill a Mockingbird* (1962), *The Promised Land* (1989), *Wild Women Don't Have the Blues* (1989), *Goin' to Chicago* (1994), *My People: The Life and Writing of Margaret Walker Alexander* (1998), *Homecoming* (1999), *The Rise and Fall of Jim Crow* (2000), and *Strange Fruit* (2002).

Web-Based Resources

American Social History Project, Center for Media Learning at New York University and Center for History and New Media at George Mason University, History Matters (*http://historymatters.gmu.edu*), is directed at high school and college faculty members and includes primary documents related to African American life. It also includes syllabi and lesson plans.

Charlotte-Mecklenburg Library, Charlotte, North Carolina (*http://www.cmstory. org/aaa2*), includes primary source materials related to local African American families.

Documenting the American South, Academic Affairs Library at the University of North Carolina at Chapel Hill (*http://docsouth.unc.edu*) offers first-person narratives and literature from southern authors, mainly drawn from their collection.

Durham County Library, Durham, North Carolina (http:www.dclibrary.net/prod1/ncc/photoarch/og016.htm), features materials related to local African American families.

Electronic Text Center, University of Virginia, Charlottesville (*http://www2.lib. virginia.edu/etext/index.html*), offers access to their collection, which include numerous documents on Jim Crow.

The Library of Congress, African American Odyssey (*http://memory.loc.gov/ ammem/aaohtml/aohome.html*) provides access to maps, sheet music, audio files, text, and photographs that are easily searchable by keyword.

Minnesota Public Radio, American Radio Works (*http://www.americanradio works.org*) offers materials to support the program *Remembering Jim Crow,* which is part of a larger project entitled Behind the Veil: Documenting African American Life in the Jim Crow South.

Missouri Historical Society (*http://mohistory.org/content/libraryandresearch/ eyesofchild.aspx*) showcases an oral history and education project, *Through the Eyes of a Child,* focused on African American neighborhoods around St. Louis.

Musarium (*http://www.musarium.com*) is an online magazine that includes the online exhibition *Without Sanctuary* and an interview with James Allen, the collector of the materials on lynching in America.

National Archives and Records Administration (http://www.archives.gov/ education/lessons/brown-case-order) features materials on segregated education, including the cases *Dorothy E. Davis et al. v. County School Board of Prince Edward County, Virginia* (1951) and *Brown v. Board of Education* (1954).

Public Broadcasting Corporation, *The Rise and Fall of Jim Crow* (http:www/ pbs.org/wnet/jimcrow), is an extensive site that was created to accompany the PBS documentary by the same name. African American World is a new site worth reviewing (*http://www.pbs.org/wnet/aaworld*).

NOTE: While searching the collections available on these Web sites, make sure to use the following search terms: "Negro(es)," "African American," "Afro-American," and "black" to ensure the best results.

INDEX

A

ABOUT THE AUTHORS

CATHERINE M. LEWIS is an associate professor of history, the director of the Museum of History and Holocaust Education, and coordinator of the Public History Program at Kennesaw State University. She is also the special projects coordinator for the Atlanta History Center. She completed a BA in English and history with honors at Emory University and an MA and PhD in American studies at the University of Iowa. She has curated more than twenty exhibitions throughout the nation and has published seven books, including *The Changing Face of Public History: The Chicago Historical Society and the Transformation of an American History Museum* (Northern Illinois University Press, 2005), *Don't Ask What I Shot: How Eisenhower's Love of Golf Helped Shape 1950s America* (McGraw-Hill, 2007), and *Race, Politics, and Memory: A Documentary History of the Little Rock School Crisis* (University of Arkansas Press, 2007) with co-author Dr. J. Richard Lewis.

J. RICHARD LEWIS is president of JRL Educational Services, Inc. He completed his BA in English at Mercer University, his MA in English at Florida State University, and his PhD in curriculum and instruction at the University of Maryland. He spent his career as an educator and administrator in Florida, Maryland, and Virginia. He has served as a visiting faculty member at Western Maryland College and Johns Hopkins University. He retired as the director of Success for All Foundation and as a researcher at the Johns Hopkins University in 2001. He has served as a desegregation consultant for the Miami Desegregation Assistance Center; the Urban Education Center in Pittsburgh, Pennsylvania; Milwaukee Public Schools; the Cincinnati Desegregation Assistance Center at the University of Cincinnati; and Memphis State University, among others. In 2007, he co-authored *Race, Politics, and Memory: A Documentary History of the Little Rock School Crisis* (University of Arkansas Press, 2007) with Dr. Catherine M. Lewis.